Advance Praise for

ENERGY-WISE
LANDSCAPE DESIGN

Sue Reed has compiled an extremely useful and readable book on ways in which we can design and manage landscapes with the goal of conserving — and even producing — energy. I have not seen another book which brings together so many useful concepts and practical information. This comprehensive book, written in a direct, non-jargonistic manner, will be of tremendous value to everyone from individual homeowners to students of environmental design.

—DARREL MORRISON, Professor and Dean Emeritus,
School of Environmental Design, University of Georgia and Adjunct Professor,
Master of Science in Landscape Design Program, Columbia University

Plants matter, and no one has articulated their role in conserving energy in our landscapes better than Susan Reed. *Energy-wise Landscape Design* is a comprehensive yet unusually readable review of the whys and wherefores of designing ecologically responsible landscapes. If you are looking for easy ways to reduce your carbon footprint while helping to sustain the ecosystems that sustain you, read this book.

— DOUG TALLAMY, author of *Bringing Nature Home*

This long overdue book is well organized, well written and well illustrated, a fine cohesive work that deserves focused reading. It will be a must-read for all design students, and a reach-for book for landscape professionals who wish to fill some of the gaps in their own education and design work.

—WALTER CUDNOHUFSKY, Landscape Architect, and Founder,
Conway School of Landscape Design

Energy-Wise Landscape Design integrates specific design solutions directed toward energy conservation with sustaining the natural environment. Too many books about energy-efficient landscapes ignore the energy values of nature itself and propose clearing trees or whole forests to open vistas for solar and wind power. Sue Reed's step-by-step suggestions make change towards sustainable landscaping doable, instead of difficult and unfamiliar.

— LESLIE JONES SAUER, author of *The Once and Future Forest*

Advance Praise continued

Sue Reed's book amounts to a conversation with the author who gently but inevitably convinces us to integrate thoughts about energy into all our concepts of action and beauty. She brilliantly focuses on the what and why of designing landscapes for the needs of users in the 21st century. This is a must read for those who want guidance for the landscapes of their existing properties or are about to build a new home. Her poetic conclusive paragraphs should be required reading for all, and especially for landscape architects and designers.

—DON WALKER, Landscape Architect and retired Director,
Conway School of Landscape Design

Sue Reed has done something wonderful in this ambitious first book — in friendly, plain language she has leaped over the mundane of the "how to" genre to infuse the reader with real awareness and understanding of basic principles of natural process and about the benefits and methods of gently milking nature for its goodness.

—BRAD JOHNSON, Landscape Architect,
Brad Johnson + Associates (BradJohnson.ca)

This is no vapid coffee-table garden book to be merely flipped through and set aside. Nor is it a depressing diatribe about inevitable environmental decline and culpability. *Energy-wise Landscape Design* is filled with practical, specific design advice that will inspire you to get up and get working to make a better home landscape for yourself and the planet.

— PAUL CAWOOD HELLMUND, ASLA, President/Director,
Conway School of Landscape Design, Graduate Program in Sustainable Landscape
Planning & Design, and co-author/editor of *Designing Greenways* and *Ecology of Greenways*

If like most people, you've just thought about saving energy in terms of what goes on inside your home, you're in for a big and pleasant surprise, as Sue Reed guides you to understand how making your property more beautiful with landscaping, done properly, can also generate considerable savings in your annual energy bills while making your home more comfortable. A big three-for-one benefit!

— JERRY YUDELSON, author of *Choosing Green: The Homebuyer's Guide to Good Green Homes*

ENERGY-WISE
LANDSCAPE DESIGN

A New Approach for your Home and Garden

SUE REED

Illustrations by Kate Dana

NEW SOCIETY PUBLISHERS

Cataloging in Publication Data:
A catalog record for this publication is available from the National Library of Canada.

Cover design by Diane McIntosh.
Inside: Photography by Sue Reed, except where noted; Illustrations by Kate Dana, except where noted.

Printed in Canada by Friesens.
First printing January 2010.

Paperback ISBN: 978-0-86571-653-7

Inquiries regarding requests to reprint all or part of *Energy-wise Landscape Design* should be addressed to New Society Publishers at the address below.

To order directly from the publishers, please call toll-free (North America)
1-800-567-6772, or order online at www.newsociety.com

Any other inquiries can be directed by mail to:

New Society Publishers
P.O. Box 189, Gabriola Island, BC V0R 1X0, Canada
(250) 247-9737

New Society Publishers' mission is to publish books that contribute in fundamental ways to building an eco-logically sustainable and just society, and to do so with the least possible impact on the environment, in a manner that models this vision. We are committed to doing this not just through education, but through action. This book is one step toward ending global deforestation and climate change. It is printed on Forest Stewardship Council-certified acid-free paper that is **100% post-consumer recycled** (100% old growth forest-free), processed chlorine free, and printed with vegetable-based, low-VOC inks, with covers produced using FSC-certified stock. New Society also works to reduce its carbon footprint, and purchases carbon offsets based on an annual audit to ensure a carbon neutral footprint. For further information, or to browse our full list of books and purchase securely, visit our website at: www.newsociety.com

NEW SOCIETY PUBLISHERS

Recycled
Supporting responsible use
of forest resources
www.fsc.org Cert no. SW-COC-1271
© 1996 Forest Stewardship Council
FSC

Contents

Acknowledgments

I AM DEEPLY INDEBTED TO MANY FRIENDS and colleagues whose counsel, feedback and suggestions helped make this book possible. Much that is good in the book is due to their guidance; anything inadequate is my responsibility alone.

To my generous manuscript readers...

Betsy Abert, gardener, designer and fellow ex-Con, for assuring me that nothing more was needed.

Walton Congdon, renewable energy expert, for checking the accuracy of the entire section on generating energy.

Walter Goodridge, my pal handyman, for editing several of my explanations about construction.

Craig Hefner, physics teacher, for shedding light on wind and weather.

Barbara Keene, who shares my delight in native plants, for your priceless feedback about designing and building the realm of plants.

Peter Martin, electrician, for correcting and improving the discussion about lighting.

Jason Schneider, old friend, for giving me the writing advice you give to your sixth-graders.

Vivian Ubell and David Sumberg, for your encouragement at the start.

Paul Waite, my kind and instructive landscape contractor, for 20 years of collaboration and our handful of magnificent successes.

Donald Walker, for refining my explanations about sun, shade, shadows, trees and wind (more on Don below).

Lauren Wheeler, for your valuable feedback about stormwater management, tree ordinances, the design of semi-urban landscapes and for doggedly insisting (okay, nagging) for years that I write a book, any book.

Rochelle Wildfong, dear friend, for giving me your essential "regular" homeowner's perspective on the whole thing....

I thank you all.

To Libby Burnham, my eternally cheerful librarian, for delivering into my hands book after book after book, thank you.

To Rhea Banker, Peter Jeswald and Victoria Lustbader, for your guidance in my first publishing negotiations, thank you.

To Emily Teller, for technical assistance (to the amazement of your husband and sons), thank you.

To Sally Naser, for unflagging support whether I deserve it or not, thank you.

To Walt Cudnohufsky, for creating the Conway School of Landscape Design and its perfect educational environment, where I thrived, thank you.

To my students at the Conway School, who for 15 years demanded the best of my knowledge and never settled for an easy explanation (and you know who you are!), thanks a lot.

To Ruth Parnall, for helping launch my career and teaching me much that I may no longer realize I learned from you, thank you.

To Randy Griffith, for your enthusiastic response to my early essays, and your guidance about using soft punctuation, thank you.

To Richard Allan, my first and still faithful client, for providing so many design opportunities and challenges, and for graciously allowing your projects' schedules to bend around my writing schedule, thank you.

To Phillip Eck, whose delightful landscape remains one of the best I've ever helped create, thank you. (You'll see your property in several places throughout this book.)

To Kate Dana, my illustrator for this book (and perhaps more), for your ability to bring technical information to life and translate it into brilliant art, thank you.

To Emma, my girl, my sunny day, for your clarity about how the world should work, and for being your marvelous self, thank you.

To Don Walker, my teacher, for long ago setting me on the path of ecological design, for explaining many vital truths that still inform all my work (and which surely appear more than I realize in this book) and for silently, without actually knowing it, inspiring me to complete this ultimate assignment, thank you.

And finally to David Schochet, my life's companion, who loves exploring the natural and human-made world with me, who welcomes my inevitable commentary and bravely challenges my pronouncements: this book would not exist without your wisdom and support...and your endlessly patient editing. Thank you.

Introduction

IF SOMEONE TOLD YOU there was one single way you could:

+ Save energy and money at the same time
+ Heat and cool your house more efficiently and effectively
+ Improve the beauty, utility and value of your property
+ Get a big benefit from a small investment, and a solid return on investments you've already made
+ While also incidentally contributing to a cleaner, healthier environment…

Would you be interested?

Have you been noticing your utility costs rising? Do you wish you could use less gas or electricity without changing your lifestyle or spending a lot of money? Do you want to stop feeling that little twinge of guilt each time you switch on a light or turn up the heat? Well, you've come to the right place.

This book shows how we can all save energy, simply by making small changes in the way we design and build our landscapes. The solutions presented here will work in every sort of landscape, whether large or small, hilly or flat, rural or urban. Many of them cost little to do, and some cost nothing at all. But every idea, action, design tip and suggestion in this book will help reduce the amount of energy — your own and the Earth's — that's spent on constructing and caring for our landscapes.

Lots of other books, magazines and websites explain how to improve the energy-efficiency of *buildings*. This is undoubtedly a good idea, but replacing windows, installing a new heating system or renovating a house may simply not be an option for many homeowners. *Energy-wise Landscape Design* presents hundreds of ways you can save energy, without touching your home or investing in new technologies (although the book does discuss some of those too).

This book explains two basic methods for saving energy. First we can arrange our gardens and grounds so they help *keep our homes cool in summer and warm in winter*. This is not to suggest that landscaping should entirely replace improving our houses. Rather, landscapes can be intentionally designed to help lessen extremes in outdoor temperature, thereby reducing our indoor heating or cooling needs. When we use plants and the landscape in this way, we also reap additional benefits: we don't need to make complex decisions or gamble on new mechanical systems that may or may not work as planned, we make no big investment, and we avoid disturbing our living areas. Plus, any plants we use for this purpose generally get better with age rather than breaking down or becoming obsolete, as can happen with equipment.

The second way to save energy takes place *in the landscapes themselves*. This is the inevitable result of creating landscapes so they're hardy, resilient, low-maintenance, self-sustaining, long-lasting and undemanding of outside resources. Imagine how much gas you'd save by mowing a smaller lawn or using your own fallen leaves for mulch instead of buying bagged and imported materials. Think about a landscape that's designed to fit the land well and satisfy multiple needs, so that building it is easy and living in it is even easier. Consider the benefits of using materials efficiently and creating landscapes that endure for decades.

Taking any one of these actions will produce at least modest savings. But imagine the cumulative effect of taking many of these steps. As individuals we'd save serious money and use far less carbon-based fuel. And if a lot of us make just a few of the landscape choices suggested in this book, the energy savings across the country will be vast.

ORGANIZATION OF THE BOOK

This book is divided into seven sections:

- Sections I through IV present ideas for *designing* landscapes with energy in mind. Sections I and II focus on arranging the landscape to make houses more comfortable in summer and winter, while Sections III and IV provide design ideas for saving energy out in the landscape itself.

- Section V explains how to *build and care for* landscapes in the most energy-efficient ways.

- Section VI discusses methods for *generating energy* at the small scale of a home landscape.

- Section VII ends the book with a discussion of energy-efficient *lighting*.

Each chapter addresses a particular energy-saving goal and includes Actions that explain how to accomplish that goal. Numerous design and construction tips then provide tangible advice for implementing those actions in real-life situations.

THE BOOK'S CONTENT

This book presents ideas for conserving two kinds of energy. First it shows how to reduce *operating energy* — the energy used in our regular day-to-day functioning — that includes fuel for mowers and machinery, electricity for outdoor lights and watering systems and even the gasoline for our cars. Second, implementing the advice in this book will also reduce *embedded energy* — the energy used to manufacture and transport equipment and materials — that we consume in our landscapes without even realizing it.

Throughout the book, complex concepts and technical information are distilled down to their essence and explained in everyday language, so they can be easily understood. Specific numbers and formulas are rare. You don't need to be a professional of any sort to follow the suggestions presented here. All the ideas are described in enough detail so they can be adapted to and applied in a variety of situations.

There are no exact recipes for success in this book. No numbered diagrams to copy and transfer into your own garden. No pretty pictures to imitate. No absolute best or perfect solutions. This is because all home landscapes are unique, no matter how similar they may appear at first glance. Even if two houses are nearly identical and sitting on adjoining twin lots, their landscapes will be different, simply because the larger world will affect them differently.

Shadows, breezes, soils and water patterns; the history and quality of construction; and most important, the lifestyle, family size and personal preferences of the people who live there: these and countless other factors determine how a landscape looks and functions. All situations call for their own unique solution, and all homeowners have their own dreams and notions of home. Any single landscape can be designed in dozens or even hundreds of different ways. This book is merely a guide to achieve any landscape design goal in a way that saves energy.

While the suggestions in this book can work in many different kinds of landscapes, some may be more well-suited to a particular landscape or region than others, or more appealing to some homeowners than others. Certain ideas may even appear to be mutually exclusive or contradictory. The point here is not to suggest you should implement every recommendation in this book. Rather, it's to remind all of us to be thoughtful about the choices we make, to be aware of their costs and, whenever evaluating a possible action in our landscapes, to consider energy efficiency as an essential part of the equation.

Finally, in addition to helping any individual homeowner consume less energy, the suggestions in this book will also lighten this country's need to import resources. And many of them will also help improve the health of the natural environment. The most important thing to keep in mind, though, is that these ideas will work for you *whether or not* you care about politics, the world economy, the environment or going green. This book assumes that saving energy, in itself, is a worthwhile goal.

Arranging the Landscape to Help Cool a House in Summer

THERE ARE MANY WAYS to cool a house. Before the current age of technology, people all over the world kept themselves comfortable, and protected themselves from the extremes of weather and climate, by working with nature. They shaped their homes and landscapes to minimize nature's harshness and make the most of its beneficence.

However, around the middle of the twentieth century, we modern humans adopted a new comfort-enhancing process, one that has continued essentially unchanged since that time. In total innocence, and without any intent to do harm, we ignored basic, well-understood methods to *prevent heat from accumulating* in our houses. Instead we put our faith in strategies that would *remove the heat after it had already accumulated.*

This new approach was made possible by the extremely low cost of energy. In recent decades, it continued in our complete ignorance of the harm caused by producing and using large amounts of energy. And it continues today, even though energy has become extremely expensive, and we know without a doubt that burning fossil fuels damages the environment.

In response to the realities of today's world, this section of the book explains several ways to keep ourselves comfortable by reducing the amount of heat our homes absorb in summer. Cooler houses are more comfortable, so they reduce our need for fans and air conditioning, potentially reducing a single home's energy costs by hundreds of dollars each year.

In addition, when a house is cooled during the day, it releases less stored heat back out to the surrounding air at night. This reduces the *heat island effect* of warm air created around buildings, which might also indirectly help neighbors feel more comfortable and save energy themselves.

This section includes four chapters that show how to help cool buildings from the outside.

The Heat Island Effect

The *heat island effect* occurs when solar heat radiated from pavement and buildings, combined with the exhaust from cars, factories and air conditioners, raises urban and suburban temperatures 2 to 10°F (1 to 6°C) higher than nearby rural areas. Elevated temperatures can impact communities by increasing peak energy demand, air-conditioning costs, air pollution levels, and heat-related illness and mortality.[1]

Wherever you live, arranging the landscape to help cool your house will lower your fuel consumption, utility payments and CO_2 emissions, while making your property more beautiful and increasing its real estate value. And it will make any house — whether it's old and leaky or tight and well-insulated — more comfortable to live in.

Designing Structures for Passive Solar Cooling

All of the Actions and Design Tips in this section will be most effective if your house itself is also designed to help deflect the sun's heat and make the most of cooling breezes. If you are planning to build a new home or renovate your existing home, keep in mind the following design principles for passive solar cooling.

South-facing walls should contain a large number of windows, for greatest solar gain in winter, but these windows should be protected from high-angle midday sun with overhangs, awnings or operable slatted shutters. Please note, this rule holds true only in the cold and temperate regions of the world. In hot regions, north-facing walls should have as many or more windows than south-facing walls, to enhance light and ventilation while reducing heat absorption.

East- and west-facing walls, which receive low-angle sunlight in morning and afternoon, should have few windows. The best way to shade them is with plants.

Windows and vents should be opened to bring in outside air when temperatures are cool (night and early morning), then closed when outdoor temperatures rise. Note that in places where the outdoor air is very humid, or if temperatures don't get much below 65°F at night, this passive ventilation may not have a significant effect.[2]

Other methods for ventilation include a solar (or thermal) chimney — a vertical shaft, usually dark-colored — that protrudes well above the roof. This stack heats up during the day, creating a draft that pulls air upward, thus producing a breeze within the living space. Note, solar chimneys may also be used to ventilate just a single room, such as a composting toilet chamber, or for pulling air through a geo-thermal heat-exchange system. (See Chapter 20 for more detail about geothermal heating and cooling.) Another method is a whole-house fan, a unit that draws air through the entire house and pushes it out through a vent in the attic.

Low-emissivity (Low-E) window glass, which can prevent heat loss from the house in winter, can also prevent some of the sun's heat from entering the house in summer. It's important to select the right kind of Low-E coating to suit your prevailing conditions (is your house in a "heating climate" or a "cooling climate?"). Be sure to get complete information from your local supplier and avoid buying windows over the Internet or from distant suppliers who may not provide the most appropriate product.

Reflective and light-colored roofing can significantly reduce cooling costs, but the greatest gain from this action will be found in uninsulated or poorly insulated buildings.

The subject of passive solar design is vast and extensively explained in many books, magazines and websites. See Appendix C for a list of resources.

CHAPTER 1

The Sun and the Wind

THE FIRST TWO SECTIONS OF THIS BOOK show how thoughtful design of the landscape can reduce the energy needed to heat and cool a building. Essential to this effort is understanding nature's processes. How do the sun and wind move, throughout the day and over the course of a year? How do they affect a building's temperature and the comfort of the people inside? This chapter explains these basic physical realities, so the advice that follows will make sense and be easy to apply in a variety of situations.

For some of you, this information may be a review of concepts already fully known. For others, it may be mostly new knowledge, or perhaps a reminder about things learned long ago but now nearly forgotten. Whatever your background, this first chapter serves as a vital starting point for the rest of the book.

THE SUN

Civilizations throughout history have paid close attention to the sun's movement across the sky. Ancient Egyptians built royal pyramids so that chambers deep inside would be briefly lit by a shaft of passing sunlight. Mayans oriented their ceremonial buildings to capture the sun's rays at certain times of the year. Many early societies linked the sun to their religious beliefs, and used their familiarity with the sun's place in the sky to guide the growing of food. For both of these purposes — the ceremonial and the agricultural — knowledge about the sun's location throughout the year was central to early people's survival.

Now, few among us depend on the sun for the basic necessities of life, and our Western religions pay it no attention at all. We modern humans have lost what used to be an intimate knowledge of the sun. This situation, however, may be about to change. As new technologies make it possible to create electricity affordably from solar energy, as government policies shift to emphasize and support renewable energy, and as we seek ways to reduce our own use of fossil fuels, many of us will become more attuned to the sun and its reliable path across the sky.

Let's start at the beginning. Contrary to what people believed for thousands of years, and despite the very convincing illusion that the sun is moving while the Earth is standing still, our planet actually circles around the sun. Every year the Earth completes one entire orbit around the sun, and we all go along for the ride. The Earth's orbit actually takes 365.25 days. To keep our calendars correct, every fourth year we add one day, February 29, and call that a leap year.

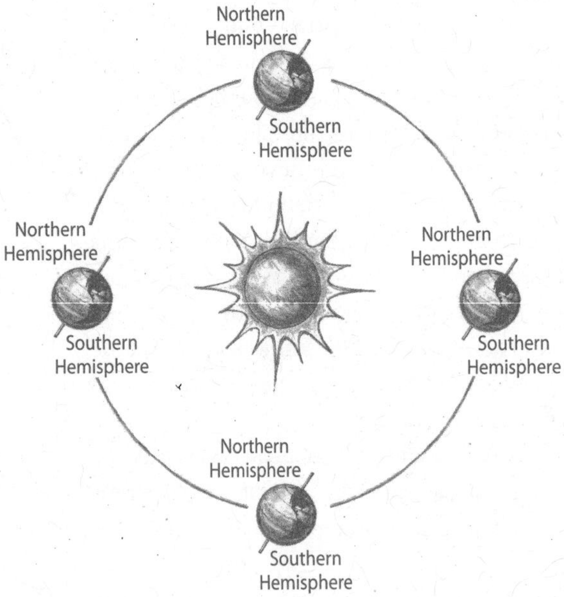

As we make this trip, hours of daylight get shorter and longer, from winter to summer and back again. This happens because the Earth is slightly tilted; its north-south axis is not straight up and down relative to its path around the sun. Imagine a spinning top or gyroscope that's leaning a bit sideways. This is what the Earth looks like as it circles the sun (the main difference being that our planet never falls over, because the spinning never slows down or stops, so far).

Because of this tilted axis, the northern and southern hemispheres (the top and bottom half) get exposed to the sun for different amounts of time, depending on the planet's position in its orbit. In one part of the orbit, when the northern hemisphere is tilted toward the sun, we have summer in Seattle and Scranton while it's winter in Australia. Six months later, when the planet has traveled around to the other side of its orbit and the northern hemisphere is tilted away from the sun, people in Chicago are shivering while in Sydney they're sunbathing. In between these seasons, the northern and southern hemispheres trade spring and fall.

During this year of orbit, wherever we live, all of us are riding the Earth around its own daily rotation. We see the sun rise and set because we ourselves are in motion, while the sun is (essentially) standing still. It's like taking a ride on a carousel as a child. Remember? Half the time you could see your mom, and then for a while you couldn't, and then, aha there she was again!

The sun follows a set pattern throughout a year, appearing to rise earlier and set later as we approach the long days of summer, then

Fig. 1.1:
We experience summer and winter because our planet's axis is tilted relative to the direction of its orbit. If the earth's axis were perpendicular to the its orbit, we'd have no seasons at all.

reversing that process as we move into winter, when the sun rises late and sets early, and the days feel much too short. Then the cycle starts again. This pattern is consistent from year to year, and we clever humans have figured out how to predict exactly where the sun will be at any hour of any day, in any month or season of the year, anywhere we live.

We can, as a society, use this information to do many impressive things. We might power a space station, create electricity in solar thermal power plants or perhaps completely replace our need for fossil fuels. But this book offers a simpler message: we as individuals can use knowledge about the sun to make our living places as energy efficient as possible. To help you get started, the information below explains basic facts about the sun's position in the sky.

The Sun's Path Across the Sky

We all sense the sun's changing patterns, whether or not we pay attention or know how to make sense of them. Are you awakened on a spring morning by the sun beaming into your bedroom, but by summer its rays at the same time of day are shining into a different room? When walking to work, do you see the sun between two familiar buildings and then realize, later in the year, that it's not there anymore? Have you noticed traffic slowing down on one stretch of road as you drive home from work, because the sun is glaring off car windshields, but a few weeks later traffic flows freely during the same trip?

All day, all year, the sun is up there somewhere, but where, exactly? How can we know or measure its location when the sky contains

Yes Virginia, the Earth Is Round.

If you don't quite believe that our planet is round, here are a few suggestions to help clarify the question:

- Watch a ship disappear over the horizon. If you can watch long enough, you'll notice: it doesn't fall off the edge, but rather it sinks gradually out of sight.
- Look at the shape of the shadow that's cast on the moon during a lunar eclipse. It's a curve. And the shadow is being cast by what?… the Earth!
- Take a trip on the next space shuttle and look back at where you came from.

Did You Know

If you're standing near the North or South Pole, the ground beneath your feet is hardly spinning at all. But if you're standing at the equator, you're spinning faster than 1,000 miles per hour.

no reference points? The answer is: we indicate the sun's position in two dimensions, using the Earth itself as a reference. One dimension is the sun's compass direction. The second is altitude, or the sun's height above the horizon.

Direction

The sun rises in the east and sets in the west, right? It turns out that this familiar truism is actually true on only two days of the year: the vernal equinox and the autumnal equinox. During the rest of the year, the sun rises and sets just *generally* east and west.

Here's what happens. On March 21, the vernal equinox, the sun rises and sets due east and west. After this moment, both sunrise and sunset shift toward the north until June 21, the summer solstice. This is the longest day of the year, when the sun rises as far to the north of east and sets as far to the north of west as it ever will. Then, as the Earth travels around toward the other side of the sun, sunrise and sunset shift gradually back toward the south (if you don't remember why, see *tilted axis* discussion above). On September 21, the autumnal equinox, the sun again rises and sets due east and west. It then continues to shift further south until December 21, the winter solstice. On this, the shortest day of the year, sunrise and sunset are as far to the south as they will ever get. (Note: in some years, these dates may vary by one day in either direction.)

This general pattern holds true everywhere on the planet. At any given time of day, however, the exact position of the sun overhead depends on the geographic latitude of the viewer. People in Ecuador see the 9 AM sun shining from a dramatically different direction than a

person in Alaska. (All of the suggestions in this book are based on a latitude of 40° north, which will be explained further in Chapter 2.)

A couple of consistent facts help us understand how to design landscapes with the sun. The first is that, in the northern hemisphere, the sun at noon *always* shines from due south, and the sun never, at any time of day, shines from due north. The second important point to keep in mind is that, because the summer sun rises so far to the north of east and sets so far to the north of west, it takes a long time to get all the way across the sky, from one end of the day to the other. And in winter the reverse is true; because the sun's starting and ending points are in the southeast and southwest, relatively close together, the sun spends a shorter amount of time in the sky overhead.

Altitude

The second measurement that tells us the location of the sun is its altitude, its height above the horizon. Sunrise happens when the sun first peaks over the horizon. From that point on, the sun's altitude above the horizon increases until noon and then decreases until sunset. The shape of its arc across the sky depends entirely on the season: the summer sun sails high overhead; in spring and fall, its arc is a little lower than in summer; and in the depths of winter, the sun doesn't get very high into the sky at all.

As with direction, the sun's altitude also depends on the geographic location of the person looking at it or the landscape receiving its rays. Figure 1.3 depicts the sun's path — both direction and altitude — at 40° north latitude.

Fig. 1.2: The position of the sun in the sky at various time of the year depends on the location from which it's being seen. This diagram illustrates the sun's direction as it's experienced in temperate regions of the northern hemisphere.

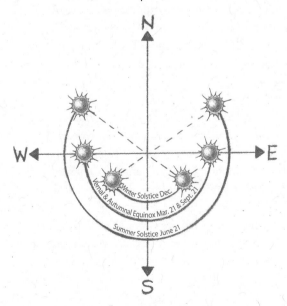

Why do we need to know about the sun's direction and altitude? The sun's position in the sky affects our lives in many ways. For the purposes of this book, the two significant issues are the amount of heat we receive from the sun and the shape of shadows cast by objects that block the sun.

Knowing where the sun will be in relation to our homes and landscapes enables us to plan the location of trees, fences, shade structures and even the buildings themselves to help keep us comfortable throughout the year. Chapters 2 and 5 present several ways to apply this information, in summer and winter, at specific times of day. If you live at geographic latitude that's very different from the 40° north used in this book, and you wish to figure out the sun's *exact* position for yourself, Appendix A demonstrates how.

It's especially important to understand the sun's path at times of the year when outdoor temperatures rise or fall beyond our human comfort range. With this knowledge, we can take steps to work with the sun to help warm our living spaces in winter and cool them in the summer.

Our Human Comfort

All warm-blooded mammals, including humans, need to generate their own heat to stay alive. This is accomplished through the metabolism of food (via digestion). Some of the heat that we produce is used to perform vital tasks — circulation, respiration, metabolism, etc. — that keep our body functioning. At times, though, our bodies generate more heat than they need, and we have to shed this excess heat if we are to feel comfortable.

All mammals have a range of body temperatures within which they can *survive* and a narrower range of body temperature for *optimal health*. For survival, human body temperature must stay between about 77°F and 104°F. However, the normal temperature of a healthy human is quite narrow, between about 98°F and 100°F. Luckily for us, we have an amazing ability to regulate our core temperature so it stays in the normal range even when surrounding temperatures reach as low as about 60°F or as high as 150°F.[1]

Most of us would not be able to live a normal life at those extremes of heat and cold. While

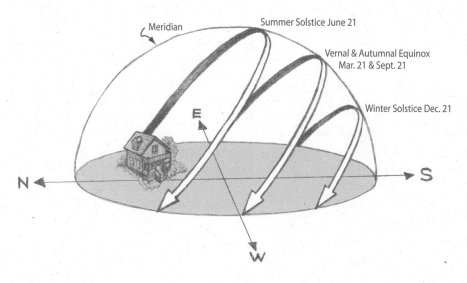

Meridian

Summer Solstice June 21

Vernal & Autumnal Equinox
Mar. 21 & Sept. 21

Winter Solstice Dec. 21

E

N

S

W

Fig. 1.3: *Throughout the year, the sun rises and sets in different locations, and it also passes higher and lower across the sky. During the summer solstice, the midday sun is higher than at any other time; the midday sun on the winter solstice is lower than at any other time of year.*

temperature preferences vary greatly from person to person and from season to season, as a general rule we are most comfortable, and most able to shed excess body heat, when the air around us is between about 68°F and 82°F. So, apart from adjusting our home's thermostat, how do we regulate our body temperature when the surrounding air is too hot or cold? The following discussion explains how.

How Heat Is Transferred

Heat energy always moves from a warmer entity to a cooler one. This happens because the molecules in warm objects are vibrating faster than the molecules in cooler objects, and nature constantly works to even out this sort

Fig. 1.4:
Because radiant energy is transferred by infrared waves, it occurs without any direct contact between two objects.

of difference, to establish a state of equilibrium. When a higher-energy molecule collides with a lower-energy molecule, a small amount of energy gets transferred from the warmer to the cooler one. The result is that warmer objects cool off a little bit (their molecules slow down) as they give their energy to colder things, whose bumped molecules then speed up and get warmer.

The following methods of heat transfer — radiation, conduction, convection and change of phase — apply to living beings, including animals and plants, and to inanimate objects such as our house, car and water pipes. Whenever heat is lost or gained, from any sort of being, object or substance, more than one of these methods may be operating at the same time.

Radiation is the transfer of heat through the emission of *infrared waves*, which can pass equally well through both outer space and our own atmosphere. These waves transfer heat by energizing the molecules of objects in their path. Radiant heat is what we feel when the sun shines on our skin, or when we stand near a fire or sit next to a warm radiator in our house. We ourselves also produce radiant heat, which others standing near us can feel.

Radiant heat is collected in our homes when the sun shines through our windows and transfers its energy to interior walls, floors, furniture, etc. This occurs regardless of outdoor temperature, and can be collected even in winter. (Of course, radiant heat can also be provided by a building's heating system, via radiators.) Any radiant heat that has been captured and stored in a building during the day will then continue to warm the room at night, through

What Is a Molecule?
Molecules are the small particles that make up all matter, and they themselves consist of even smaller particles called atoms. A water molecule contains two hydrogen atoms and one oxygen atom (H_2O). Oxygen is made of two oxygen atoms bonded together; adding a third oxygen atom creates a molecule of ozone. Molecules are held together by strong chemical/electrical bonds that may be broken under certain conditions.

re-radiation, unless it's allowed to escape back outside toward cooler temperatures.

Radiant heat can be blocked with opaque barriers like walls, shutters, awnings, drapes and the dense foliage of plants. Even translucent window shades and a moderate amount of foliage can reduce the amount of radiant heat entering a building. Radiant heat can also warm the exterior of a building, and if the walls are uninsulated, this heat will be transferred to the interior by conduction.

Conduction is the transfer of heat through *direct contact* between a warm object and a cooler one. This is the heat that hurts our bare feet if we walk on hot pavement in the summer, or burns our hand if we accidentally touch a hot wood stove. Conduction also happens to our bodies if we take a cold shower: heat leaves our body very quickly, and we shiver in response (shivering, which generates heat, is how our body tries to protect us from too much heat loss). The rate of heat flow by conduction increases with greater differences in temperature between two objects.

Through conduction, the warmer side of a wall (outside in summer, inside in winter) will transfer its heat to the colder side of the wall, resulting in a net cooling of the warmer surface. This is the reason that exterior walls are insulated: to slow or prevent the movement of heat from one side to the other. Shading or sun-lighting the exterior of a building can affect conductive heat transfer by reducing or increasing the temperature difference between the two surfaces.

Convection is the transfer of heat due to the *motion of fluid or air*. Both water and air become less dense as they're heated (i.e., their

Fig. 1.5: *Both this window shade and the foliage of a nearby tree will block the transfer of radiant heat through the window glass. The tree will also help keep the house's exterior walls cool.*

Fig. 1.6: *When objects of two different temperatures come into contact, the warmer object loses heat to the cooler object, causing it to warm up. Given enough time, and no further addition of energy, both objects will eventually be the same temperature.*

What Is Infrared Light?

Infrared waves are part of the electromagnetic spectrum, which is the range of all possible radiation frequencies. This spectrum extends from extreme long-wave radiation, such as radio waves, to extreme short-wave gamma radiation. It includes wavelengths that may be thousands of meters long and those that are smaller than an atom.

Infrared light lies in this spectrum between the waves of visible light and microwaves. Longer infrared wavelengths, called "far infrared," are about the size of a pinhead. They are thermal, which means they produce heat. Shorter wavelengths, called "near infrared" are too small to see and not hot at all; they are the ones used in a TV remote control.

molecules become more dispersed), which causes them to rise. The same process also happens in reverse: water and air sink as they cool. In both cases, the movement generates a convection current, sometimes called a draft, or wind. These currents may also be created by putting pressure on the fluid or vapor, as with forced hot-air heating systems.

Convection currents are complex and hard to predict, but for our purposes, the basic concept is this: moving air carries heat away from its source, whether that source is a living body, a stove burner, a hot-air radiator or a whole toasty house. Our focus is on how to shape landscapes to make the most of convection, so summer breezes can help cool a house (and ourselves, inside), and chilly winds steal less heat from our homes. A more complete discussion of wind patterns relative to landscape design is presented on pages 16-19 and below.

Change of phase is a natural process in which *energy is consumed or released*. The following is an extreme simplification of a process that's scientifically quite complex.

Water molecules exist naturally in three different forms — solid, liquid and vapor — that in science are called *phases*. They move back and forth between these phases depending on how much energy they contain. In their solid phase (ice), most of the molecules contain little energy and move around so little that they seem to be motionless. Water molecules in their liquid phase have a moderate amount of energy, with some of them moving slowly and others moving fast, but most of them somewhere in between, which keeps the water in its liquid form. In the vapor phase, water molecules move so fast that they escape the bonds of their liquid form and spread out into the surrounding air, creating humidity.

Heat is transferred anytime water changes phase. When substances move from a slower phase to a speedier one, energy is consumed. This happens both when liquid becomes vapor (evaporation) and when ice becomes liquid (melting). In the other direction, when liquid becomes solid or when gas becomes liquid, energy is released. The physics involved in

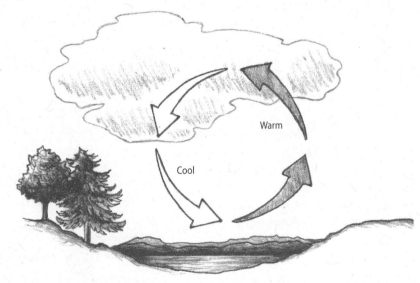

Fig. 1.7: *Convection currents, driven by the sun's uneven heating of the earth's surface, are the primary cause of large-scale weather patterns. They also explain the flow of cool and warm air inside a building.*

Warm

Cool

these reactions is complex, and it's all based on nature's unceasing effort to create equilibrium.

For our purposes, however, the relevant principle is this: evaporation consumes energy. When we perspire, the energy that's used to turn our sweat into vapor comes from both the surrounding air and our bodies themselves, which cools us. The same thing happens when plants' leaves transpire — energy is taken from the surrounding air and from the plant itself. If there's a large amount of foliage available and able to transpire, the result is a cooling not just of the plants themselves, but also of the surrounding air.

The Role of Humidity in Our Comfort

Humidity is the amount of water molecules (in their vapor phase) in the air. When the air is hot, our bodies try to cool us by perspiring. Yet, when air is humid, water molecules don't evaporate as easily as they do in dry air. As a result, some sweat stays on our skin, and we feel sticky. Our bodies' regulatory mechanism doesn't work well in humid air.

This is why we may feel comfortable in very high temperatures when the air is dry, while at the same temperatures when the air is very humid, we feel uncomfortable (hence the great appeal of air conditioning, which lowers temperature *and* humidity). On the flip side, when the air is too dry, our bodies may lose valuable moisture. Dry skin is uncomfortable, but loss of moisture from our mucus membranes may actually be harmful to health, reducing resistance to colds and other infections.

Just as we are most comfortable when air temperature is between 68°F and 82°F, we also have a comfort range for humidity. Moisture levels that feel best to us are around 40% to 60% relative humidity. When the air around us

Fig. 1.8: *Lush foliage pulls energy from the air as it transpires, further cooling this already shaded patio.*

United States Humidity Zones

In the course of a year, humidity levels rise and fall due to fluctuating temperatures and seasonal weather. Yet there are overall patterns that hold true from year to year. More than half of the continental United States is considered to be a humid zone, including a region that reaches from the east coast to just west of the Mississippi River, and a swath of northwestern states. The central plains, Rocky Mountains and southwestern states are considered dry-subhumid, semi-arid or arid. These categories are based on a ratio of annual precipitation and potential evapo-transpiration.[2]

is too damp or too dry, we can shape our landscapes to help keep humidity levels close to our comfort range. How? By taking advantage of and directing the wind.

THE WIND

Wind is a natural humidity reducer: it provides energy that speeds up evaporation (in both people and plants), and it increases the rate of air exchange between the inside and outside of a building. In humid regions of the US, we can design landscapes so the cooling breezes of summer will help cool us and our homes. In drier regions, and during winter when the air is dry, we can position landscape features so they block or deflect wind, to minimize the amount of valuable moisture that's swept away. Adding more plants in dry regions will also increase humidity, as they transpire moisture into the surrounding air. Chapters 3 and 6 provide more detail about all of these actions. Before getting into a discussion of how to use the wind, let's focus now on just how it's produced and what it does.

What Causes Wind?

Can you picture that familiar cartoon image of wind being blown by a big, puffy-cheeked face in a cloud? You know…storms come from an angry face and sweet breezes flow from a genial face? Actually, the reality is much less fun, though like a lot of nature, it's beautifully elegant.

Wind is produced by the uneven heating of the Earth's surface. This unevenness happens for two reasons. First, our planet contains many scattered areas of land and water, which absorb the sun's energy at different rates: land heats up (and cools off) faster than water; snow and ice reflect more sunlight than dark forests and oceans. And second, the angle at which the sun

What Is Air Pressure?

Air molecules actually have weight, though it's a very small weight, and together they press down on whatever is below them. A column of air that's one inch by one inch in size, that extends from sea level to the top of the atmosphere, exerts 14.7 pounds of pressure. At sea level, air pressure is greater than it is at high elevations, where there's less atmosphere above to press down.

When warmed air rises, it causes low pressure. Cooler, descending air causes high pressure. Different masses of air over land and water have different amounts of pressure depending on whether they're warming or cooling, hence rising or sinking. When one mass of air (a large volume of air with relatively uniform temperature and humidity) moves and encounters another mass with different properties, the transition zone between them is called a *front*.

A cold front happens when a cold air mass moves in and replaces a warm air mass. This causes warm air to rise quickly, often producing rain or thunderstorms (or snow in the winter), as temperatures and humidity of the rising air drop. A warm front happens when a warm air mass moves in to replace colder air, resulting in higher temperature and humidity. Both types of fronts usually generate or are associated with increased wind.[3]

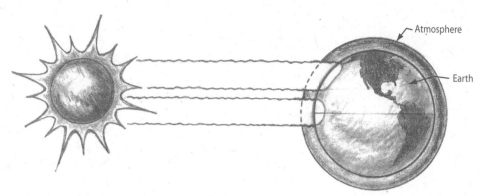

Fig. 1.9: *A lower angle of incidence produces less heat than a steeper angle, both because the sun's rays "land on" a larger area of the earth's surface and because they must penetrate a greater amount of the atmosphere.*

strikes the Earth's surface affects its warming power. The sun's rays strike the regions near the equator at a steeper angle than further north and south. Low-angle sunlight spreads out over a larger amount of the Earth's surface than high-angle rays, and it also has to pass through a longer stretch of atmosphere before reaching the ground. Both of these conditions reduce the warming power of low-angle sunlight.

The Earth's surface is warmed by the radiation from the sun. Air that touches the Earth is warmed by conduction, and warmed air rises (convection). When warm air rises, it creates an area of low pressure in the space left behind. This pulls in cooler air to take its place, and the result is a breeze and, on a larger scale, wind. The same process happens when cool air descends. Essentially, wind is just another form of solar energy, because the pressure and temperature changes that produce wind are caused by what? Yep, the sun.

Prevailing Winds

Ascending air currents rise up above the Earth's surface, and then at an altitude of about six miles, the spinning of the planet begins to exert

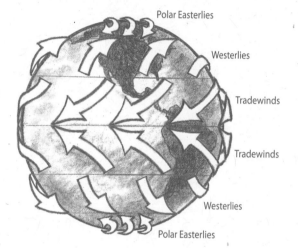

Polar Easterlies
Westerlies
Tradewinds
Tradewinds
Westerlies
Polar Easterlies

a force on them. The science of wind is so complex that people spend lifetimes learning it. But modern meteorologists and ancient mariners alike would agree: large air masses move in predictable patterns around the globe. These prevailing wind patterns take the form of trade winds, westerlies and easterlies.

The continental US is generally most affected by westerlies, winds blowing primarily from the west toward the east. Throughout the year, wind and weather in this country most often come from the west, usually from the

Fig. 1.10: *Global wind patterns are caused by warm air that rises near the equator and is then pulled sideways by the earth's rotation.*

southwest in summer and the northwest in winter. Many regions of the continent experience variations in this pattern, especially in the southeast where hurricanes bring eastern winds, and in desert regions where wind direction changes frequently. Much of Florida and the southern tip of Texas are so far south that they are most strongly affected by the trade winds that blow generally from northeast toward southwest.

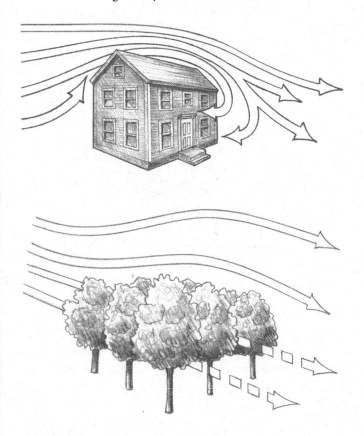

Fig. 1.11: *Solid barriers deflect more air than porous barriers, but they also generate turbulence. By contrast, barriers that let some amount of wind slip through may block less wind than solid barriers, but they will also create less turbulence and have a greater wind-calming effect on a larger area.*

Thermal Air Currents

Have you ever watched a hawk circling over a distant ridge without moving its wings? Have you yourself ever flown in a small aircraft over hills or mountains and felt the plane being tossed and bumped? On a summer evening, have you noticed wisps of fog drift across a low valley road? All of these conditions are due to local thermal air currents, which occur as air heats up on a sunny day and cools in cloudy weather or after sunset.

The thermal currents that affect our landscapes and homes are small-scale air movements magnified by mountains, hills and even gentle slopes. Warm air rising from the ground seems to intensify as it follows the rising terrain upward, and cool air flows downhill almost like a river. These currents happen in both summer and winter, and we can design our landscapes to take advantage of or blunt their cooling effects.

Sea Breezes and Land Breezes

In regions near a large body of water, daily breezes will usually be created by warm air rising from the land and pulling cooler air in from the adjacent water. These sea breezes may extend for several miles inland. At night, as the land cools more quickly than water, breezes flow toward the relatively warmer lake or ocean.

How Can Wind Be Deflected, Reduced or Intensified?

Wind flows like water. And, like water, it can't be completely eliminated or stopped, but instead must be cooperated with and accommodated. Wind can be pushed to one side by obstacles such as hillsides, buildings, solid fences and windbreaks. Or it may be divided into smaller streams by porous obstacles in its path such as plants, slatted walls or penetrable structures.

The Venturi Effect

When a river narrows to pass between canyon walls, its speed picks up; so too with air. This is the Venturi effect: when air or any fluid flows through a constricted space, its velocity must increase.

We can intensify the power of wind in summer by designing the landscape to make the most of this effect, by arranging things so they create funnels or leave small spaces for wind to squeeze through. In winter we can arrange windbreaks and other barriers to prevent this effect, so they don't accidentally increase wind speed.

REGIONAL CLIMATE

The continental United States contains thousands of small climate regions, each with its own unique combination of temperature, wind, humidity and weather patterns. Numerous

maps depict these regions in different ways, using different classifications and terms: humid continental, semi-arid, desert, alpine, tropical, marine, Mediterranean and many more, depending on the purpose of the map. For the sake of clarity, this book distills these many individual climate regions into four broad categories, each characterized by a general group of conditions. The US Department of Energy's Energy Efficiency and Renewable Energy website provides a map that illustrates these regions.[5]

What Is Turbulence?

Turbulence, a chaotic or unstable eddying motion, is a very complex phenomenon that's hard to calculate and even harder to predict with accuracy (hence the frequent errors in weather predictions). Basically, when wind flows over or around an obstacle, air pressure increases in front (windward) of the obstacle and then decreases behind it, causing a slight vacuum or low-pressure area on the downwind (leeward) side. This change in pressure pulls air downward from above or inward from the sides, creating wind eddies.

Wind Chill

Wind chill temperature is a term that indicates how cold people and animals feel when outside. Wind chill is based on the rate of heat loss from exposed skin caused by wind and cold. As wind speed increases, it draws heat from the body, driving down skin temperature and eventually the internal body temperature. Therefore, wind makes the air *feel* much colder.

The only effect wind chill has on inanimate objects, such as car radiators, water pipes and buildings, is to more quickly cool the object to the current air temperature. Objects will *not* cool below the actual air temperature. For more detailed information, visit the National Weather Service website.[4]

Temperate Region: the largest region in the continent, a broad band that stretches across the middle of the country. In this zone, summer and winter feel about the same length. Summers are hot and winters are cold, with winds blowing generally from west to east, and rain is moderate to abundant. In these regions, design has to address ways to minimize both summer heat and winter cold.

Cool-Cold Region: encompassing the northern Plains states and the top of New England. This zone experiences perhaps the largest range of temperature, from minus 30°F in winter to over 100°F in summer. Here, winters feel like the longest season, with short days and the sun low in the sky. Design for energy efficiency here focuses more on reducing winter cold (with trees, landforms and structures) than on cooling in summer.

Hot-Humid Region: the entire southeastern portion of the US, comprising about a sixth of the whole continent. This region is characterized by high summer temperatures, high rainfall, high humidity (that makes the heat feel worse) and comfortable winters. Because the air is often so moist, temperatures fluctuate only moderately between day and night. The goal of energy design in this zone is to maximize shade and air movement in summer. Many of these actions also apply to the coastal Northwest, where ocean winds produce a prevailing humidity through much of the year.

Hot-Arid Region: the southwestern sixth of the US, stretching from eastern Texas to the Pacific Ocean. Like the hot-humid zone, summers here are long and hot. But an entirely different climate pattern produces extremely dry air, intense fluctuations between day and night-time temperatures and winters that are cold and dry. Design in this region focuses on providing shade but also on deflecting dry winds and increasing humidity when possible.

Most of the recommendations in this book focus on the Temperate Region, for two reasons: this region occupies the majority of the continental US, so suggestions about dealing with these conditions will apply to the largest audience; and designing to minimize the extremes of both winter and summer is more complex than designing primarily for just one season (either winter or summer), as is the case with the other regions. Throughout the book, highlighted *Regional Notes* explain particular actions that apply to the Cool-Cold, Hot-Humid and Hot-Arid environments.

CHAPTER SUMMARY

This chapter has explained basic facts about the sun and wind. The sun's passage across the sky every day throughout the year, the ways in which heat gets transferred from warm objects to cooler ones, the source and pattern of wind movement. Understanding these physical realities allows us to manipulate them, so we end up feeling more comfortable inside our homes and buildings, thereby reducing our need for external sources of energy. Chapters 2 through Six discuss several ways to work with both the sun and wind, so we can shape our landscapes and arrange the major components of our grounds to help cool our homes in summer and warm them in winter.

CHAPTER 2

Shading the House

FOR THE PURPOSE OF SAVING ENERGY, one of the most effective things you can do is to directly shade your house in the summer. Shade lowers the amount of solar radiation that reaches your house's walls, windows and roof, potentially reducing their temperature by 20°F to 45°F.[1] When the air is hot outside, a cooler exterior means the interior will be cooler too (because less heat is conducted through the walls), and the people inside will be more comfortable.

Shading a house from the sun's heat is a simple idea, but achieving it is actually a bit complex, because the sun never stands still. All day long, with every passing hour, the sun shines from a new place in the sky, from a new direction and at a new height above the horizon. Along the way, its rays get stronger, then weaker, and objects cast shadows of different

Fig. 2.1:
Not so long ago, when houses were generally built without insulation, and air conditioning was unheard of, the customary way to cool a house was to plant shade trees. Many of us benefit from this wise investment even today.

lengths, in different directions across the landscape. Of course, to shade your house you could just plant trees everywhere around the house or build your home in the woods. For most of us, however, these choices are either impossible or undesirable. The solution needs to be more subtle.

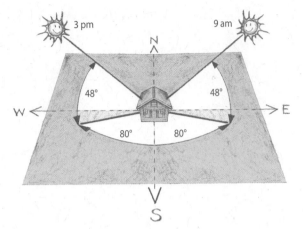

Fig. 2.2: *Hour by hour, the afternoon sun repeats the arc of the morning sun, sliding toward the western horizon in an exact mirror image of the way it rose from the east.*

Residential Consumption of Energy

Air conditioners consume more electricity than any other appliance. According to a 2001 report by the Department of Energy, central air conditioners accounted for 14.9 percent of total household energy consumption (and room air conditioners used another 1.9 percent). Other major uses, by percent, were: refrigerators (13.7), space heating (10.1), water heating (9.1) and clothes dryers (5.8). All appliances together consumed 42.2 percent of the total.[2]

This chapter's Actions provide guidance about shading buildings during late afternoon and early morning, mid-morning and mid-afternoon, and at midday. Because the sun is always moving, there's no single method for shielding a house from its heat. The job is made easier, though, by the fact that wherever you live, the sun's path is predictable, and has been thoroughly charted. This enables us to know precisely where the sun is in the sky, and to formulate general concepts about how to block or reduce the amount of sunlight that reaches a house at any time of day, throughout the year.

Also, even though the morning and afternoon sun shines from different locations in the sky, both its altitude above the horizon, and its compass angle relative to south, are the *same on either side of midday*. So for example, on June 21 in Philadelphia, the sun at both 9 AM and 3 PM is 48° above the horizon, and 80° away from south (toward the east in morning, west in afternoon). The same pattern holds true for 8 and 4, 10 and 2, and all other pairs of hours, relative to midday.

One final note: To get the most out of the advice in this and other chapters, it'll be useful for you to know the direction of north and

Daylight Savings Time

When daylight savings time (DST) is in effect, from March through October (in the US, Canada and Europe only), clocks are turned forward by one hour. This effectively moves an hour of daylight from the morning to the evening. Daylight savings time has nothing to do with the natural lengthening of day that happens in summer as the Earth circles the sun. The total amount of light in a day is the same as it would be in standard time, but during DST, the hour when the sun is highest in the sky is called one PM instead of noon.

Fig. 2.3

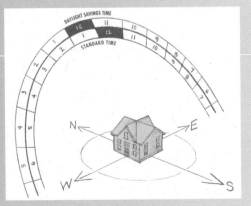

south on your property. If you don't know this, or if you know it only generally but want to be more specific, Appendix A explains how to locate true north. Be aware that, on most of the planet, compass needles point to *magnetic* north, not *true* north.

HOUSE-SHADING ACTIONS

The sun's position in the sky shifts slightly from one day to the next, all year long. For the sake of simplicity, the information in this section is based on an average of the sun's position *throughout the three months of summer*. See Chapter 1 for a more complete explanation of the sun's movement.

All of the shading solutions presented here are based on the sun's path as seen from a geographic location of 40° north latitude. If you live further north than this, the sun will be lower in the sky at all hours of the day, causing objects to cast longer shadows than discussed in this chapter. In locations farther south, the sun will be higher and shadows will be shorter. To find out exactly what's happening with the sun at your latitude, contact a landscape architect or solar energy evaluator, or follow the steps in Appendix A.

ACTION: Provide Shade During Early Morning and Late Afternoon

Four hours before and after midday, the summer sun shines down on the landscape from a direction that's *directly east and west*, and from an angle *about 35° above the horizon*. When this low-angle sunlight strikes a house, it penetrates easily through unshaded windows and warms the air far into the house's interior.

Locations at 40° North Latitude

40° north latitude passes through or near these major cities:

Philadelphia, PA	Denver, CO	Istanbul, Turkey
Columbus, OH	Sacramento, CA	Naples, Italy
Kansas City, MO	Beijing, China	Madrid, Spain

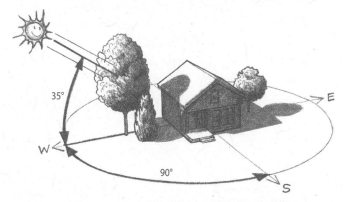

Fig. 2.4: *This diagram represents the sun's position when viewed at a geographic location of 40° north latitude. Here, four hours before and after noon the sun shines from due east and west (i.e. at a compass angle of 90°), and from an altitude of 35° above the earth's surface.*

The slanting sunlight of late afternoon also strikes the vertical walls of your house more strongly than it strikes the ground. So, although sunbathing at this time of day may be safe because the sun is low in the sky, your house's western walls and windows are receiving more direct sun than they do at midday. (See Angle of Incidence, page 17.) The heat of this stronger sunlight, when absorbed by uninsulated or dark-colored walls, will also be conducted to the interior.

By the time many people arrive home from work, after an unshaded house has been baking for hours, the late-day low-angle sun streaming directly into western windows may make the house feel unbearably hot. This could be the time when you're most likely to turn on your air conditioning. But if the western sun is blocked or filtered (and especially if the house has been shaded all day), your living space might be cool enough for you to skip the air conditioning. Shading your windows with outdoor plants can be more than twice as effective as curtains or window blinds at reducing heat absorption.

The following Design Tips show how and where to plant trees and large shrubs to help keep your house cool in late afternoon. If you wish to block early morning sun, which can be especially important in hot regions, these Design Tips apply equally well to the east side of the house.

Where Does Absorbed Heat Go?

Some of your house's absorbed heat may naturally be carried out open windows, on convection currents that draw heat from the lower to the upper floor. But it won't radiate back out to the warmer exterior, and much of it will stay trapped inside, raising interior temperatures by as much as 10°F to 20°F. This is the same way that greenhouses stay warm in cold weather: short-wave solar radiation (light) passes easily through glass, but long-wave thermal radiation (heat) doesn't pass back out.

Design Tip: Where to Place the Plants

First, determine your own west or east shading zone. (See Appendix A for how to find north and south in relation to your house and property.) Then, decide *generally* where within this zone you want to have trees or shrubs. This decision will depend on the location and shape of existing landscape features like patios, gardens and lawns, and on the shape of your house, the position of windows, the need for privacy, etc.

Because the sun at this time of day is approximately 35° above the horizon, *objects cast shadows that are about 1.5 times their height*. If you want the shadow to cover windows or the entire wall, you'll need to position the object or plant closer to the house than the shadow's length. There's no exact formula for positioning plants for shade, because their height, shape and density vary so much, but the following diagrams will help you to determine appropriate solutions for your landscape.

- A 20-foot tall tree will cast a shadow about 30 feet long. If the tree is growing 20 feet from the house, its 30-foot shadow will extend partway up the outer wall of a one-story house.

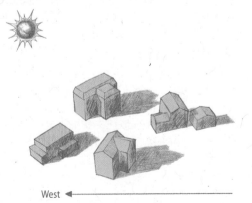
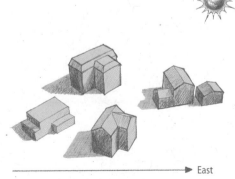

Fig. 2.5:
The configuration of your house and its orientation relative to the sun will determine the shape and location of your shady and sunny outdoor spaces.

West

East

- A 40-foot tree growing 20 feet from the house will shade the entire height of the wall.
- Two or three trees growing together can shade most of the width of the wall.
- A 10-foot tree or shrub will cast a shadow about 15 feet long. If this tree is planted 10 feet from the house, its shadow will reach only up to the lower third of the wall. To shade a higher portion of wall, plant small thin trees or large shrubs as close as 4 to 5 feet from the house; you may lightly prune a shrub's branch tips to keep them from touching a wall.

Remember to think also about the height of the lower branches; a high canopy will let sunlight pass below. When pruning a tree, be careful to preserve its lower branches if you want more afternoon shade, or remove them if you want more sun. Appendix B lists trees according to their mature height and general growth requirements.

If your landscape already contains trees and you'd like to know how tall they are, Appendix A explains a method for measuring their height. It also describes how to calculate the lengths of shadows cast by objects of various heights at different times of day throughout the year.

Design Tip: What Kind of Plants to Use

The best plants to use for shading the house are deciduous species, which lose their foliage in the fall, just when we begin to need as much heat and light as possible to reach our houses. These plants then regrow their foliage in spring, just as we start to appreciate coolness and shade again.

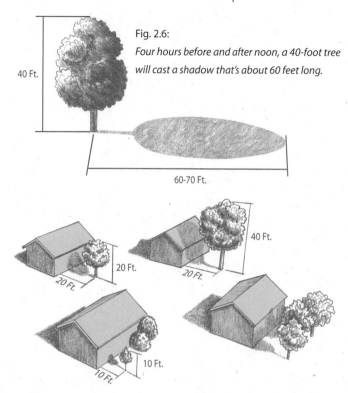

Fig. 2.6:

Four hours before and after noon, a 40-foot tree will cast a shadow that's about 60 feet long.

Fig. 2.7:

Trees cast shadows of predictable lengths, which allows us to position trees strategically, to create shade where it's wanted.

Evergreen plants are an acceptable second choice for shading the east and west sides of a house. Depending on their size and shape, evergreens here may cool the house in summer without blocking valuable winter sunlight, which never shines from due east or west during the winter in temperate regions. Evergreens in this location may, however, cast undesirable shadows in spring and fall, when the sun rises and sets true east and west, so deciduous trees are generally preferable in these locations.

Design Tip: Other Things to Keep in Mind

If the ground near your house slopes up or down a significant amount, this will affect the

Fig. 2.8: *Shadows lengthen on downhill slopes and shorten on uphill slopes.*

length of shadow cast by trees or shrubs on these slopes. A shadow that's cast *down* a slope will be longer than if the ground were flat. And conversely, shadows being cast *up* a slope will be shorter than they would be on flat ground.

By evening, any trees to the northwest of your house will throw very long shadows toward the house. Their shade at this time is welcome of course, especially for outdoor gathering spaces, but it won't have a strong effect on cooling the house.

ACTION: Shade the House During Mid-afternoon and Mid-morning

Two hours before and after the middle of day, the summer sun shines down on the landscape from a direction that's *about 60° to the east or west of south*, and from an angle *about 55° above the horizon*. Sunlight at this time feels hot, especially in the afternoon, when the air has already been warmed by almost eight hours of sun.

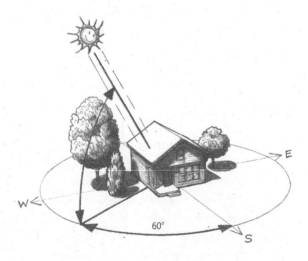

Fig. 2.9: *Two hours before and after noon, the sun shines at a compass angle about 60° to the east or west of south, and from an altitude of 55° above the earth's surface.*

The best way to cool the house — its walls, windows and even its roof — at this time is with tall trees planted near the house. Trees on the southwest will give the greatest benefit, helping to keep the house cool in the afternoon when the day's accumulated heat is still increasing. Southeastern shading is especially valuable in hot regions, to reduce heat gain as early as possible; in temperate regions, morning shade is generally less influential than afternoon shade.

Trees need not be taller than the house to be effective. Remember sunlight in the morning and afternoon doesn't fall from directly overhead. If a tree is near your house and only some of its canopy is taller than the house, the upper part of its shadow still will be cast onto the roof. The greatest benefit, however, will result from having the tree's crown entirely higher than the house, with some branch tips extending over the roof.

There are no exact formulas for where to position these trees, because all trees grow at different rates and have different widths, depending on their species and individual character, the type of soil and other conditions on the site. In addition, houses of different heights need trees of different heights to shade them. The following Design Tips will guide your process and help you make the best choices for your unique situation and preferences.

Design Tip: What Plants to Use

Only deciduous trees should be used for mid-morning and mid-afternoon shade. Never plant evergreens near the house on the southwest and southeast, because their persistent foliage will block desirable morning and afternoon sunlight in spring and fall, and they will dramatically cool the house in winter.

Trees Near Your House?

Some people are uncomfortable with the idea of any tree branches hanging over their roof. Witness the majestic maples, though, that arch over many old farmhouses; they show the commonly accepted wisdom of an earlier time. If trees are healthy and properly cared for, and weak-wooded trees are avoided, a lush dark canopy of foliage shading your house will cause no harm.

Fig. 2.10: *Shadows can be cast on the roof of a building by trees both big and small: it all depends on height and distance.*

Design Tip: Where to Place the Plants

First, determine where southeast and south-west shading zones are in relation to your house. Then decide generally where in those zones you'd like to place a large tree. As with the previous Action, this decision will depend on several factors, including what else is going on in your landscape (sitting areas, gardens, lawns, etc.), the shape of your house, the position of views, the need for privacy, etc.

The sun in mid-morning and mid-afternoon is about 55° above the horizon. The following diagrams will help determine how far away from the house to plant a large tree. Select a tree with an approximate mature height and with growth preferences that match the conditions where you intend to plant it (shady, moist, sunny, dry, etc). For ideas about suitable trees, see Appendix B.

Design Tip: Low Branches

Consider also the height of a tree's lower branches. A low canopy will shade more of the ground and possibly more of the house in summer. Yet in winter, a high canopy will let more desirable (low-angle) sunlight pass below. If the arrangement of your landscape requires that a shade tree be positioned closer to the south than to the west or east of your house, consider removing or thinning the tree's lower branches to let low winter sun reach the house walls and windows. See Chapter 5 for a more detailed discussion of winter sun.

As stated earlier, shading the house with trees is not an exact science. One fact that's definitely true, though, is that in the northern hemisphere, the sun never shines directly from the north. In the weeks before and after the summer solstice, the sun does rise slightly (about 30°) to the north of east, and similarly it sets slightly to the north of west, but unless trees on the north side of your house have a very wide canopy, they will not significantly shade your roof during late morning or early afternoon.

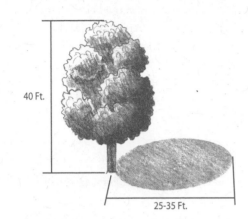

Fig. 2.11:
Two hours before and after noon, a 40-foot tall tree will cast a shadow about 30 feet long.

40 Ft.

25-35 Ft.

40 Ft.

20 Ft.

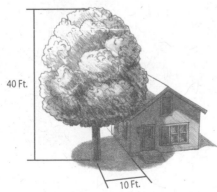

Fig. 2.12:
When located southeast or southwest of your house, 40-foot tree located 10 feet away from the building will offer significantly more cooling effect than the same tree 20 feet away.

40 Ft.

10 Ft.

Hot-Humid and Hot-Arid Regions

Keep in mind that an important aspect of summer cooling in hot and humid environments is maximizing air flow. For trees on the southeast and southwest sides of a building, use trees with high canopies, or prune up their lower branches, to let breezes reach the house. Also, minimize dense shrub masses near the building, because they will both block wind and generate their own (small amount of) humidity. Conversely, in Hot-Arid regions, it's a good idea to plant low shrubs near the house, to help raise humidity. Chapter 3 covers this subject in more detail.

Design Tip:
What Size Trees Should You Buy?

When you're deciding what size tree to buy, bear in mind that you can buy a very large tree (20 to 25 feet tall, or more) for a very large amount of money, and if it survives the transplant, this tree can give you instant shade. On the other hand, if you're not in a big hurry, planting one or several small trees is a safer and more economical choice. See Chapter 14 for guidance about planting trees.

A ten-foot tree will endure being moved much more easily than a large tree, and it'll establish itself more quickly, and start growing faster, than a larger specimen. A few small or medium-sized trees may cost the same as one large one, but in 10 to 15 years, they'll actually have caught up with the single large one, and then there will be several of them instead of just one. This is also a more energy-sensible choice, because smaller trees require less energy than large ones to grow in a nursery, dig up, transport and replant.

Fig. 2.13:
Because they're relatively small, these 1-inch caliper sweet birch trees will adjust quickly to their new location. (For more information about proper planting techniques, see Chapter 14.)

How Trees Grow.
Trees grow taller primarily by forming new twigs at the tips of existing branches, or at the tip of the central trunk, called the *leader*. These twigs thicken each year and eventually become branches. Some few tree species do produce twigs directly from their trunks as well as from the branch tips, but on all trees, the branches that are growing at a certain height will remain at that height, unless they die or are removed. A tree's branches do not get farther from the ground as the tree grows.

Transplanting Wild Trees
Taking trees from forests or natural areas is not a good idea. It deprives those environments of their essential components, removes food and habitat and disturbs an ecosystem's functioning. In addition, the roots of wild trees have usually crept far beyond the vicinity of the tree, zigzagging around various unseen obstacles below the ground. Digging a healthy root ball in the wild is nearly impossible and frequently results in the death of the tree.

Fig. 2.14:
*At a geographic
location of 40°
north latitude,
the noon sun
shines from due
south (as is true
everywhere in
the northern
hemisphere),
at an altitude
of about 75°
above the
earth's surface.*

A good solution may be to buy one medium-sized or large tree and a few small ones. This way, the trees together will make an attractive, naturalistic composition, and if for some reason the large tree doesn't thrive, the smaller ones will compensate.

Design Tip: Large Trees Already Near Your House?

Wonderful large trees may already be growing near your house, casting precious shade. If some

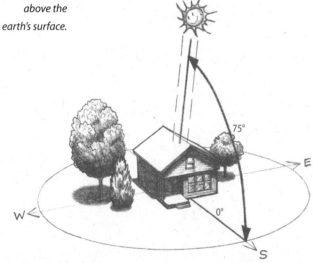

of them appear to be declining in health, try to preserve these valuable assets if possible. Much can be done to nourish and prolong the health of mature trees. It makes sense and will save you money in the long run to have a professional arborist assess, prune, cable or otherwise care for desirable shade trees.

If existing trees are growing directly south of your house in a place that blocks desirable winter sun, thin higher branches and consider removing lower branches to maximize solar gain. See Chapter 5 for a fuller discussion of working with the sun in winter.

Hot-Arid and Hot-Humid Regions

Since gaining warmth from winter sun is less important in these regions, planting large trees south of the house is less problematic and usually a good idea. If these trees will interfere with solar gain from a roof-mounted solar array, consider using a ground-mounted array (see Chapter 17).

ACTION: Shade South-facing Windows and Walls

In temperate regions of the northern hemisphere, the midday sun shines from *due south* at an angle *about 75° to 80° above the horizon.* The sun's rays at this time are nearly vertical, and stronger than at any other time of the day. Solar energy absorbed by a roof, especially if it's dark-colored and un-insulated, may be a source of tremendous heat gain in your house.

At this time of day, shadows cast by objects in the landscape are extremely short. The shadow of a 40-foot tree might be only 10 to 20 feet long. Any trees intended to shade the house on its south side must be either very close to the house, or very wide or very tall.

As an example, to shade a second-story roof, a 40-foot tree with a canopy that's 30 feet wide would need to be growing no more than 10 feet from the house. While many homes have large trees growing quite close to their walls, *planting* large trees within 10 feet of the house is not recommended, for these reasons:

- For stability, a large tree should be able to extend its roots out in all directions.

- Trees' bare branches in winter can deflect up to 50 percent of the sun's energy, unless their canopy is entirely above the roof and allow low-angle sun to reach the house.

- Strong tree roots can harm a weak foundation.

During midday, high-angle sunlight doesn't penetrate far into the house. However, the sun's heat at noon is intense, and minimizing any solar gain can make a big difference in the comfort of your south-facing rooms. The following Design Tips show how to reduce the amount of heat absorbed by your house in summer *without* planting trees directly south of the building.

Design Tip: Build an Overhang

An overhang or narrow porch along your south wall should extend out from the house just far enough to deflect the high midday sun. In temperate regions, a 3-to-6-feet deep structure will completely shade a south wall. Extending further than that may prevent desirable winter sunlight from entering your windows, so be careful not to build too deep a porch on your south wall.

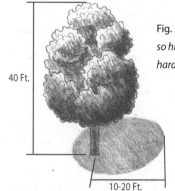

Fig. 2.15: *Because the sun at noon is so high in the sky, a 40-foot tree casts hardly any shadow at all at this time.*

40 Ft.

10-20 Ft.

Hot-Humid and Hot-Arid Regions

Hot-humid regions are hotter in summer and less cold in winter than temperate regions, so deflecting the midday sun is more important than preserving winter sunlight. Wide overhangs and deep porches that wrap three sides of the house are historic solutions. They help cool buildings' interiors, and their added shade in winter is largely irrelevant. In hot-arid regions, wide overhangs may also be helpful, but it's important to find the right balance between summer cooling and winter warmth.

One especially effective way to shelter a south wall is to build an arbor or pergola, either attached to or near the house. These structures can be designed to block the high-angle rays of midday in the summer while allowing the lower-angle midday sun of winter to pass through.

Design Tip: Use Vines

Deciduous vines trained to grow across the roof of an arbor or pergola will help cool the air below the structure. Vines growing up a trellis on a south wall will have the same effect. However, vines can be very quick, aggressive

One Beautiful Example

A small tree that is particularly effective in this situation is serviceberry (*Amelanchier*). This tree's several smooth-barked trunks ascend gracefully to a final height of 20 to 25 feet, along the way spreading gently out into slender side branches that hold sprays of tiny oval-shaped leaves. In early spring, the tree is engulfed in a white cloud of flowers, which in June become reddish-blue fruits that are relished by orioles, jays and catbirds. Winter sunlight penetrates easily through its thin branches.

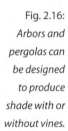

Fig. 2.16:
Arbors and pergolas can be designed to produce shade with or without vines.

growers needing lots of attention to keep them in check, so they're not for everyone and not appropriate in every situation.

Design Tip: Plant Shrubs or Small Trees Near a South-facing Wall

If building an overhang from the south wall of your house isn't possible or practical, another strategy is to position deciduous shrubs or small trees close to the wall. Especially in front of windows, the best plants to use are species with delicate branches and foliage that's concentrated just slightly above the window. Like a soft, living overhang, this arrangement will moderate the sun's energy without blocking light and views.

Design Tip: A Note About Evergreen Trees

In general, summer shade should not be provided by evergreen trees, because their foliage in the winter will prevent the sun's warmth from reaching the house. This is especially true

Kinds of Vines

Vines grow in one of three ways: by tendrils, by twining and by clinging. Tendrils are thin flexible stems that try to wrap themselves around anything they contact. Grape vines use tendrils to climb up trellises and arbors. These tendrils are weak and easily broken, so commercial grapevines often may need support, while grapevines in the wild may be very easy to extricate from the trees where they're growing.

In contrast, twining vines wind their entire stems around any available object or support. If a twining vine such as bittersweet, wisteria or honeysuckle wraps itself around another plant, that plant will eventually be strangled by the vine's encircling embrace, or it may be pulled down by the weight of the vine's mass. Most of the vines that are considered invasive are twining vines.

Clinging vines climb by attaching little feet, called holdfasts, to the surfaces they touch. These vines, including Virginia creeper and Boston ivy, cling easily to rough surfaces.

The best vines to use for directly shading a south wall or overhead structure are vines that cling by tendrils, followed by twining vines. Clinging vines should not be grown on or near a wood-sided house. Vines are notorious for vigorous growth, so whatever type of vine you use, be prepared to keep a close eye on its spread.

on the south side of your house. A good rule of thumb for evergreen trees south of the house: they should be placed a distance of at least twice their mature height away from the house.

The one exception to this rule is very tall evergreen trees near the house. If their canopies are high overhead and they have no lower branches or foliage, as is often the case with white pines, these trees will cast desirable midday shade in summer (when the sun is high overhead) without blocking warmth in winter (when the midday sun is only 30° above the horizon). The problem with this situation is that these trees would have to be planted very near the house to have this effect, and growing young pines against a house is undesirable. However, if you have tall old pines near your

Fig. 2.18: *While keeping tall pines near a house might not be for everyone, it does create overhead shade in summer, color near the house in winter, and a dramatically beautiful appearance all year long.*

house, you may wish to keep them for this purpose. And if you plan to build a house on property that contains high-canopy pines, you may wish to build near them.

On the southeast and southwest sides of the house, when the afternoon winter sun is even lower than at midday, evergreen trees should be farther away than twice their height. It's safe to plant evergreens directly west/northwest and east/northeast of your house, because the winter sun never shines from that direction. See Chapter 5 for more about solar gain in winter.

CHAPTER SUMMARY

This chapter presents several ways to help cool a house in the summer, by shading roofs, walls and windows. The summer sun rises early and

sets late and, because its position in the sky shifts constantly from morning to afternoon, different strategies work best at different times of the day.

In early morning and late afternoon, trees cast long shadows and may have a cooling effect even when planted fairly far from the east or west side of a building. By mid-morning and mid-afternoon, shadows are shorter; at this time of day, trees need to be closer to the house, on the southeast or southwest, to be effective. The high noon sun, shining from due south, creates short shadows. At midday, the best cooling is provided by small trees (or large shrubs) very near a house's south wall, overhangs or porches, and large trees with branches that extend over the roof.

This chapter also offers specific advice about what kinds of plants to use, how to determine their best location relative to a house, and particular situations to avoid or manage with care.

Although shading a building is one of the best ways to cool it, this may not be possible in many regions, or even in many small landscapes. Fortunately, there are several other methods we can use to reduce summer heat in our living spaces: by cooling the air and the ground near our homes. These strategies are presented in Chapters 3 and 4.

Shading an Air Conditioner

A good way to save extra energy in the summer involves shading air conditioning (AC) units that are placed in your windows, or whole-house AC units with freestanding heat exchangers outside the building. Shading these appliances, even when located to the north, can increase their efficiency by 10 percent.[3] Use small trees rather than shrubs to create this shade, and be careful not to plant dense shrubs too near AC units, as this might interfere with their proper functioning.

CHAPTER 3

Cooling the Air Around the House

THIS CHAPTER PRESENTS the following Actions:

+ Add trees and many other plants to your landscape.
+ Capture cooling breezes.

Shading the house as described in the preceding chapter will significantly reduce your indoor air temperatures and decrease the amount of time you'll need to run fans and air conditioners. But did you know that the same trees and shrubs that cool your house by shading it will *also* cool the air around your house, just by growing there? This marvelous natural air conditioning happens through a process called transpiration.

Here's how it works. Plants grow by using sunlight to convert carbon dioxide and water

Fig. 3.1: *Trees near a house will shade the building and, almost equally important, they'll cool the air above, below and all around them.*

into oxygen and carbohydrates. They then use these carbohydrates to produce cellulose and other building materials, which in turn give each plant its form. This is photosynthesis. Much of this miraculous process takes place in a plant's leaves.

In the leaves is also where transpiration happens. Small pores on a leaf's surface (stomata) open during daylight hours to take in carbon dioxide from the surrounding air and to release oxygen. When the stomata are open, excess moisture that's not needed for photosynthesis diffuses out, or transpires, through these openings into the drier air.

A single mature tree with a 30-foot crown transpires approximately 40 gallons of water per day. This can reduce nearby air temperatures by 2°F to 9°F.[1]

How does transpiration cool the air? This phenomenon seems almost as miraculous as the process of photosynthesis, but its chemistry is simple. Evaporation is a process that requires energy, because it involves the breaking of chemical bonds. Water molecules *change phase* from a liquid state to a gaseous state (evaporate) because they've become so energized (moving faster and faster) that they escape water's cohesive forces. The energy that powers this process comes both from the plant itself and from the heat energy in the surrounding air (technical term: *the latent heat of vaporization*). Heat is actually taken out of the air to make transpiration happen, and the result is a natural cooling of the air.

This is why the air around trees, even above them, is cooler than elsewhere. While the air below trees is cooled by shading, the air above and around them is cooled even more, simply by the evaporation of moisture. These effects are difficult to quantify, but researchers using computer simulations estimate that 65 to 90 percent of a tree's cooling energy reductions are caused by transpiration.[2]

Perspiration and Transpiration

Mammals perspire to maintain a healthy body temperature. When we're hot, we sweat. Water forms on our skin, and our bodies use their own heat to evaporate (or change the phase of) the water. This takes heat away from the body, helping us feel cooler. If we don't drink water to replace what's been lost through sweating, we dehydrate, lose energy, and eventually, if we don't take in water, we will die. Plants transpire for the same reason — to cool the plant and preserve its vitality — and with the same effect.

During transpiration, moisture is pulled up from the roots (where water and dissolved minerals have been absorbed through osmosis), as the plant works to restore hydrostatic pressure in its leaves. We've all seen what happens when water lost through transpiration can't be replaced: leaves wilt, photosynthesis stops, and eventually, if moisture doesn't become available, the plant will die. This is a good reason to keep the ground as moist as possible by covering it with low vegetation and mulch, as described in Chapter 14.

ACTION: Add Trees and Many Other Plants to Your Landscape

Cooling the air with transpiration is simple, and it can be accomplished in many ways. It can be done on a large scale or just a little bit, at a great or small expense. It can be done anywhere, in any part of any state. The way to cool the air is simply to have as many large, healthy transpiring plants as possible in your landscape.

Transpiration happens in all kinds of plants; it's just a part of their living. Your vegetable garden and flowering shrubs transpire, and so do the potted plants on your patio. Even your lawn transpires. Air temperatures above lawn may be 10° to 14°F cooler than temperatures above bare earth.[3] But because of their tremendous amount of leaf surface, trees transpire and cool the air more than any other kind of vegetation in a home landscape.

Hot-Arid and Hot-Humid Regions

Plants' ability to transpire depends on water being available in the soil. In arid regions, some trees can tap deep sources of moisture, but it's important to mulch the ground around valuable shade trees, to keep the soil as moist as possible. (See Chapter 9 for advice about watering wisely.) In humid regions, using strategies to cool the air through transpiration are offset by a resulting increase in humidity, which decreases comfort. A better solution involves maximizing air movement, discussed later in this chapter.

DESIGN TIP: PLANT TREES

For maximum cooling, plant large trees near the house. To help cool the entire landscape,

Transpiration and Humidity

The moisture that vegetation pulls from the ground and releases into the air can raise humidity levels immediately nearby. This effect might be unwelcome in humid regions and during muggy summer days anywhere, or it may be extremely welcome in arid environments.

plant trees and shrubs on as much of your property as is practical. It's especially good to position these plants as upwind as possible. Follow the Design Tips in Chapter 2 for advice about where to position trees for proper shading of the house. See Chapter 8 for a discussion of reducing the size of your lawn and Chapter 14 for guidance about planting trees and shrubs.

If you want to make an even larger impact, encourage your neighbors to plant trees, and work with your town to protect natural areas and plant trees in public spaces, around parking lots, along roadsides, etc.

Fig. 3.2: *Although no trees directly shade this house, the site's abundant vegetation (no lawn here!) contributes to an overall cooling effect through transpiration.*

Fig. 3.3: *In shade for most of the day in summer, these air conditioning condensers operate at maximum efficiency until late afternoon, when they stand in direct sun for several hours; planting a small tree or large shrub to shade these units would improve their efficiency.*

Design Tip: Air Conditioners

If possible, avoid placing air conditioning units in south and west windows. Air conditioners warm the air with the heat of their motors and with the hot exhaust that is simply a product of their functioning. After all, the hot air in your house has to go *somewhere*.

ACTION: Capture Breezes

Winds and breezes can increase our summer comfort significantly. In temperate regions, they cool both by increasing evaporation and by lowering humidity. In hot dry regions, they may decrease our comfort by carrying away too much moisture, but for most of the country, it's a good idea to arrange our landscapes so they capture or increase the cooling benefits of breezes.

Air flows in complex and often unpredictable patterns. Like water in a rocky stream,

Albedo, Climate Change and Trees

Albedo is the fraction of solar radiation reflected back into the atmosphere from the Earth's surface (from the Latin *albus* for "white"). Deep ocean and dense forest reflect little solar radiation and have low albedos. Light surfaces such as fresh snow and polar ice reflect a lot of radiation and have high albedos. The overall albedo for the Earth, with its variable cloud cover, is about 30 percent.

A surface's albedo depends on many factors, including latitude, season and temperature. Typical albedos for some of the Earth's various surface covers are: asphalt pavement (2%), oceans (3%), northern cities (7%), conifer forest in summer (8%), conifer forest in winter (13%), deciduous forest in summer (15%), grassy field (20%), deciduous forest in winter (21%), desert (25%) and fresh snow (90%).[4]

The effects of albedo on global warming are complex. In general, though, dark surfaces absorb radiation and tend to warm the atmosphere, while lighter surfaces bounce energy back into space, helping to cool the atmosphere. So, does it make sense to add more trees to our landscapes if their low albedo might increase global warming? The answer is yes, and here are three reasons why.

First, trees evaporate moisture from the soil into the air. So, even though the albedo of forests is similar to asphalt, transpiration in forested regions helps lower air temperatures. Plus, ☛

fast-moving air can be diverted by large barriers, or deflected and stirred into turbulence by small objects in its path. Unlike water, though, air movement can't be dammed or completely stopped; its force is too immense. Wind and breezes must keep going, somewhere, somehow.

Global winds like the trade winds, and unexpected winds such as tornadoes and hurricanes, can't realistically be managed by landscape design. (See Chapter 1 for a more complete explanation of winds.) Wherever you live across the globe, your region experiences prevailing wind patterns that you can understand and work with. In the temperate regions of the US, for example, summer breezes generally arrive from the southwest, while winter winds approach from the colder northwest. You may already know what direction the summer wind blows from in your region. If

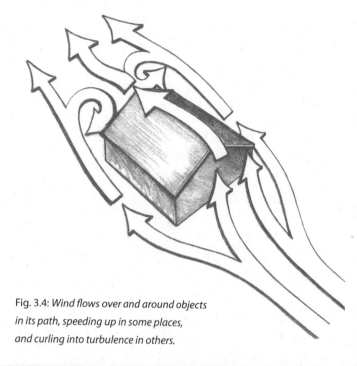

Fig. 3.4: *Wind flows over and around objects in its path, speeding up in some places, and curling into turbulence in others.*

transpired moisture often forms clouds. While the effect of clouds on climate change is extremely complicated, the prevailing conclusion of scientists at this time is that clouds at all levels in the sky appear to reflect and radiate away from the Earth more energy than they retain. The result is a slight net cooling of the Earth's climate.

A second factor to consider is what the new tree cover will replace in your residential landscape. Trees have a lower albedo than lawn, but a higher albedo than pavement and buildings. Some amount of lawn may be covered (or replaced) by trees and shrubs, but the winter albedo of deciduous trees is essentially the same as grass, and in summer the difference between the albedo of lawn and tree is so slight that any negative effect will be small.

Finally, the extent of land potentially covered by new trees planted in temperate landscapes is tiny compared to the extent of open ocean that covers our entire planet. Trees properly placed in your landscape, which will cool the house in summer and help warm it in winter, will also reduce your participation in the burning of fossil fuels for power. The resulting reduction in greenhouse gas emissions may slow the melting of polar ice and minimize the expansion of low-albedo, atmosphere-warming oceans.

In conclusion, the possibility that more trees on the Earth might cause a slight rise in global temperature is far outweighed by the substantial benefits resulting from shade and transpiration. ∎

not, it's easy to discover simply by paying attention for a few weeks, posting a temporary flag in the yard or watching a weather vane. Whatever their prevailing direction, you can take simple actions to help these fairly predictable winds cool your house in summer.

Design Tip: Direct Prevailing Breezes Toward the House

After determining where summer breezes generally come from in your own landscape, place dense groups of plants in rows that are *parallel*

to that direction. Solid fences too, if you need them for privacy or enclosure of a space, should be oriented parallel to the wind whenever possible. Avoid placing any large obstacle that will block or deflect the arriving breezes away from the house or a space for outdoor use.

Hot-Arid Regions

In regions where the wind brings more heat and dryness than relief, the recommendations in this chapter may not apply. Consider instead following the guidelines in Chapter 6 for deflecting the wind in winter.

When air or any fluid flows through a constricted space, its velocity speeds up. To take advantage of this Venturi effect, arrange plants, fences and even outbuildings so that they are parallel to the breeze and angled slightly inward toward the house, creating a sort of a funnel. Keep in mind that landforms, too, can channel

Observations from a Tropical Tourist

When visiting tropical homes, Americans and Europeans usually sit where the furniture arrangement directs them to sit. By contrast, residents and local visitors seem to automatically gravitate to the coolest and breeziest parts of a house, whether or not there's furniture in those places to sit on.

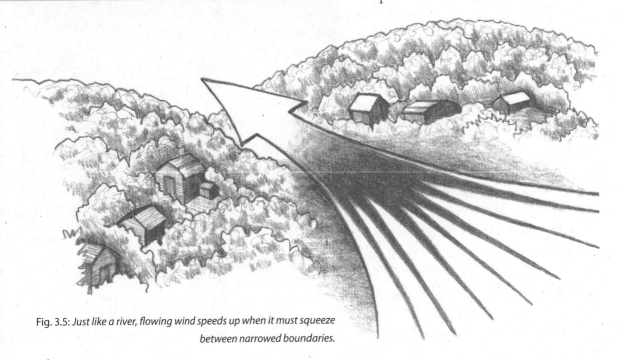

Fig. 3.5: *Just like a river, flowing wind speeds up when it must squeeze between narrowed boundaries.*

air flow. As the air passes through the smaller and smaller space between these objects, it speeds up, increasing its cooling power.

Creating a funnel of plants or other structures may be difficult to accomplish in small landscapes, but it can have a significant effect in large and open properties. A related effect that's easy to do even on small properties is to trim up the lower branches of any trees that stand between the breeze and the house. The wind's velocity will increase as it squeezes between the ground and the dense foliage above.

Finally, if you wish to build a porch or outdoor gathering place, consider placing it on the breezy side of the house, so it will be a haven of cool comfort when the house is too warm. Take care not to enclose this space with any fence, wall or dense vegetation that will block the wind.

Design Tip: Make the Most of Thermal Air Currents

Chapter 1 discusses breezes that are created when the sun heats the air, creating rising air currents during the daytime (especially noticeable in summer!). Similarly, warm air rising up and flowing down slopes can generate air currents and miniature winds that you may actually be able to feel when you're in their path. These thermal air movements are minor compared to wind and prevailing breezes, but even a small amount of landform near your site can enhance air currents and make a difference in your comfort.

Therefore, celebrate and accentuate any slopes on your landscape instead of leveling or removing them. If possible, position outdoor

Fig. 3.6: *The window between the ground and this tree's lower branches provides both a delightful view and a funnel to accelerate summer breezes.*

Fig. 3.7: *This strategically positioned dining patio is cooled by thermal breezes moving up and down the steep lakeside slope.*

gathering places midway on a slope, so you'll feel rising breezes in the morning and sinking breezes in the evening. If your yard stands in the path of thermal air currents, avoid building solid structures that will block their flow. Consider arranging solid or semi-solid elements in the landscape directing cool evening currents toward the house, in the same way that you might funnel prevailing breezes.

CHAPTER SUMMARY

This chapter shows how we can cool our homes by working with two of nature's most basic processes — transpiration and wind — both of which naturally cool the air.

Simply in being alive, plants cool the air by transpiring moisture through their foliage. The energy that fuels this process comes in part from the heat of the surrounding air, resulting in lower air temperatures. To make the most

of this free cooling effect, we need only to keep our landscapes full of vegetation: the more and the larger the better (within the limits of regional rainfall and soil conditions).

The second strategy for cooling the air is to take advantage of wind and breezes. This can be accomplished by understanding the direction of prevailing winds and placing objects in the landscape to funnel those winds toward our living spaces. We can also work with the natural rising and falling air of thermal currents, by placing buildings, windows and outdoor spaces to receive those currents, and by taking care not to put plants or other landscape features in places that will block them.

To get the greatest benefit from the air-cooling actions explained in this chapter, we should also take steps to keep the ground near our homes as cool as possible. Read on to find out how!

CHAPTER 4

Cooling the Ground Near the House

THERE ARE TWO REASONS to keep the ground surface in your landscape as cool as possible. First, by preventing the absorption of daytime heat, you'll reduce the amount of heat that the ground gives back to the air and buildings at night (through convection and conduction). This will help your house cool off more quickly. Second, many of the actions you take to cool the ground will also keep the ground moist, which will keep your plants healthy so they can continue to shade the house and cool the air, as previously described in Chapters 2 and 3.

To minimize the absorption of the sun's energy, this chapter explains the following Actions:

+ Shade the ground with living plants.
+ Cover bare ground with non-living mulch.

Fig. 4.1: *Mulch and plants (in this case, white snakeroot and ferns) keep the ground cool and moist, helping plants grow, producing yet more shade and cooling the air.*

- Minimize lawn area.
- Minimize pavement, especially near the house.
- Use "cool" pavement when feasible.

Dense Ground Cover

Quite often, plants sold as ground cover are quite aggressive spreaders, hence their usefulness for this purpose. Keep in mind, though, that the fastest-spreading plants often have extremely dense root systems that hungrily suck moisture and nutrients out of the soil, depriving other plants of sustenance. The widespread gardening convention of entirely carpeting the ground with a green mantle may actually harm nearby trees, shrubs, wildflowers and ferns. Instead of planting the most common ground covers that send their roots out in every direction, consider using a variety of plants that can share the soil: some with large leaves, others that grow in wide clumps, etc.

The Sun's Angle of Incidence

The intensity of solar radiation is determined by the angle at which the sun's rays strike the Earth's surface, called the sun's *angle of incidence*. If the sun is positioned directly overhead, at 90° above the horizon, the incoming rays strike the surface of the Earth at right angles. If the sun is 45° above the horizon, they touch the Earth's surface at that angle, causing the rays to be spread out and received over a larger surface area than the area struck by sunlight at a 90° angle. This spreading out reduces the intensity of the radiation of lower-angle sunlight by as much as 30 percent as compared to overhead sunlight.[1] (See figure 1.9)

ACTION: Shade the Ground with Living Plants

As previously mentioned, shading your house with plants can lower its surface temperature substantially. Shading the ground, however, can have an even greater cooling effect, because in summer the Earth's surface is also being cooled from below.

The Earth's warmth several feet below the surface remains at a fairly steady temperature throughout the day. More significantly, it also stays at this temperature throughout the year. This stability is the result of the insulating effect of the ground itself, which is both slow to warm up and slow to cool down. In summer the ground just a few feet below the surface may often be 30° to 35°F cooler than the air. Therefore, any efforts to keep the sun from heating the soil from above will be aided by this natural internal coolness below.

The most important place to cool the ground is the south side of your house. In landscapes across North America, midday sunlight shines from high in the southern sky. Because the noon sun is so high in the sky, its radiation at that time is more concentrated than in the morning or afternoon.

Design Tip: What Plants to Use

All kinds of plants have the potential to help shade the ground. There's no single best way to accomplish this action, and your decision about what to do will depend on several factors, including how much space you have, the shape of your property in relation to the house, the proximity of other buildings, regional rainfall amounts and your personal taste.

Also, different kinds of shade have different benefits and disadvantages. Trees cast a large amount of shade on the ground, but their shadows shift across the landscape with the passage of the sun, and some trees' canopy may be too high up to significantly cool the ground where you want. The shade cast by shrubs and low plants is close to the ground, but you need a lot of small plants to shade as much ground as a single large tree. The best solution for your whole property will probably include a mixture of plant types — trees, shrubs, ferns, perennials, even mosses.

As explained earlier, the best place for large trees near the house is to the southwest and southeast of the building. When the summer sun is shining from these directions, it is moderately high in the sky. At this high angle of incidence, the sun's rays are easily absorbed by the earth (or by an upturned leaf, or a tanning teenager). So any shading from these directions, to help deflect sunlight away from the ground, will have a great benefit.

The best trees to plant for the purpose of cooling the ground are species with dense foliage and wide-spreading canopies, such as maple, oak, hickory or hackberry. To get the greatest ground-cooling benefit, keep trees' branches as low to the ground as possible, without sacrificing other landscape values such as views, privacy and health.

When planting trees to shade the ground, keep in mind the importance of shading any pavement near your house. Dark-colored pavement absorbs more heat than any other kind of ground surface. Placing trees so their canopies arch over your driveway or stone patio will be especially beneficial.

Fig. 4.2:
Here, mountain laurel and mountain andromeda combine with hemlock and birch trees and a carpet of haircap moss, to shade every bit of ground.

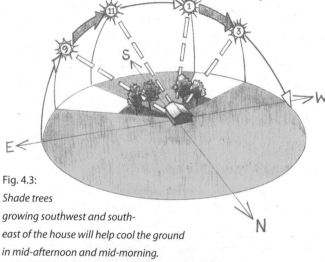

Fig. 4.3:
Shade trees growing southwest and southeast of the house will help cool the ground in mid-afternoon and mid-morning.

Fig. 4.4:
Shaded pavement can be 10-20° cooler than unshaded pavement.

Smaller trees, shrubs and short plants may simply be arranged as you like, in accord with your landscape needs. Even creeping vines and mosses will help. The main idea is to choose and arrange plants so they cover as much of the ground as possible.

ACTION:
Cover Bare Ground with Mulch

To augment the cooling effect of living plants, spread a layer of non-living material over any bare ground in your landscape. This mulch will cool the landscape by preventing sunlight from reaching the ground. It will also absorb and hold rain against the surface of the soil.

Nature produces vast amounts of mulch, simply through the shedding of leaves, needles, twigs, flower blossoms, fruit and other parts of plants that fall away in the course of their living and dying. A forest floor is a great example of nature's own mulching: a rich carpet of fluffy debris covers the entire ground surface, gradually decaying and all the while holding its

Fig. 4.5:
A thick patch of
hay-scented ferns
beneath this
grove of trees
helps hold fallen
leaves in place.
(Note: this fern
can be a very
aggressive
spreader and is
not recommended
in perennial
gardens.)

spongeful of cool moisture against the earth. See Chapter 14 for detailed advice about different kinds of mulch, and when and how to use them.

Hot-Arid Regions

As noted in Chapter 3, mulch is especially important in places that receive little rainfall, both to cool the ground and to preserve precious moisture that supports trees needed to shade the house.

ACTION:
Minimize the Extent of Mown Lawn

Mown grass has a vast, interwoven, thirsty root system that sucks moisture from the soil. Unless you live in a region with abundant rainfall, or you irrigate regularly, or your loam is deep and rich, the ground that supports your lawn will dry out and heat up on sunny days. Yes, it may cool down at night, but because lawn soil is generally too shallow to hold much moisture, the daytime sun will warm the ground very quickly. This will stress the lawn grass, diminish its health and may lead to a decline in coverage, starting a cycle of further desiccation and decline.

Hot-Arid Regions

In regions where rainfall is scarce, a lush lawn may cool the ground and the air more than bare soil, but using precious potable water to create large amounts of lawn does more harm than good. It lowers the water table, diminishes the amount of water available for other more important purposes and can lead to pollution and salinization of the water supply.

Also, because lawn grass is perpetually kept short, sunlight can easily penetrate to the soil below. As a result, while the ground below a lawn is generally cooler than bare earth or pavement, it's hotter there than under any other kind of living surface.

There are two solutions to this problem. The first is to build up the depth and richness of your lawn soil, by pursuing healthy lawn care practices; steps for accomplishing this goal are presented in more detail in Chapter 14. And the second is to have just the amount of lawn area that you need, so that as much of your landscape as possible can be kept cool with trees, shrubs, meadow and mulched gardens.

Fig. 4.6: *A small patch of front lawn provides a bit of space for gathering and respects societal expectations, but rich gardens occupy most of the yard.*

Design Tip: Just Enough Lawn

To determine just what is the right amount of lawn for you, start by thinking clearly about what *jobs* you want and need your lawn to do for you. Do you use your lawn as a place for kids to run around, play ball, just romp and be free? Do you entertain on your lawn, or grill, play croquet, sunbathe? Is your lawn a place for pets to cavort, or perhaps to relieve themselves? Do you want your lawn to make a particular sort of impression on neighbors, friends or family members?

No one can say what the right amount of lawn will be for you. But if you wish to help cool the ground by keeping your lawn area to a minimum, an important question to consider is whether some of the jobs you ask of your lawn could just as easily (or perhaps even more easily) be accomplished in other places, in other ways. Chapter 8 provides several suggestions for alternatives to lawn.

Organic Lawn

The subject of organic lawn care is large and still growing. Its basic premise, however, is that the most vigorous and self-sustaining lawns come from healthy soil. What does this mean? Healthy soil is rich and crumbly, and it contains a wide array of nutrients and micro-nutrients, along with millions of tiny micro-organisms that help make those nutrients available to lawn grass.

In organic lawn care, instead of feeding your lawn from above with fertilizer from a bag, which contains just the barest minimum of nutrients needed for grass to survive, the best way to keep your lawn (and your pets and kids) healthy is to feed the grass from below, by nourishing the soil. The resulting deep and rich soil holds moisture better than the soil of conventionally grown or chemically fed lawns, so it stays cooler and keeps the grass growing steadily, even through hot and dry periods.

This flowering dogwood tree, growing just 20 feet from the house, helps enclose an intimate patio while also shading a hot corner.

ACTION: Minimize Hard Surfaces, Especially Near the House

If you've ever blistered your feet on a hot road, you know, without any further research or data, that pavement absorbs the sun's energy. Exactly how much solar energy is absorbed, and how hot a paved surface may become, depends on the mass, density and color of the paving material and the temperature, season and time of day. In general though, paved surfaces exposed to midday sun will be hotter than others, because at that time of day the sun's nearly vertical rays are strongest. Longer hours of exposure will also lead to greater heat absorption, and more heat emitted at night.

Studies in Arizona show that on a 100°F day, the surface temperature of pavement may reach 150°F during peak sunlight conditions.[2]

Design Tip: Patio/Terrace

Avoid building a large paved sitting area on the south side of your house. If your house is designed so that a door on the south wall is the only reasonable access to the outside, consider building just a small porch, deck or landing at that door, then placing the larger gathering space off to one side. A patio on the southeast or southwest may be shaded by the same trees that you're using to shade your house, whereas planting trees directly south of your house, to shade a hot space, will block desirable solar gain in winter (see Chapter 3).

If you must place your outdoor space on the south, consider building it with light-colored materials that will reflect rather than absorb heat. Gray or tan stone is cooler than dark blue or black, fine pebbles or pea-stone are cooler than a flat-tone surface. Avoid white materials, if possible, to prevent glare.

Minimize the amount of driveway and parking pavement near the house, especially on the south and west sides. (This may not be possible on small lots where the driveway only fits in one place.) If you need a lot of space for parking extra vehicles, try to find a place for it that's as far as possible from the house. Also consider breaking up large stretches of pavement into

Decks

A wood deck may be cooler than a stone surface, due to its lower thermal mass and greater reflectivity if light colored. Using wood as a landscape construction material, however, has several energy disadvantages. This subject is covered in detail in Chapter 15.

smaller spaces for fewer vehicles, perhaps with shade trees between them. Smaller dispersed parking arrangements have the added environmental benefit of reducing concentrated rainfall runoff and adding more soft places near the pavement that can absorb the runoff. (Chapter 12 provides more detailed information about designing driveways.)

ACTION:
Use "Cool Pavement" on Driveways

Driveways, parking spaces and stone terraces absorb more heat than any other kind of ground surface. In cities, this can cause the *heat island effect*, in which day and nighttime temperatures may be up to 10°F hotter than in nearby rural areas. The same effect may happen, though to a lesser extent, in your home landscape.

Many strategies are being explored to reduce the heat island effect in urban and suburban settings. Two of these strategies — increasing the ground surface's reflectivity and increasing its permeability — can be applied in your own property.

Design Tip: Increase Reflectivity

By the time evening arrives, a white car that's been sitting in the sun all day will feel cooler inside than a black car. For the same reason — light colors reflect heat while dark colors absorb it — light gray or tan pavement will be cooler at the end of the day than black or dark gray pavement. (Thicker materials will generally hold heat longer than thinner ones, but for standard thickness home driveways and stone surfaces, the lighter the color, the cooler the pavement.)

Fig. 4.8: *Cars tuck into several small nooks in this woodland parking lot, preserving both the beauty and the cooling benefits of the trees.*

Fig. 4.9: *Light-colored surfaces are cooler than dark ones.*

Pavement as Heat Storage

Progress is being made in using hot asphalt surfaces as a source of energy to heat homes and offices. The process involves laying flexible water pipes under the surface before the pavement is put in place. This idea makes a lot of sense for new construction of larger paved areas, and the time may come when it's a standard procedure for residential pavement too, but at this point the process isn't efficient for small or low-traffic areas.

So, to reduce the amount of heat stored in your driveway, build it with light-colored materials. The coolest, most-reflective materials for your driveway include:

+ Concrete (most suitable in the south, where the ground doesn't freeze)
+ Asphalt mixed with light-colored aggregate (stone particles)
+ Granite block
+ Light-tinted precast concrete pavers
+ Loose pea-stone (best in low-traffic areas)
+ Compacted sandy gravel (best for extra parking spaces, low traffic areas)
+ Crushed seashells (where locally available)

How Concrete Is Made

Concrete consists of Portland cement mixed with water and various sizes of stone particles called aggregates, which is then laid or poured into its final configuration and allowed to harden (technically, to "cure," which is a chemical process, not a drying). The creation of Portland cement involves heating limestone and clay to between 2,500° and 3,000°F. Because of these extremely high temperatures and the huge amounts of concrete used across the planet, concrete production has a tremendous impact on the atmosphere. The manufacture of concrete is responsible for about 5 percent of all human-caused CO_2 emissions worldwide.[3]

Hot-Humid and Hot-Arid Regions

Because white or light-colored material can cause glare in the high sun of these southern regions, and black material absorbs a tremendous amount of the day's heat, choose medium-colored pavement materials instead.

Whenever possible, choose the material that's produced or made in your own region, to minimize the energy cost of transport. And give preference to materials that require the least amount of energy in their manufacture.

Concrete production, for example, consumes extremely high amounts of energy; it should be used in landscape construction only when no other alternative makes sense. However, almost all paving materials come with a relatively high "embedded energy" cost. Asphalt is a petroleum product; pre-cast blocks and pavers are made of concrete; granite and other paving stones have been removed from the Earth and transported to your home with huge effort and expenditure of energy. There is no perfect solution. But you can make a positive difference, especially with paved areas exposed to a lot of sun, by choosing light-colored materials and by making your paved areas only as big as they need to be (see Chapter 12).

Design Tip: Increase the Permeability of Hard Surfaces

In the same way that moisture transpiring from a plant's foliage cools the air (see pages 35-36), water evaporating from the ground will also have a cooling effect on nearby temperatures. New ideas and technologies are making it possible for pavement to be made so that rainwater can percolate into the ground below, then cool the ground and air as it evaporates up through small voids in the surface.

Permeable (or porous) pavement is made of asphalt or concrete that's formulated to contain many tiny spaces between its component particles. Below the pavement lies a bed of crushed rock with even larger voids, where rainwater is temporarily stored until it gradually seeps into the subsoil. This new system was originally developed as a way to reduce storm-water runoff in urban or sensitive areas; its cooling effect is a fortuitous side benefit.

Porous paving works well for commercial parking lots and other large projects. At this time it is best used in regions where the ground doesn't freeze and winter pavements aren't treated with sand that may clog the pores. The cost of this type of pavement may be prohibitive for most small-scale projects like your driveway. To learn more about the uses and construction of permeable pavement, see references listed in Appendix C.

If you wish to make your driveway permeable, both to help keep storm water on site and to allow for evaporative cooling, here are some reasonable options:

- Use a loose gravel or stone surface.
- Use block pavers on some portions of the driveway.
- On extra parking spaces or places that won't be plowed in winter, use plastic grid pavers filled either with gravel or gravel and loam that supports the growth of lawn grass.

Fig. 4.10:
This driveway saves energy by being both light-colored and porous.

- Construct the driveway surface so that rainwater drains off to a place where it will be easily absorbed.

CHAPTER SUMMARY

When we minimize the ground's absorption of the sun's energy, we reduce the amount of heat that radiates from the ground later in the day and into the night. This results in cooler buildings and greater comfort, and hence a reduced need for fans and air conditioning.

This chapter presents several ways to design landscapes specifically to keep the ground as cool as possible. The most effective of these is shading the ground with plants and various kinds of mulch. Others include: keeping lawn area to the smallest size possible and maintaining rich, healthy soil below; minimizing hard surfaces such as pavement and bare earth near the house; and choosing surface materials that reflect rather than absorb heat, or stay cool by letting rainfall percolate through.

All the chapters in this section have focused on designing our landscapes in accord with the sun, wind and nature's processes, specifically to help cool our homes during the heat of summer. Section II now addresses the subject of making similar sorts of choices to help warm buildings in winter.

Arranging the Landscape to Help
Warm a House in Winter

OUR SOCIETY AS A WHOLE has moved away from the idea of working with nature. As discussed in Section I, many of us use fans and air conditioning to remove accumulated heat in our homes, rather than working with nature to prevent heat buildup. In winter we rely on technology and fossil fuels to keep us warm, neglecting many methods that were used for centuries to orient living places toward the sun's warmth in winter and away from chilling wind.

We could take many actions inside our homes to help us consume less energy during the cold seasons: replace old windows, improve insulation, seal cracks, install a new furnace and programmable thermostat, to name a few. All will increase a building's efficiency and will help save money in time. But many of these actions also involve complex decisions, large financial investments or major disruptions — or perhaps all three — and they may just not be practical or possible.

This section focuses on *improving the comfort and energy efficiency of our homes through the design of our landscapes*. Many of these energy-saving actions cost nothing at all. They simply require awareness and paying attention to our choices. Others may require a small investment, but they will also increase the value of your property and enrich the lives of everyone who lives there.

Heating costs in winter are different for every home, depending on lifestyle and heating demands; the efficiency of the heating system; the condition of the building itself (insulation, air-tightness, etc.); the number, condition and location of windows; and geographic location, orientation and microclimate.

This section deals only with microclimate, the temperature and wind conditions immediately surrounding your house. Chapter 5 explains how to capitalize on the sun's warmth and light, and Chapter 6 presents ways to reduce the chilling effect of winter winds.

Keep in mind that *strategies for increasing energy efficiency in winter are nearly a complete mirror image of strategies for cooling our homes in summer.* In summer, we aim to deflect the sun's heat and capture cooling breezes. In winter, we welcome solar energy and deflect cold winds. Achieving these apparently contradictory goals is possible, however, because of two simple realities: the path of the sun is high and wide in summer, but low and narrow in winter; and summer winds come generally from the warmer southwest, while winter winds blow from the cooler northwest. This fortunate situation allows us to devise solutions for each season that don't interfere with solutions for the other, even though they take place in the same landscape.

Designing Structures for Passive Solar Heating

The proposed Actions will be most effective if your house is also designed to take advantage of the sun's heat and reject cold wind. When planning to build a new home or renovate your existing home, keep in mind the following design principles for *passive solar heating*.

Orient buildings on an east-west axis, so their longest wall faces south, providing space for many windows to receive maximum winter sun. In general, the glass areas should be 7 to 10 percent of the floor area, though this may be higher if they contain Low-E glass. North-facing walls should have the fewest windows, followed by the west wall, then the east. In hot regions, however, north-facing walls should have the most windows. An east-west building axis also allows a pitched roof to be a solar collector, either with skylights, photo-voltaic modules, integrated photovoltaic shingles or hot water heat panels or tubes.

Compact floor plans make buildings easier to heat. A two-story house has less roof area exposed to the cold than the same living space spread out across one floor, and heat rising from the first floor may help heat the upstairs.

Low-emissivity (Low-E) coatings on windows reduce heat loss by as much as 30 to 50 percent, according to the US Department of Energy. This microscopically thin coating allows sun energy to enter but reduces the amount of heat traveling back out the windows. Different types of Low-E glass work best in different climates, so be sure to research the best choice for your region. Visit www.eere.energy.gov and click on Consumer's Guide to Energy Efficiency and Renewable Energy.

There are three types of passive solar heat gain:

Direct Gain: your house is its own solar collector. The walls and floors absorb the sun's heat that is released into the living space at night, a process enhanced by the use of thermal mass (heat-retaining materials such as stone, masonry or water). These gains are greatest in the hot-arid regions and the Rocky Mountains, where there are extreme temperature swings between day and night. Thermal mass offers less significant benefits in the hot-humid and temperate zones.

Indirect Gain: an exterior wall of the house is the solar collector. This south-facing structure, or Trombe wall, consists of a transparent surface over a dark-coated wall, with an air space in between. Heated air rises within the wall and enters the house by convection through vents at the top. This warmed air circulates by natural flow (and sometimes fans) and then sinks as it cools, returning through vents at the base of the wall.

Isolated Gain: a separate sun space collects heat that then moves into the larger living space through conduction (via a shared wall) or convection (via fans or air currents). This room, greenhouse or sunporch, which is shut off at night to prevent heat loss, requires attention to ventilation to avoid overheating in summer.

Appendix C provides a list of resources about passive solar design.

CHAPTER 5

Taking Advantage of the Sun's Heat

O NE OF THE EASIEST THINGS you can do to reduce your fuel costs in winter is simply to use as much of the sun's energy as possible to heat your home. All living beings, from the most primitive of animals to the most sophisticated humans, know that no matter how chilly the air may be, sunlight generates heat. Doesn't your dog always curl up in a patch of sunlight on the floor? In winter, don't you walk on the sunny side of the street if you can?

Even in the bitterest cold, the sun's rays penetrating (radiating) into your house will warm the air, and even the walls and furniture. This radiant heat will enable your heating system to run for shorter amounts of time. All the coal, oil and natural gas we use to power our heating systems are essentially just ancient, compressed sunlight that has been saved deep

Fig. 5.1: *Increasingly, new homes are being designed and positioned with solar gain in mind.*

in the Earth and made available to us at great expense. Doesn't it make sense to simply skip over all that processing, transporting and handling and instead take advantage of energy that comes straight from the sun right now, for free?

Working with the sun to warm our homes in winter requires a basic understanding of the sun's movement across the sky. As already mentioned, the sun's position in the sky has been charted in great detail (to find out more about

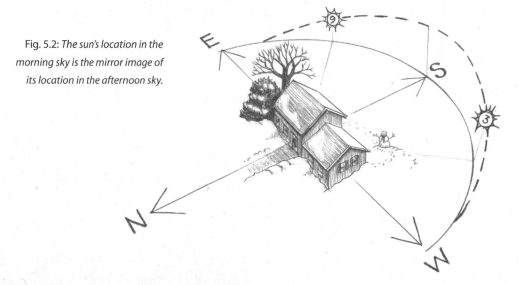

Fig. 5.2: *The sun's location in the morning sky is the mirror image of its location in the afternoon sky.*

Ancient Sunlight

Whatever kind of system provides heat for your house, the energy that powers that system probably came originally from the sun. Coal, oil and natural gas all derive from the buried remains of living organisms whose existence was made possible by sunlight. (Note: wood heat uses sunlight more recently stored, and propane is primarily a by-product of oil production.)

Most of this country's electricity is now created by a further transformation of these fossil fuels. The only exception to this general rule is electricity derived from hydropower or from nuclear fission. A very tiny amount of electricity may also come from renewable sources such as wind, solar

thermal power, biomass and systems that capture the energy of ocean tides. At the start of the 21st century, however, the vast majority of our energy still comes from organic (carbon-based), sun-powered compounds extracted from deep below the ground.

Chart of US energy consumption by source, as of 2007[1]

Non-renewable sources	Renewable sources
Petroleum 37.5%	Biomass 3.6%
Natural Gas 23.3%	Hydropower 2.4%
Coal 22.5%	Geothermal 0.3%
Nuclear 8.3%	Wind 0.3%
Propane 1.7%	Solar/other 0.1%

the sun in your own location, see Appendix A). This information enables us to know ahead of time where the sun will be, so that no matter where we live, we can plan our actions to make the most of its energy.

Another handy fact that helps in our planning (also mentioned in Chapter 2) is that both the sun's compass angle and its altitude above the horizon are *the same on either side of midday*. So, for example, on December 21 in Philadelphia, the sun at both 9AM and 3PM is 13° above the horizon and 43° away from south (toward the east in the morning and toward the west in the afternoon). The same pattern holds true for 10AM and 2PM, and 11AM and 1PM.

HOUSE-WARMING ACTIONS

As in the first section, the information presented here is based on an *average of the sun's position throughout the months of winter*. It's also primarily applicable to places located about 40° north of the equator. If you live in regions farther north or south than this, assume that the sun will be (respectively) lower or higher in the sky, at all hours of the day, than what's shown here.

The basic goal in this chapter is to help capture and hold as much of the sun's energy as possible, by taking the following Actions:

- Allow maximum sunlight to reach the house at midday (i.e., when the sun is shining from due south).

- Make the most of morning and afternoon sun (i.e., around 9AM and 3PM, when the winter sun shines from the southeast and southwest).

Why Is Winter Cold?

For the millions of us who live in regions about 40° above the equator (a latitude that stretches through Philadelphia, Sacramento, Beijing and Istanbul), the winter sun describes an arc, from dawn to dark, that's never more than about 90° wide, just one quarter of a circle. And worse, in these regions, the noon sun stands a mere 30° above the horizon. Brrr!

ACTION: Allow Maximum Sunlight to Reach the House at Midday

The sun is highest in the sky during the hour before and after noon. Earlier and later in the day, the sun's rays touch the ground at a lower angle of incidence (see Figure 1.9), causing their energy to be spread over a larger area, which diminishes their warming power. Even though the winter sun is relatively low in the sky as compared to summer, *midday* in winter is still the time when the sun's energy is great-

Fig. 5.3:
This home was specifically designed and sited to make the most of midday sun in the winter, while also being shielded from winter winds by dense evergreens to the north.

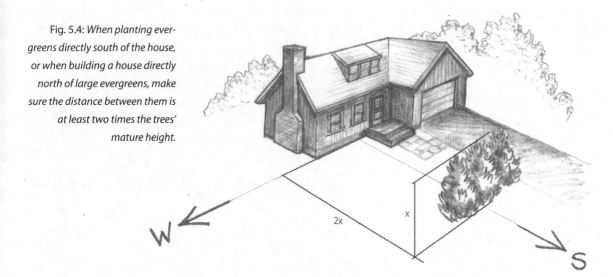

Fig. 5.4: *When planting evergreens directly south of the house, or when building a house directly north of large evergreens, make sure the distance between them is at least two times the trees' mature height.*

est, and it's the most important time to make sure your house receives as much sunlight as possible.

Recall from Chapter 2 that the best ways to cool a house during midday in the summer, when the sun is high overhead and shadows are short, involve shading a south-facing wall with overhangs, vines and deciduous shrubs near the house. For larger shade trees to be effective during midday, they'd have to be growing quite near the house, and with some exceptions, this is generally not recommended. Luckily, excluding trees south of the house is also just the right thing for winter.

Cool-Cold Regions

In environments where maximizing warmth in winter is more critical than cooling in summer, it's important to maintain a swath of open space, from the southeast to the southwest of the house, so nothing will block the winter sun.

Design Tip: Trees

Evergreen trees can block nearly all of the sun's light and energy. If you wish to have evergreens in your south yard, either to increase privacy or just to create an appealing scene, be sure to plant them a distance from the house that's at least two times their mature height.

Planting large evergreens (pine, hemlock, spruce, etc.) closer than this, on the assumption that you'll keep them pruned at a desired height, is not a good idea. Pruning is one of those tasks that often gets neglected, and beyond a certain point, it can become very difficult, or damaging to the trees, or expensive if you need to hire a professional with suitable equipment. Plus, if you should move to a different house, placing this burden on the new owner seems a bit unfair. For a list of evergreens and their mature height, see Appendix B.

If deciduous trees are already growing near the south side of your house and you wish to keep them, either for aesthetic or sentimental reasons, you can maximize the amount of sun that reaches the house by:

- removing their lower branches, so the low-angle winter light can reach the house below the lowest branches and

- pruning out some interior branches. (The Information Box on page 161, in Chapter 14, provides advice about how to prune a branch.)

Design Tip:
Other Landscape Features

Overall, any open space directly south of the house will allow the greatest amount of sunlight to warm your living space, both by direct radiation and by reflection off the ground. This will be true in places where snow covers the ground as well as in regions without snow, where lawn or meadow grasses remain exposed all winter. The soft tan color of dormant grasses will also reflect a certain amount of sunlight up into south-facing windows.

A stone terrace or driveway south of the house will collect heat during the day and gradually release it after the sun goes down (a sort of outdoor thermal mass). Intentionally positioning these dark-colored, heat-retaining features south of the house is generally not recommended unless they can be shaded in summer, but if they already exist in your landscape, they can provide a modest benefit in winter. Positioning a driveway near a south-facing wall, or clearing the snow off a south-facing patio, helps absorb and re-radiate heat.

Fig. 5.5: *This spruce hedge is a classic example of "wrong plant, wrong place." Probably originally planted for privacy from the road, these trees have grown so tall that they prevent every bit of midday sun from warming the house in winter. At the same time, the absence of lower branches not only provides little screening, but actually directs views toward the exposed windows.*

Fig. 5.6:
Even though deciduous trees drop their leaves in the fall, their bare branches can also reduce the amount of sunlight that reaches your house, in some cases by as much as 20-30%.

Fig. 5.7: *By removing the snow from this southwest-facing patio, the home-owners benefit from its stored radiant heat, and they also get to use their outdoor space earlier in the spring.*

Daylighting

During the winter, sunlight at all times of the day shines at such a low angle that it can easily penetrate far into the interior of rooms. Not only will this help warm those rooms, it will also provide valuable light at this dark time of year, to help decrease our need for artificial light and the electricity it requires.

ACTION: Make the Most of Morning and Afternoon Sunlight

The Earth's tilted axis in relation to its orbit around the sun causes the winter sun to be lower in the sky than it is in summer. Similarly, early and late-day sun is even lower in the sky than midday sun, and even weaker in its power. However, if you've ever opened your east-facing curtains on a December morning to take the chill off the room, you know from first-hand experience that even early morning sunlight has warming power.

A basic understanding of the sun's path and position, explained in Chapter 1, is especially important when working with the sun in winter. From November through January in the northern hemisphere, morning and afternoon sunlight never shines from due east or west. Instead it comes from the southeast and southwest, and it is in these parts of the landscape, relative to the house, that we should also remember to avoid placing any trees or structures that will block the sun's rays.

Design Tip: Place Trees Properly

In winter, evergreen trees on the southeast and southwest of the house will cast very long and dense shadows during the morning and afternoon. A single evergreen's shadow may come to a point at its tip, causing little reduction in sunlight, but if you wish to plant a tall evergreen hedge or group to the southeast or southwest of your house, remember to position trees as far away as possible, ideally at least 3.5 times their mature height.

Deciduous trees, too, will cast long lacy shadows at these times. However, the low-angle sun of morning and afternoon will shine below the branches of most large trees, so any shade trees in this location (which are ideal for summer cooling) will cause little reduction in solar gain.

The branches of smaller deciduous trees and tall shrubs near the house may slightly diminish the sun's warmth, so consider thinning some interior branches of these plants, if they're located near any windows on the southeast, south and southwest sides of your home.

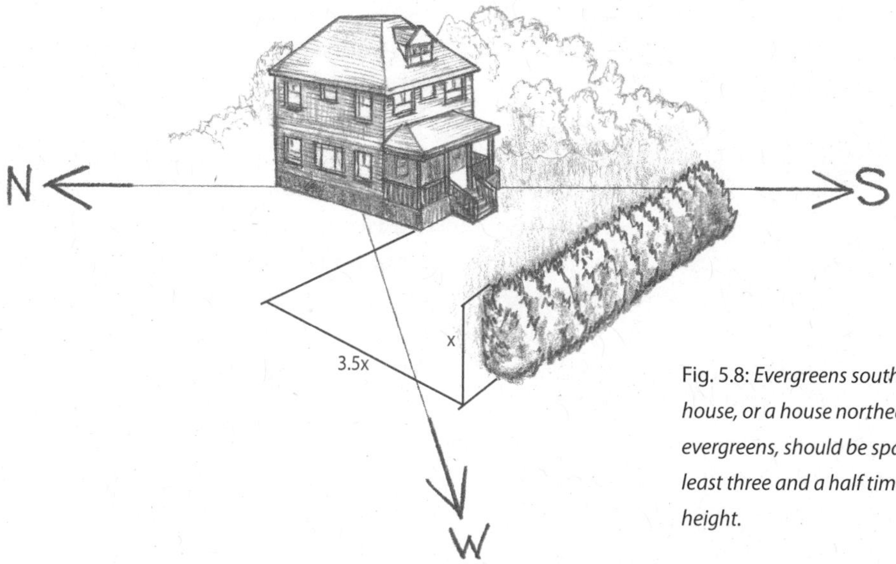

Fig. 5.8: *Evergreens southwest or southeast of the house, or a house northeast or northwest of tall evergreens, should be spaced apart a distance at least three and a half times the trees' mature height.*

Design Tip: Other Landscape Features

Morning and afternoon sunlight is at such a low angle that horizontal surfaces in the landscape will reflect more than they absorb. If it makes sense in the overall design of your property, consider placing open spaces (lawn, meadow, etc.) and outdoor sitting areas (terrace, deck, etc.) on the southeast or southwest side of the house, to help to bounce sunlight into any windows on those sides. This effect will be heightened if the surfaces are light-colored.

Similarly, any vertical surfaces in these parts of the landscape are more likely to absorb warmth than to reflect it, especially if they are made of a dense material and are dark in color. Consider building a stone wall around a garden or patio, extending a stucco wall from the house to define an entry courtyard, or other similar actions, to make the most of valuable early and late day solar energy.

Fig. 5.9: *In the right place, the right tree very near a house will cause little reduction in winter solar gain.*

CHAPTER SUMMARY

The actions in this chapter aim to help us capture as much of the sun's free heat in winter as possible, to reduce the amount of time we run our furnaces, boilers and heating systems. In the reverse of shading actions taken during summer, the goal here is to maximize the amount of sun that reaches our rooftops, walls and windows. Fortunately, across most of this country, deciduous trees cooperate in this goal by dropping their leaves in autumn, just when we're starting to need the sun's warmth.

In addition, while the cold of winter is the result of short days and low sun, these two facts also make it easier to capture whatever sun energy is available: the sun's shorter path across the sky limits the area in which our actions will make a difference. The six hours in midday, three hours on either side of noon, are the only time we can get significant warmth from the sun, so this chapter addresses only those times of day, with actions that apply only to the southeast, south and southwest sides of a building.

The main message here is to position landscape structures and trees — both deciduous and evergreen — so they don't block the sun or cast shadows on our houses during the middle of day. Next, Chapter 6 presents ways to arrange our landscapes to help minimize the cooling effects of winter wind.

Reducing the Chilling Effect of Winter Winds

WINTER WINDS TAKE HEAT AWAY from your house by increasing the rate of air exchange between warm indoor space and the cold outdoor air. Strong winds can force cold air through small cracks and reduce the effectiveness of your insulation. If you have a very tightly constructed house, the heat loss may be minimal. But all houses leak a little bit, and some leak a lot, especially around windows and doors, along the foundation and through tiny unseen gaps in walls.

Air infiltration is proportional to the force of the wind on a building, so reducing wind velocity will reduce heat loss. In other words, deflecting or blunting the force of winds against your house will bring less cold air in and pull less warm air out. This has the potential, depending on the condition of your house, to significantly reduce your heating costs.

Across much of the United States, winter winds blow primarily from the northwest and north (see Chapter 1 for more detail about how wind works). While wind is a powerful force of nature that can't be fully stopped or controlled, knowing where it's likely to be coming from is a big help as we work to limit its chilling effect. All of the following actions share one common goal: to reduce the force of wind that blows against your house, by placing different types of obstacles in its path.

This chapter presents the following Actions to help deflect winter winds:

+ Plant a windbreak.
+ Plant a buffer near the house.
+ Position structures to divert wind.

ACTION: Plant a Windbreak

Before the age of convenient insulation and tight windows, even before houses were insulated at all… before the age of central heat, when homes were heated only with wood, and

Fig. 6.1: *A mature windbreak — tall evergreens positioned to the north of a house — help deflect winter winds away from the building.*

Fig. 6.2: *Hemlock trees mixed with viburnums and other shrubs make this yard private while also protecting it from north wind (note the direction of the tree shadows at noon).*

Windbreaks for Farms

Much has been written specifically to help farmers protect their fields and livestock from winter wind and snow. To find out more on this subject than is provided in this book, check with the US Department of Agriculture or with a university Agricultural Extension Service.

then later with coal… in those days before easy energy, people all across the country planted trees to deflect cold winds away from their homes. You can see evidence of this wherever you live. Just take a short trip — by bus, train or car — through nearby countryside or into a town that's been around for a hundred years or so, and if you pay attention, you'll see plenty of these windbreaks.

They may be very old by now, maybe three or four tall evergreens towering over a tidy little farmhouse. Perhaps there's only one tree left, because the others got too old and had to be cut down. Maybe all the lower branches are gone (which can actually increase wind speed via the Venturi effect; see below). Or they may be dense hedges of evergreens planted tightly along the edge of a field or yard, with the individual plants all grown into a solid wall. In every case, you'll know they are windbreaks because you'll find them north of the home that they were planted to shelter.

Design Tip: What Kind of Plants to Use

Most windbreaks consist of evergreen trees that are arranged either in a straight row or in a somewhat linear grouping. For agricultural purposes and on large properties, long and wide hedgerows will provide substantial protection. For those of us with moderate to small landscapes, a windbreak that's a more informal grove, perhaps containing a mix of mostly evergreen and a few deciduous trees, may be preferable to a solid evergreen hedgerow. This second type of windbreak will also provide diverse habitat for wildlife, and may help maintain good relations with neighbors.

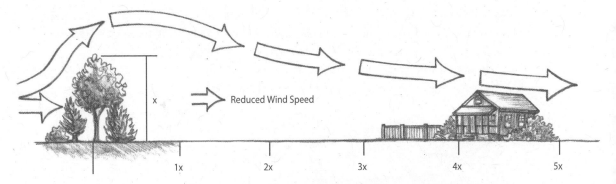

Reduced Wind Speed

1x   2x   3x   4x   5x

Fig. 6.3: *To get the greatest benefit from a windbreak, determine the mature height of trees being planted and position them 3-5 times that distance away from (upwind of) the house.*

Keep in mind that shade will eventually cause most evergreens to lose their lower foliage and branches, so it may be preferable to separate the two types of trees somewhat, allowing plenty of light to reach the evergreens. Or consider including some broadleaf evergreens (mountain laurel, rhododendron, etc.) at the outer edges of the grove, which will eventually help fill in some of the lower spaces, to keep the windbreak intact.

Design Tip: Windbreak Location

Whatever its makeup, all windbreaks should be located in the landscape to the north/northwest of the house. There's no absolute formula that fits every situation, but in general it's best to plant evergreens at a distance from the house that's about 3 to 5 times the height of the mature trees. Windbreaks can actually reduce the force of wind for a distance up to 30 times their height (downwind), but the greatest protection comes in the region closest to the windbreak, within 1 to 5 times its height.[1]

Cool-Cold Regions

In cold environments, deflecting winter winds is one of the most important landscape design actions. Keep in mind that this can be accomplished with landforms and structures as well as with dense masses of evergreen trees or shrubs. To prevent trapping cold air near a house, avoid building berms or other landforms on the downhill side of the building.

Design Tip: A Note About Turbulence

Evergreen trees and shrubs can block nearly all the sun's light, but they can't completely block out the force of wind. And this turns out to be a good thing in most windbreaks.

Turbulent air has a higher velocity than calm air (this is explained in more detail in Chapter 1, pages 19 and 40). Porous windbreaks, which let a portion of the wind pass through their small perforations, will reduce turbulence and extend the total length of the protected area (though wind speed immediately behind a solid barrier is slower than behind a porous one).

The space behind a solid windbreak is also where blowing snow may be dropped, as the wind no longer contains enough energy to carry a snow load. Slightly porous barriers drop less snow directly behind them; instead it gets carried further away from the windbreak, to be spread more thinly over a larger area.

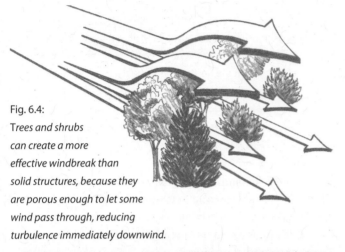

Fig. 6.4:
Trees and shrubs can create a more effective windbreak than solid structures, because they are porous enough to let some wind pass through, reducing turbulence immediately downwind.

Fig. 6.5: *This dense hedge curves around the north and west sides of the yard, providing excellent protection from winter wind, while the deciduous trees allow sunlight into the house in winter and shade it in summer.*

Design Tip:
Summary of Windbreak Design

A windbreak will provide greatest protection when it:

+ is oriented across the direction of the wind, rather than parallel to it (in most of the continental US, this means the windbreak is aligned generally east to west).

+ is longer than the object or structure it's intended to protect, by at least 10 to 20 feet in both directions, or longer if possible, to diminish the effects of turbulent winds swirling in around from the ends of the windbreak.

+ forms a slight convex shape from end to end; this will be more effective than a straight line or a concave curve that catches the wind.

+ contains branches and foliage close to the ground.

+ contains shrubs as well as trees, which will help trap snow, enhancing ground-level protection.

+ is quite dense while also allowing some slight leakage through perforations, as in a snow fence, hedge or grove of trees.

+ contains no large gaps that will actually increase the speed of wind as it squeezes through.

Design Tip: Shaping the Ground

The taller a windbreak, the longer its area of downwind protection. If possible before planting a windbreak, consider reshaping the ground itself to raise the height of trees planted there. In the long run, when the trees reach full maturity, the gain will be negligible. But at the start, it will make a difference.

Reshaping the ground, however, must be done with care. The soil where roots will grow must be good quality soil that's fertile and rich, while the interior of the mound should be lower quality soil, to conserve the high-humus topsoil. And because tree roots grow in the top 12 to 18 inches of the soil, any raised ground must slope very gently back to the original surrounding ground, providing space for tree roots to slope downward as they grow, into the natural ground. Steep-sided berms should be avoided. If your site is too small to make this idea work well, don't do it.

Construction Tip: Planting a Windbreak

When planting a windbreak, leave space between the young trees to give them room to expand as they grow. If they're too close together, their interior branches won't get enough sunlight, causing them to eventually die (which will increase the Venturi effect), and need to be replaced. One method to ensure long-term success, is to plant the rows of trees in successive years, so they reach their mature height at different times, with the lower foliage of younger trees filling in the spaces left by thinning foliage of their older neighbors.

Talk to your supplier about the expected spread of a mature tree. In the end, the inner branches of any group of evergreens will have less foliage than the outside, but when trees are young, they need as much foliage as possible to support growth. Expect to wait at least 5 to 6 years for an evergreen windbreak to offer moderate protection and about 10 to 20 years for it to reach full maturity. (See Chapter 14 for more guidance about planting trees.)

Wind Tunnels

Whether in winter or summer, breezes that are funneled between gradually smaller spaces will pick up speed. This is the same phenomenon that happens when a river runs faster as is passes between narrowed banks. It's important to avoid accidentally increasing the chilling effect of wind blowing toward your house. In cold regions, never orient a windbreak so it increases the force of winds blowing from the north or northwest, and avoid placing scattered trees that can actually increase turbulence and wind speeds.

What Will the Neighbors Think?

Bear in mind that if you have a neighbor to the north of your property, any trees you plant in the northern portion of your landscape may cast shadows on the southern portion of their landscape. Consider working cooperatively to find the best solution for everyone involved.

Fig. 6.6: *Trees planted too far apart will only increase wind turbulence in the spaces between them. Note the wall of evergreens growing south of this house, perhaps too close.*

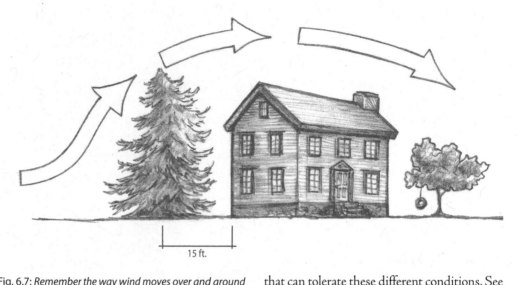

15 ft.

Fig. 6.7: *Remember the way wind moves over and around obstacles. Dense, large evergreens growing within 10-15' of your house's northwest side will deflect winds up, over and past the building. This will be especially true with one-story homes, but taller trees will also shelter taller buildings.*

Caution
Whenever planting anything on your property, be aware of overhead power lines and avoid planting anything that will grow to a height that interferes with those lines. Also get informed about buried power, gas, water or cable lines and avoid digging anywhere near them. Contact your local DigSafe organization for a free delineation of all underground utilities on your property.

Also, be prepared for the trees' foliage on the north-facing side of a windbreak to be less dense than on the south-facing side, due to less direct sunlight. It's important to select plants that can tolerate these different conditions. See Appendix B for a list of trees and shrubs you can use in windbreaks.

ACTION:
Plant a Buffer near the House

If your property isn't large enough for a windbreak placed some distance from the house, or if for other reasons you just don't wish to have a large grove or row of evergreens out in your landscape, you can still deflect winter winds by planting evergreen trees and/or shrubs quite near your house. This *buffer* can amount to wrapping one side of your house in a nice toasty muffler: it creates a pocket of calm air between the wind and yourself.

A wind buffer near the house can provide excellent protection without being as extensive as a windbreak planted further away. Even just a few tall evergreens can make a difference. This option may be more affordable and feasible than a windbreak, and it also provides the added benefit of creating a privacy screen near the house.

Design Tip: Tree Buffers

All plants on the north side of a building will receive only limited sunlight during the growing season, because the building itself blocks the southern sun. Hemlocks are among the most shade tolerant of evergreen trees, and they are particularly well-suited to this purpose because they keep most of their lower branches even in moderate shade. Note that the native eastern hemlock species (*Tsuga canadensis*) is currently susceptible to damage by the hemlock woolly adelgid, which does not appear to affect western hemlocks (*Tsuga heterophylla*).

When planting trees near your house, be sure to consider the ultimate spread of their branches, and plant things far enough away to prevent their contact with the house. Remember, it will not be healthy to prune off a tree's south-facing branches (the branches facing your house), as these will be especially valuable for the growth and health of the tree. Most hemlocks' branches will extend about 15 to 20 feet. Be aware that until the tree reaches at least to the level of your eaves, you may experience some turbulence in the space between the buffer and the house. Eventually, though, most evergreen trees will grow taller than your house and provide substantial protection.

One note of caution: since winter winds in much of the US come from the north and northwest, trees growing near the house must be kept healthy, with good strong roots, to minimize the possibility of blowdown. The

Fig. 6.8: *Avoid planting the wrong evergreens too close to the house. This hemlock, which might have been planted to create privacy from a neighbor, has now grown so large that it's harming the house.*

most important factor in tree health is soil that's moist and well drained.

Design Tip: Shrub Buffers

A dense group of evergreen shrubs near your house walls will provide some minor reduction in heat loss from winds. To be effective, this buffer will need to be planted so that, when mature, the outer tips of their branches are 1 to 3 feet from the wall. Between the shrubs and the house will be a pocket of relatively calm air, especially if the shrubs are evergreen, which can slightly reduce the amount for air infiltration due to wind blowing against your house. Many shade-tolerant shrubs are well-suited to this type of buffer, particularly rhododendrons and yews.

ACTION: Position Structures to Deflect Wind

In some situations, the best way to deflect winter winds may be with structures such as a fence or building. You may already be planning to build a decorative fence around your outdoor sitting area, a stone wall between your driveway and entry courtyard, a privacy fence surrounding your pool, a picket fence to keep goats and chickens out of your vegetable garden. You could even be planning to add a potting shed, three-season porch or garage. If so, keep wind protection in mind as you consider the best location for these new structures.

Design Tip: Buildings

Whatever you build, keep in mind that if it crosses the path of prevailing winter winds, the same principles that apply to vegetated windbreaks apply as well to these structures. These principles are:

+ The height of the obstacle directly affects the length of protected area, with the greatest protection occurring within 1 to 5 times the height, and lesser amounts of wind reduction extending downwind as much as 30 times the height of the barrier.

Driveway Siting Tip

If building a farm road or driveway in an open field, especially if across the direction of prevailing winter wind, raise the driveway surface a foot or so above surrounding terrain. This slight slope will accelerate the wind as it blows across, helping to keep snow clear.

+ Solid structures will slow the wind more than permeable structures, but they will also cause more turbulence immediately downwind (on the leeward side) and shorten the protection zone.
+ Solid structures will cause snow to accumulate on the windward side, usually at a 45° angle, and snow to be dropped near the leeward side, usually within a distance about 5 times the height of the barrier. A porous barrier allows some snow to pass through and be gradually dropped at greater distances away. This thinner spreading of snow results in easier snow removal and faster melting in spring.

Design Tip: Fences

The power of wind increases with the cube (or third power) of its speed. This means that when wind speeds double, their force is eight times stronger. Therefore, any fence or structure that will receive the full brunt of winter winds must be built to withstand a significant pressure.

Solid fences should be built with extra cross pieces and, ideally, with the nailed side of boards facing the prevailing wind direction, so that in strong wind those boards are pushed in toward their supporting structure and are hence less likely to be ripped off. Also, posts for solid fences should be sunk further into the ground than would be customary for non-windbreak fences (porous fences will not be subjected to the same degree of wind pressure).

In locations where it's important to deflect wind but also to minimize snow accumulation near a fence, such as along a driveway, road or parking area, porous fences are a good choice. They should have openings of about 2 to 3 inches, and the spaces may run either vertically or horizontally. Traditional picket fences, or any fences that are about 25 to 50 percent permeable, are ideal for allowing snow to pass through.

CHAPTER SUMMARY

This chapter explains basic methods to reduce the force and speed of winter winds that blow against your house and rob its heat. All the actions are variations on one theme: placing different types of obstacles in the path of the wind can blunt its force and deflect its direction. However, not just any obstacle in any location will have a positive effect. Some landscape features may accidentally increase the speed of the wind (through the Venturi effect) or cause turbulence that makes matters worse rather than better, especially relating to snowdrifts. This chapter explains the best types of windbreaks and buffers, along with how to design and position them for greatest effect.

This concludes the portion of the book that's devoted to *saving energy by cooling and warming our homes*. From this point forward, all the energy-efficiency actions in this book *apply to the landscape itself*. They include steps for saving fuel directly, through designing for low maintenance and easy care, along with ideas for reducing embedded energy costs, by designing and building for durability and by using efficient techniques and suitable materials.

Fig. 6.9:
Wind speeds up slightly as it passes through the small openings, helping to carry the snow load and prevent snow from accumulating, both on the windward and leeward sides of the fence.

Designing the Realm of Plants

THIS SECTION MOVES BEYOND METHODS for saving energy by arranging our landscapes to help keep our houses more comfortable in summer and winter. The following chapter presents ways to reduce the energy we consume in our *landscapes themselves*. From the most obvious step of creating smaller lawns that require less mowing, to more subtle actions like gardening with regionally native plants, creating ecosystems that are largely self-maintaining and making the most of natural rainfall, our landscapes contain countless opportunities to design for energy-efficiency.

One of the most important steps we must take to achieve this aim, right at the start, is really not an action at all. Rather, it's a shift in attitude. And it's more of an ongoing process than a single action.

Here's what's involved. We shape our gardens and landscapes for so many complex reasons: to make a social statement, to satisfy cultural expectations (spoken or unspoken), to recreate a cherished image, to express personal or social values. The list could go on and on. But far and away the primary reason for most of our landscape choices and activities is a desire to create beauty, however we define it. And this is where the shift needs to happen. *To our definition of beauty, whatever it might be, we need to add a new component and a larger understanding.* We simply need to expand the idea to include an appreciation for how much energy is being spent to produce or sustain any particular visual effect.

This is not to suggest that the things we've always found beautiful should now be considered ugly simply if they consume a lot of energy. Instead, it just means we ought to *merge a new sensibility with our old one*, so our appreciation is tempered and informed by knowledge about the true cost of our choices. It's like thinking a car is beautiful until you discover its seats are uncomfortable and it gets lousy gas mileage, or believing a coat is gorgeous until you realize it's made from the fur of an endangered animal, or feeling an exotic dish is delicious until you learn what it contains. The point here is simply that we humans *constantly* use our brains to referee our unconscious choices and preferences. And we can do the same with the decisions we make about our landscapes.

The three chapters in this section present ideas for creating landscapes that are both beautiful *and* energy efficient. Chapter 7 discusses the many benefits of creating healthy working ecosystems. Chapter 8 shows how to save energy by reducing the size of our lawns and replacing them with other things, while Chapter 9 explains steps we can all take to conserve energy by using water wisely.

Creating Healthy Working Ecosystems

A N ECOSYSTEM IS A WEB OF RELATIONSHIPS. Whether vast, modest or tiny in size, it's a place where different creatures co-exist, interacting in ways that are often invisible or meaningless to us humans. In the natural world, healthy ecosystems may change dramatically from year to year, but they're inherently self-sustaining in the long run. They make the most of the resources that are available to them, and except when exposed to great disturbances, they preserve an overall state of balance. If we bring some of this self-maintaining balance into our home landscapes, we will spend less energy, time and money taking care of them.

Of course, no garden can be entirely maintenance free. Weeds and unexpected seedlings will always appear in places we don't want them, and some plants will grow in shapes that

Fig. 7.1:
This naturally-occurring patch of ferns and Solomon's plume creates a carefree garden beside the driveway and road.

need to be modified. *Our purpose here isn't to create untended wildness in our home landscapes, but instead to welcome into our gardens more of nature's processes,* to help keep our gardens and landscapes healthy, which will lighten our load and consume less energy in the process.

In thriving ecosystems, four categories of creatures perform four vital tasks:

- Producers (plants) convert sunlight into their own bodies, which is food for all the rest of us.
- Consumers (animals) eat these plants.
- Predators (animals) eat other animals.
- Decomposers (organisms) break down the remains of plants and animals.

A healthy working ecosystem needs all four of these components. The goal is to have not just a lot of creatures, nor simply a wide variety of them. Rather, the healthiest systems contain several kinds of creatures that perform all the necessary functions, each in its own unique way. This is the meaning of biodiversity. And the result of this diversity is a system that's *resilient, productive and self-supporting.*

It's *resilient* because if one species fails, others can carry on performing the same function, so the system can recover quickly from disturbances. And a diverse ecosystem is better able to resist alien invaders. How is a diverse ecosystem *productive?* Life is essentially the conversion of the sun's energy into the actual bodies of living creatures. Different plants and animals use this energy more or less efficiently, and if there's a lot of different species in a system, chances are higher that some of them will be more efficient energy-users. This will result in the whole system containing more total biomass.

Healthy ecosystems are *self-supporting* because all the energy that's available to them keeps getting recycled by the creatures that live there. Plants grow by taking in rainfall, soil nutrients and the energy of sunlight. Hundreds or thousands of insects, birds, fish, frogs, lizards and mammals eat these plants (and sometimes each other), then all the plants and animals eventually die and return their nutrients to the soil to be used again. Nothing besides rain, and in some cases not much of that, needs to be added from the outside.

Keeping ecosystem gardens healthy usually gets easier with time. Once established, they need no fertilizer or other amendments, they'll get less weedy, they'll keep getting richer and more diverse with little help from us. And their

Fig. 7.2:
A rich assortment of plants (in this case, beech and birch trees, mountain laurel, azalea and viburnum, and a carpet of woodland ferns) promotes health and resilience in any landscape.

Biomass Defined

Measured as the total annual output of plant material from an ecosystem, productivity is visible in the lushness of leaves, stems, branches, roots, shoots, seeds, fruits and woody growth. In short, productivity represents the growth that supports all animal consumers, their predators, and ultimately the myriad creatures of decay.[1]

higher productivity equals more and bigger trees in your forest; lush waving grasses in your meadow; carpets of spring wildflowers; shrubs full of fruit we can eat (or share with birds); more fish in your pond.

Because many of the interactions in an ecosystem are unseen, and because we don't really know what's going on, we've tended to ignore them. Historically, as a society, we've gardened mostly for beauty, partly for our own health and not at all (or at most a very tiny bit) for the health of nature. But actually we do need the diversity, resilience and productivity of healthy ecosystems, and you can create them yourself, in your own landscape. This chapter presents the following Actions that will show you how to achieve this goal:

- Use regionally native plants.
- Select plants that contribute to the work of nature.
- Match plants to soil conditions.
- Add nothing; just remove unwanted plants.

ACTION: Use Regionally Native Plants

There's been a lot of discussion, over the last several decades, about the idea of gardening with *native plants*. This book is not the place for a full exploration of that topic and the various advantages of gardening with native plants. Several other resources, listed in Appendix C, address this subject extensively. Whatever your opinion, however, there's no question that using native plants in our landscapes is a way to save energy. How? The answer has three parts, each requiring a bit of explanation, but in the end the story is beautifully elegant.

Part One of the Story

Let's back up a bit and define native plants (and animals). A native species is one that has evolved over thousands and millions of years, in association with other species that share the same growing conditions. Some people use the term "native" in reference to a particular physical location: you might read about plants that are native to a county, state, region or even a whole continent. The most common definition says natives are those that lived in a certain place prior to the arrival of a non-native human population and its inevitable disruptions. While this formulation may be true, it only partially captures the essential idea of native species.

What really matters in the definition of native plants is not their hardiness, the conditions they can tolerate, where they could grow, nor how long they've grown in a particular place. The main thing that makes a species native is its *history of interactions* with the other residents of its habitat.

In nature, when plants and animals live together, they *co-evolve* (this includes sparrows, ferns, newts, praying mantises, mushrooms). They continually influence each other, in ways that might be perfectly obvious, beautifully subtle or completely mysterious. When one

Fig. 7.3: *Monarch butterflies freely pollinate the flowers of shrubs like this Arrowwood viburnum. Two months later, birds will gobble up the fruit this butterfly helped create.*

sort of plant suddenly appears in the midst of other creatures it has never encountered, and who have never encountered *it*, all bets are off. The services it used to provide may or may not be useful in its new home; the bugs and caterpillars who used to dine on its leaves may or may not recognize it as food; birds may or may not appreciate the seeds it produces at a strange time of year. This new plant may either be of no benefit at all to its neighbors, or it may actually be a detriment, overwhelming the whole neighborhood, taking up more and more space in the absence of the predators, climate extremes and diseases that originally kept it in check.

Part Two of the Story

Now we have to talk about insects. To most people's surprise, humble insects, those bugs that we generally either hate or ignore, actually sustain a vast food web that in turn supports birds, mammals, whole ecosystems and ultimately us humans too. How is this possible?

Fig. 7.4: *Thousands of species of native bees pollinate flowers more effectively than the familiar (non-native) honeybees.*

According to a 2006 Cornell University study conducted by entomologists John Losey and Mace Vaughan,

> Insects are food for the wildlife that supports a $50 billion recreation industry, and provide more than $4.5 billion in pest control. They also provide crop pollination valued at $3 billion and clean up grazing lands, saving ranchers some $380 million a year. And these are very conservative estimates that probably represent only a fraction of the true value.[2]

The key here is that insects provide essential services that would have to be performed in some other way if the insects themselves were missing. Whatever that other way would be, it would inevitably consume energy — resources, time, money — to perform work that's now being done for free. (A side note to gardeners who believe all insects are bad and must be eradicated: 65 percent of pests are controlled by other insects.)

Part Three of the Story

So, why are we talking about insects? Here's why. Plants and insects are involved in a relentless dance of eating and being eaten: the plants develop various mixtures of chemical compounds that are either unappealing, indigestible or toxic to insects, and the insects in turn develop ways to overcome these obstacles. As a result, many insects are really very picky about what they'll eat. Yes, there are a few species of generalists who can munch on almost anything. But the majority of insects are specialists, whose little tummies can't digest just any old leaf, and these bugs won't touch the foliage, not even one nibble, of plants they can't digest. They know it could kill them.[3]

Adding to the elegance of this story: most insects not only *prefer* certain types of food, they actually *require* that particular food. And here's the kicker: the food that most plant-eating insects need is the food with which they have co-evolved for millennia: the foliage of native plants! If we want to benefit from all the important work that insects do, we have to provide them with their required sustenance.

To learn more about the value of insects in our landscapes, explore the excellent book, *Bringing Nature Home*, written by Douglas Tallamy, Professor and Chair of the Department of Entomology and Wildlife Ecology at the University of Delaware in Newark, Delaware.

Design Tip: Incorporate Native Plants in Your Landscape

Native plants can be used in our domestic landscapes in the following four different ways. On any single property, it may be possible to use one, two or all of these approaches.

Simple Substitution

In the substitution method, native plants (the product of natural processes) replace conventional garden plants (plants that have been imported, hybridized, cloned or otherwise manipulated by the horticulture industry). Everything else — design goals, plant arrangements and visual effects — can remain the same as in traditional landscapes. This is the simplest approach to using native plants, and it's one that can be done by anyone. Seek out

Fig. 7.5: *Monarch caterpillars eat only milkweed foliage; without this essential food supply, monarch butterflies could not exist.*

Insects and Native Plants

Bill Cullina, horticulturist and author of three books on growing and propagating native plants, sums up the issue beautifully. He writes:

> Native plants are often promoted as low-maintenance, problem-free alternatives to finicky garden hybrids. While it is absolutely true that a plant that has evolved in your particular climate and soils will be hardier and more adaptable than many exotics from half a world away, it will likely be eaten by more types of insects, mammals and birds than a plant growing far from its native home. This is precisely the point. While you may have to learn to live with some tattered leaves and blemished flowers, you can also free your garden and yourself from the pesticides that are undeniably and needlessly polluting our soil, air and water while at the same time promoting a bit of ecological balance.[4]

Fig. 7.6:
This Silverbell tree, native to the Appalachian forests, tucks nicely into a semi-shaded corner.

suitable native plants at nurseries and garden centers, and, if none are available, request them.

Nature-inspired Associations

Another method involves designing gardens based on the aesthetic and biological patterns found in nature. What's involved is understanding

Plant Hardiness Zones

Like conventional garden plants, native plants also are inherently tolerant of a certain range of temperature; some species can thrive in a wide range of conditions while others are quite particular. Cold is one of the most limiting factors in a plant's survival, so the US Department of Agriculture (USDA) has compiled maps showing plant hardiness zones or regions characterized by the same average lowest temperature. As you would with any type of gardening, check the hardiness zone of any plant you wish to use in your landscape. And keep in mind two things: temperature is only one of many factors that determine a plant's survival, and plant hardiness zones are shifting northward slightly as a result of global warming, so be sure to check the most current map available (these maps are easy to find on the Internet).

- which plants typically grow in association with each other,
- the physical conditions that support them and
- how plants naturally distribute themselves, i.e., in dense groups of just one species, in interwoven drifts, as a fairly uniform sprinkling of many species together, as individuals here and there.

Nature-inspired gardens can work in one tiny corner of your property, in a few chosen places or throughout your entire landscape. One of the best ways to create these gardens is to be sure to include the *layers* that are characteristic of most ecosystems. The layers of a forest consist of the canopy overhead, shorter trees and large shrubs, small shrubs and tall herbaceous plants that reach up to about our eye level and the ground layer of plants mostly below our knees (moss, ferns, sedges and short herbaceous plants). Grassland, savanna, mountaintop, marsh, desert and every other sort of garden that nature dreams up has its own characteristic set of layers. And within each of these layers, plants and animals are interacting in ways that don't happen elsewhere above or below.

Gardening with nature-inspired associations is a bit trickier than simple substitution, and it requires more knowledge. However, much of the necessary information is becoming available to the general public, and soon this type of gardening will be as commonplace as the strict, patterned rows of annuals that used to be in the gardens of Versailles. Appendix C lists resources for finding out more.

Conservation Patches

Conservation patches, although similar to nature-inspired gardens in that they contain plants in natural associations, are semi-wild zones where plants grow in their own freely chosen arrangements, with minimal input from us humans. They might be a hedgerow of shrubs that sprang up between neighboring properties, a grove of trees in the back corner of your lot, the steep shrubby bank between your yard and the road, a thicket of ferns creeping along a ditch or inching out from a shady woods or countless other possibilities.

Sara Stein, the author of *Noah's Garden* and *Planting Noah's Garden*, calls her own patch a pocket woods. She recommends that we all try to preserve or create some small piece of semi-wildness in our landscapes to create *corridors* that link one ecosystem to the next. This will help all plants and animals thrive, so they can continue to perform ecological services we can't imagine, and ultimately make our human lives better.[5]

Fig. 7.7: *In this nature-inspired garden, bloodroot, leucothoe and maidenhair ferns fill the ground layer; maple-leaved viburnum (flowering here) occupies the middle layer; and a striped maple tree arches above, its lower leaves visible at the top of the picture. (In the forest, even taller trees would canopy over all of this.)*

Fig. 7.8: *Dozens of flowering dogwood trees, self-sown from one or two original plants, now form a semi-wild grove in the front yard of this New England home.*

Invasive Plants

Many plants grow so fast, and spread their roots and seeds so far that they out-compete and sometimes completely overwhelm humbler plants. Quite often, these aggressive plants are species that have been imported from other parts of the world (or even this continent) and consequently freed from the natural processes — competition, predation, disease, pests, etc. — that originally kept them in balance with their neighbors.

The subject of invasive plants is vast and extensively covered in many books and Internet websites. Frequently, the main concern with these plants is that they are harmful to the environment. Whether or not you care about the environment, it's important to keep in mind that controlling and removing invasive plants requires a lot of energy, both carbon-based and your own. And some of these plants — Norway maple, winged euonymous, Japanese wisteria, multiflora rose, kudzu vine, mile-a-minute vine, oriental bittersweet, buckthorn, to name only a few — can be quite destructive. Invasive plants can prevent the growth of desirable plants, or by physically swallowing up or pulling down established vegetation, they can completely thwart many of our other energy-efficiency actions. Appendix C lists some of the most aggressive invasive plants and suggests some ways to work toward removing them.

Restorations

Some situations call for the establishment, or re-establishment, of entire natural ecosystems, with a full complement of producers, consumers, predators and decomposers. This is generally the work of landscape specialists. For regular landowners facing the task of repairing a denuded or degraded landscape, the option of simply standing aside and letting nature take its course may or may not be effective, for two reasons. First, this process can take much longer than we might care to wait, up to 50 years or more in some cases. And second, we live in a time when many natural landscapes are subject to invasion by aggressive non-native plants that can quickly dominate a patch of land or a whole region, sometimes without being noticed until it's too late. Restorations should probably be undertaken with the advice of someone who understands the plants and natural processes taking place on a piece of property, someone who can offer a range of ideas and solutions.

The discussion above is an adaptation of ideas originally articulated by the ecological landscape architect, Darrel Morrison, in various classes, discussions and conferences throughout the 1990s. Some of his concepts appear in a chapter he wrote for the book *Dynamic Landscape Design* by Nigel Dunnett.[6]

ACTION: Select Plants That Contribute to the Work of Nature

When we garden, many of us tend to choose plants for their size, shape, texture, color and other visual qualities. A growing number of us also garden with the goal of providing nectar for butterflies and hummingbirds, fruit for birds, nesting materials and cover for small mammals. Yet plants can be so much more than just a pretty picture, and gardening to support wildlife is still primarily meant to satisfy our own *human* needs and wishes, however noble.

To create a functioning ecosystem, we need to move beyond these human-oriented goals and to garden with plants that participate in the countless, invisible, essential interactions of the natural world. Exchanging pollen, releasing pheromones, dissolving minerals, absorbing nutrients, supporting bacteria, evaporating water, dropping seeds: the list of tasks is vast and endless. Describing it in even partial detail would require a book much larger and different than this one. In fact, we can never really know the whole story. But still, we can try to join in the play.

The key to selecting plants for their contribution to nature is simply to look past your garden's visual compositions and seasonal

Fig. 7.9:
Some tiny nibbler gave this Solomon's seal its lacy edge, creating a natural work of "food art."

displays, to see what else is going on, and to *welcome* it. The list below offers a tiny sampling of the many intricate, elaborate and oh-so-clever roles that plants perform in nature. When you're gardening, or planning your garden or just reading about gardens, keep your mind and eyes open to opportunities like these:

- Ferns shade the ground, preventing the growth of weeds, but before the fronds get tall each summer, tiny spring wildflowers thrive in the spaces between their stems.

- Cushions of moss catch the falling seed of nearby mountain laurels, their moist bed and acidic soil providing a perfect medium for the seeds to germinate.

- The clover that drifts among lawn grass (if you let it) takes nitrogen from the air and *fixes* it on its roots, where it later becomes available in the soil for other plants to use. (Nitrogen, which most plants can't get directly from air, is needed to make protein.)

- Tall perennials bloom late in summer, so their seeds ripen in the fall and often remain on the plant far into winter, when birds can dine on yummy seed heads peeking above the snow.

- The hollow stems of grasses and perennials, lying on the ground over the winter, provide a nest cavity for native bees (who pollinate flowers longer, more diligently and over greater distances, than honeybees, which are alien species imported to the US).

- Stands of young saplings and brush provide an excellent home for many kinds of birds that won't thrive in either a mature forest or an open meadow (and certainly not in a suburban lawn). This includes bobwhites, turkeys, warblers and many songbirds.

- Woodland perennials with large leaves (wild ginger, bloodroot, trillium, mayapple, so many more) shade the soil so it stays cool and moist, creating ideal conditions for other woodland plants.

- Shrubs with many small stems (called *suckering*), such as dogwoods, azaleas and viburnums, have correspondingly dense and bushy roots that hold soil and keep banks from eroding.

ACTION:
Match Plants to Soil Conditions

Soil is the place where plants grow. It consists of tiny bits of rock, which have been broken down from mountains and larger rock, mixed with a few bits of decaying plant and animal life. This is where plant roots absorb dissolved nutrients that will be turned into the plant's stems, leaves, flowers and fruit.

The following discussion is not a complete tutorial on soils, which are amazingly complex and the subject of countless books, studies and whole university departments. Rather, this is a basic introduction to one vital part of our landscapes, in the simplest terms. Basically, the ability of soil to support plant life depends on three interrelated qualities that all soils embody, in varying degrees.

The Nature of Soil

Soil's character, like people's, comes from a blending of parent material and surrounding environment. The result is an unpredictable mix of what it started with and what's been added later, though the different influences are easier to see and analyze in soil than in humans.

Moisture-holding Capacity

Moisture-holding capacity, sometimes called texture, is mostly a result of how small the soil's rock bits have become. Soil with the tiniest particles, called *clay*, is so tightly crowded that few air spaces remain. Water clings to the abundant surface area of so many minuscule particles, and the air spaces are so small that water can't drain out very easily. In soil with the largest particles, called *sand*, the bits fit together more loosely, so there's lots of space between them, allowing water to flow easily through. Medium-sized particles, called *silt*, hold soil well but also drain well.

The amount of organic matter mixed in with the rock particles of soil will also affect how well it drains or holds moisture. Decaying remains of plants — seasonal fallen leaves, grasses lying on the ground, spent flower heads, seed husks or just the countless plants that die throughout any year — all return their bodies to the ground, where fungi and small creatures that we never see mix them into the soil below. The sponginess of organic matter helps sandy soil hold moisture and clayey soil release it.

To find out what sort of soil you have, take a pinch of dirt between your thumb and forefinger then dunk this into some water. Keep your fingers closed while you do this. Then remove them from the water and rub them together, feeling the consistency of what's still there. If it's gritty and firm, the particles are large and your soil is mostly sand. If it's slippery and soft, you have a lot of tiny clay particles in your soil. All the consistencies in between gritty and slippery represent varying sizes of particles, with silt being the most average consistency. It's not an exact science, but you get the idea.

Fig. 7.10:

Sand is soil particles 0.05mm to 2mm in size; silt particles are 0.002mm to 0.05mm; particles smaller than 0.002mm are considered clay.

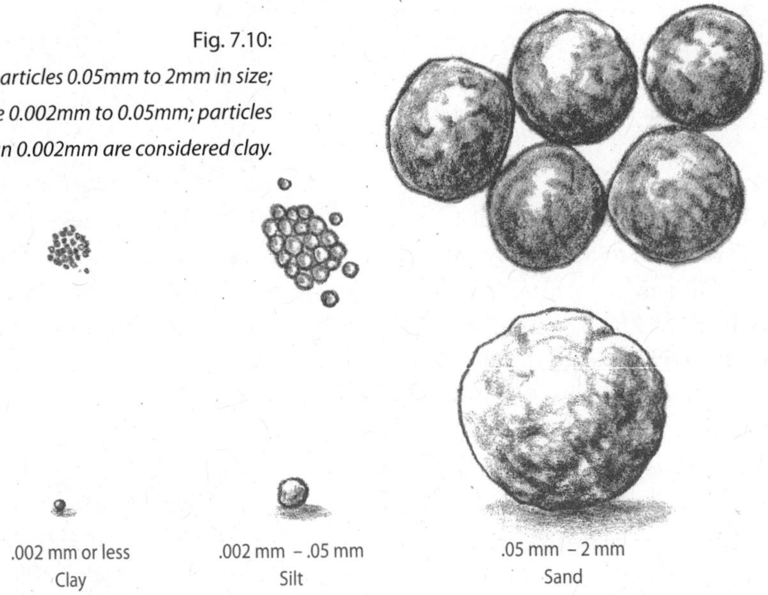

.002 mm or less
Clay

.002 mm – .05 mm
Silt

.05 mm – 2 mm
Sand

Design Tip: Select Plants That Can Thrive in Existing Moisture Levels

Plants everywhere have evolved to tolerate, and even thrive in, soils that range from very damp to very dry. If we select these plants that match the kind of soil in our landscapes, we will spend less time and energy adding things to the soil to help it drain more quickly or more slowly, and we'll spend less time and energy watering thirsty plants. This is the basic principle behind xeriscaping that's so popular in the American southwest, where water is scarce and gardens are designed specifically to need less water. But the concept is equally valid everywhere.

Soil Acidity or Alkalinity

A soil's acidity is largely determined by the nature of the rock that it came from (its parent rock). This original mineral nature remains in the soil no matter how much the rock has been cracked, split and repeatedly crushed, no matter how small its particles become. If the bits of rock that make up the soil are mostly of a limestone origin, the soil will be alkaline (often called sweet or lime). Soil that started out mostly as quartz or granite will be more acidic.

In chemical terms, a soil's acidity is a measure of the activity, or *reaction*, of its hydrogen ions. This measure is indicated on a pH scale from 1 to 14 (pH stands for the *power of hydrogen*). On this scale, 7 is neutral, numbers below 7 indicate acidic soil, and numbers above 7 represent alkaline soil. But what do these numbers mean for non-scientists?

Basically, in acidic soils (low pH), many of the nutrients that are important for plant

growth don't dissolve easily and so become unavailable or difficult for plant roots to absorb. Conversely, in more alkaline soils (a higher

Fig. 7.11: *The blue flag iris (native to eastern Canada and the northeastern US) (above) thrives in moist wetland soils. This delicate treasure can often be overwhelmed by the aggressive yellow iris (a European plant) (below).*

Testing for pH

A simple pH test, available at any garden center, will reveal your soil's approximate acidity level. For even greater accuracy, send a soil sample to the agricultural extension service of any regional university, or to a specialized soil testing laboratory.

pH), most of these essential nutrients become more soluble, hence more available to plants. As William Cullina explains in the introduction to his book *Growing and Propagating Wildflowers*

> Lime-loving plants evolved under conditions of relative abundance, and they quickly suffer deficiencies when the soil is too acidic. And conversely, acid-loving plants have adapted to living with scarcity and low nutrient levels, so they can be easily overwhelmed by excess.[7]

Design Tip: Select Plants to Match Existing Soil pH

Fig. 7.12: In this pocket of acidic soil thrive mountain laurel, sheep laurel, mountain andromeda and canby pachistima.

We can choose the plants that already know how to survive and thrive in the particular soil acidity of our own gardens and landscapes. By doing so, we will skip the whole question of adding just the right amount of this or that amendment, and we'll avoid the problems caused by adding too much or too little or the wrong thing altogether. We'll prevent needless trips to the garden center and perhaps, in an ideal (or fantasy?) world, reduce the amount of natural resources (calcium, aluminum, sulfur, etc.) that are mined from the Earth for the purpose of manufacturing "soil amendments."

Soil Fertility

Soil fertility is a measure of the nutrients in soil. This includes macronutrients like oxygen, carbon, hydrogen, nitrogen, phosphorus and potassium and micronutrients such as calcium, magnesium, sulfur, boron, chlorine, copper, manganese, molybdenum and zinc. In nature, these nutrients in soil come from the mineral makeup of the parent rock itself, from the decay of once-living plants and animals, and from added organic matter such as manure. Fertility in all soils is increased by the presence of worms, bugs, fungi and bacteria that break down organic matter and make it available to plants.

As with soil moisture and acidity, plants everywhere on the planet have evolved to live perfectly well in varying levels of soil fertility. Some plants, such as bog- or desert-dwellers, actually prefer low-nutrient conditions. The ferns and spring wildflowers of eastern forests need richness and high fertility. When plants receive too many or the wrong nutrients, their internal processes can be damaged. The result may be distorted growth, late development or extreme production of either foliage or flower, or the plants may simply wither and die.

Design Tip: Only Add Fertilizer When Necessary

Adding fertilizer may be required in garden soils that have lost most of their nutrients due

to abuse, overuse or poor care, but it should not be necessary in stable, healthy soils that are allowed to recycle their own nutrients. This is not to suggest that you should never add fertilizer. Instead, as a first step, *if you're wondering about the fertility of your soil, have the soil tested.* As mentioned above, garden centers provide this service, but their results are only approximate. A better choice is to send soil samples to an agricultural extension or soil-testing service.

Any nutrients added to soil that are not quickly absorbed by plants will leach into the soil below and make their way into the water table. These excess nutrients can later harm other plants, animals and humans, which will require energy to alleviate and repair. *Add fertilizer only in direct response to a soil test* and follow the specifications exactly. The best fertilizer to use contains 50 percent water-soluble nitrogen, which breaks down very slowly, reducing excess leaching.

Design Tip: Select Plants to Match Existing Soil Fertility

To minimize the need for fertilizer, choose plants that can tolerate the natural nutrient levels of your soil. Most garden catalogs and plant lists supply information about a plant's growing requirements, along with its size and other visual qualities. For greater accuracy, check these recommendations against a reliable reference book (many are listed in Appendix C).

ACTION: Add Nothing; Just Remove Unwanted Plants

No matter what kind of landscape you have, whether it's mostly lawn, established gardens, healthy natural areas, degraded ecosystems or

Fig. 7.13: *Bunchberry dogwood flourishes in the swamps, bogs and coniferous forests of Canada and most northern US states, and grows only in nutrient poor (usually moist) soils. It will not thrive in average garden soil.*

Imported Soil

Quite often in new landscapes, the usable soil that originally covered the ground has been removed, or moved around and rearranged or completely replaced by soil from somewhere else, with the result that soil in garden beds has completely different qualities than the native soil. When selecting plants, be sure to pay attention to the characteristics of all the different soils in your landscape.

a whole beautiful forest, consider a drastic new approach to gardening: don't add anything. Please note, adding nothing is not the same as doing nothing. It's not a recommendation for laissez-faire gardening. Rather, it's simply a suggestion to let everything *new* be added by nature itself — which is smarter by far than we are at figuring out what can grow and thrive in any particular place — and then to remove whatever you don't want.

Again, as with the earlier discussion about restoration, this action may not work in entirely new landscapes that are devoid of all vegetation. Nor will it be suitable in places where towns or homeowner's associations require a certain appearance or aesthetic standard. And it can be tricky if your landscape is surrounded by invasive plants, especially if you have a lot of bare ground where weeds will thrive. However, if you have the right sort of site and an adventurous, open-minded attitude, this kind of gardening will require less energy than any other. See Appendix C for resources about eliminating invasive plants.

CHAPTER SUMMARY

This chapter explains the value of bringing some of nature's self-maintaining balance into our home landscapes, so that taking care of our gardens and grounds requires less of our own time and the world's energy. Several ideas for accomplishing this goal are presented, including: using regionally native plants, either in simple substitutions for conventional garden plants or in more complex, nature-inspired patches; taking advantage of the services provided by insects; and choosing plants for their role in the larger work of nature as well as for their beauty.

In addition, the chapter describes the importance of matching plants to a site's soil conditions rather than dramatically altering the soil to suit pre-determined notions that are unconnected to the physical realities of a region or landscape. Designing in accord with this advice will save a significant amount of energy, both in the direct cost of soil amendments and in later costs associated with maintenance and watering.

To save even more energy, read about ideas for reducing lawn area and using water wisely, presented in Chapters 8 and 9.

Fig. 7.14: *This thicket of mountain laurel was saved during construction of the new deck, to hold the steep bank, conceal the tall deck supports, and delight the owner with its reliable blooming. Tree saplings that occasionally sprout up are removed, to maintain views and sunshine.*

CHAPTER 8

Reducing (or Eliminating) Lawn

W HO CAN SAY WHY A CERTAIN IDEA takes hold in our imagination and can't be dislodged, no matter what we see, hear, feel and know about how that idea really doesn't make sense. This is the case with the North American lawn. Despite all reason, we feel that a lawn is essential to our social standing. Many of us actually believe that a neat green lawn somehow indicates good citizenship. To create and maintain our lawns, we think nothing of spending huge amounts of time, money, energy and resources; we care nothing about polluting air, water and soil. We administer lawn treatments right on schedule, based on the stern instructions from their manufacturers, as if these substances were medicine prescribed by a doctor.

In the ultimate irony, to keep grass free of weeds, we blithely spread bags full of chemicals that harm the health of ourselves and our children, our pets and our friends, not to mention a whole world of wild creatures we never see or consider. The installation of lawn is automatically included in builders' contracts for constructing new houses. Local bylaws, zoning ordinances and homeowners' associations dictate that our landscapes contain lawn. When it comes to lawn, our overriding cultural belief is still the more the better. But why?

Lawns started out as an English phenomenon. Fields of short grass swept across the estates of wealthy lords, who either paid servants to keep them shorn with scythes or kept flocks of sheep to clip them down with their constant nibbling. English rainfall kept them beautifully watered. In early America, by contrast, most front yards were a place to grow food, herbs, chickens and maybe a few ornamental flowers. Often, they were simply packed dirt. Eventually, however, in that classic human way, Americans in the early 1900s started wanting to imitate the English lawn that they read about, heard about and sometimes even saw for themselves in their travels. We just simply had to have this symbol of wealth and status, in even the humblest of our landscapes.

Trouble was, our native grasses didn't make good lawn: they were too clumpy and too slow to emerge in spring. To solve this problem, seed companies developed and manufactured new grass mixes that would "green up" early and make a nice smooth carpet. The fact that most American climates didn't (and don't) provide enough rain to support English-style lawns was an inconvenience, but soon rubber hoses and sprinklers took care of that problem. And the biggest difficulty — no nibbling sheep, no scythe-wielding servants! — was solved by the invention of the lawn mower. So then, in the mid-1900s,when the American Garden Club felt inspired to convince homeowners that keeping a lawn was a civic duty,[1] we were all set to go: we could proudly blanket our landscape with acres and acres of half-inch-tall, sterile green carpet.

Questioning the beauty and social importance of lawn may lead to interesting conversation and perhaps some heated disagreements, but this book is not the place for that debate. In contrast, the gargantuan amounts of energy consumed by the construction and care of lawns is clear to all, and beyond dispute. And that *is* the subject of this book.

In addition to the gasoline we use to keep lawns neat and tidy, consider also the huge embedded cost of American lawns, the uncountable barrels of fossil fuels required to:

- manufacture fertilizer, pesticides, herbicides, fungicides and an infinite variety of seed mixes for every type of soil and climate;

Fig. 8.1: *In imitation of historic wealthy landscapes, a vast expanse of empty lawn is the prevailing "prestige aesthetic" across much of North America. Ironically, in the older landscape pictured here (top), the grass is allowed to grow long each summer and then harvested as hay.*

- produce, advertise, sell and transport millions of lawn mowers, tractors, trimmers, edgers, sprayers, tillers, aerators, seed-spreaders, sod-lifters and leaf-blowers — all the essential tools of the lawn business;
- power the equipment that shapes the ground and prepares the soil for seeding and the trucks that transport all the materials;
- support an entire industry that's devoted to developing, promoting, marketing and selling lawn grass and its necessary accompaniments.

Is lawn a good idea for your landscape? The answer is likely to be a mixture of yes, maybe, in some places and it depends. Do we need so much lawn? Probably not. Can we afford to keep maintaining vast expanses of empty, lifeless, sometimes toxic green carpet? Definitely not.

This is not to suggest that all lawn everywhere is useless and should be removed. Rather, we should consider just how much lawn we really need, to satisfy our practical needs and make our lives better. Ask yourself questions like: what is my lawn for? how do I use it? how much time do I want to spend caring for it? is it for me, my kids, my parents and friends? or do I have lawn just because that's the *normal* thing to do and I can't think of anything else? If you want to reduce or even get rid of your lawn, to save energy that could better be used for other purposes, the following Actions will give you some ideas for getting started:

- Stop mowing some portions of lawn.
- Replace some lawn with other things.
- Design a lawn-free landscape.

ACTION:
Stop Mowing Some of the Lawn

Your landscape might contain portions of lawn that aren't thriving, either because they're too shady or damp, or because the soil in those places is depleted and thin or for other reasons. Your property may include some areas of lawn that you just don't use, that you look out at and spend your weekends mowing, wondering why you bother. All of these places are perfect candidates for this simple action: stop mowing them.

What will happen then? It depends on a number of variables, including the moisture and fertility of your soil, the type and health of grasses previously growing there and what else is growing nearby, waiting to blow in and germinate in any spaces available. Certainly the appearance of this liberated zone will immediately soften and look more furry. After a few weeks or months, the grasses that make up most lawns (probably some mix of Bermuda grass from Africa, blue grass from Europe, and North American bent grasses and fescues) will probably get so tall they fall over; maybe they'll even ripple and wave in the breeze! If the season is

Fig. 8.2:
Considering the difficulty of mowing this very steep hillside, wouldn't a wildflower meadow here make better sense?

Fig. 8.3: *One year after this lawn was "liberated," it brought forth Black-eyed Susan, fleabane, St. Johnswort, milkweed, little bluestem grass and many more appealing surprises.*

hot and dry, these grasses will probably go dormant and become tan in late summer.

In a year or two, or maybe less, you'll see new things turning up amongst the grasses. Violets, trout lily and bluets might appear in the spring; columbine, pussytoes and black-eyed Susan may show off in summer; asters, goldenrod (see sidebar) and maybe even gentian or some native grasses could turn up in the fall. Yes, some weeds that you really don't want might also take root, and taking care of this new landscape might require a bit more attention than you're used to giving your lawn. But if you acquaint yourself with the worst weeds and invasive plants, and if you remove them when you see them, before they get too established and comfortable, you'll be fine. To find out more about identifying invasive plants in

The Myth of Goldenrod Allergy

Remember back in high school, when there would be some sort of scuffle in the hallway, and a teacher would show up, glance around and quickly blame the tall kid who was innocent but just happened to be standing beside the little bland kid who'd long ago perfected the art of not getting caught? It's the same with blaming goldenrod for allergies. Contrary to widespread and persistent myth, goldenrod is not the cause of allergies. Its pollen is simply too big to be carried on the wind and then invisibly inhaled up your nose. After all, goldenrod pollen is so big you can actually see the individual particles! They are what make this flower so gorgeous; they're what bees tote around on their little bodies and carry home to feed their young.

What's actually happening when many people feel allergies in late summer and early fall is that ragweed — a widespread but little-known and barely recognized weed that grows along nearly every sunny roadside — blooms at the same time as goldenrod. Ragweed is pollinated by wind, not by bees, so its pollen is tiny, lightweight and essentially invisible to us. And since we're blind to ragweed — both the plant itself and its miniscule pollen — but we clearly see the goldenrod, we blame the most obvious possible culprit. That blame, however, is misplaced, and as a result, many people disdain or even hate goldenrods (yet we do nothing to control ragweed). Ironically, in England, goldenrod is a treasured garden perennial.

lawns, and the best techniques for removing them, see the UMASS Turf IPM fact sheet listed in Appendix C.

Another guaranteed result of not mowing will have nothing to do with the grass itself. If your liberated lawn is visible to other people, you will definitely receive comments. They may be curious, neutral or critical, but they will come. The ideal of the American lawn is so precious that any change or perceived violation to our set way of doing things will inevitably provoke a response. If you're concerned about social judgments, consider liberating only small or insignificant areas of lawn at first. This probably means *not* your front yard. If you don't care what anyone says, then by all means let the front yard get shaggy.

Design Tip: Mow a Tidiness Strip

One way to reassure worried neighbors that you actually planned and care about this new kind of landscape, that you're not just being slovenly and un-American, is to maintain a mowed strip around the edges of the lawn. The more we display front yards that are diverse, biologically alive and beautiful in a different way, and perhaps the more we explain our motivations to curious neighbors, the more this kind of landscape will be understood and accepted.

Design Tip: Maintenance Practice

How should you take care of your liberated lawn? It depends on what sort of result you're aiming for. If you want it to be a meadow of mixed grasses and flowers, you'll have to mow it at least once every year or two, to exclude the trees and shrubs that might otherwise pop up.

If you're ready to let nature take over and create a conservation patch (see page 81), you can just sit back and watch and never mow it again. Chapter 14 explains various lawn maintenance techniques and the long-term maintenance of meadows. If you'd prefer to keep it looking basically like lawn, but just a little taller and looser (this is a choice to mow less, rather than to stop mowing), see the low-mow discussion below.

ACTION: Replace Some Amount of Existing Lawn with Other Elements

If you're ready to permanently let go of some portion of lawn, to never or rarely mow it again, a variety of other landscape elements can take its place.

Fig. 8.4: *A single pass of the mower gives this landscape a socially-approved tidiness, and keeps the wildness of tall grasses and flowers safely at bay, yet close enough to enjoy.*

Lawn Regulations
Be careful about liberating your lawn in towns or neighborhoods where lawn laws and weed inspectors exist. Check with building codes, zoning ordinances and homeowner association by-laws.

Fig. 8.5:
*American
elderberry
flourishes in
a damp spot
at the back
of this yard.*

Design Tip: Other Plants

You might consider converting lawn into a grove of trees, a hedge or stand of shrubs, a wildflower meadow, vegetable garden, fruit trees or berry bushes or even some type of plant community that's typical of your region (tallgrass prairie, savanna, cactus desert, marsh, pine barren, etc.).

This approach can be especially helpful in places where the soil or light conditions don't really support lawn grass to begin with, so the lawn already looks somewhat thin or unhealthy. Perhaps your property has a corner that's deeply shaded by a neighbor's trees, and you just can't get grass to grow there: this is a perfect place for mosses, ferns or some beautiful trees of your own! Is one part of your lawn damp and mushy, where rain flows and snow melts, and water stands in shallow puddles long afterward? This is an ideal place for wetland shrubs and wildflowers.

Also, rather than keeping these semi-wild areas confined and neatly trimmed, let their edges expand on their own. A strip of unmown land along the edge of a semi-wild zone will soon be colonized by new baby plants.

Planting other things in place of grass may involve suppressing or removing the existing lawn. But if you aim to plant trees or shrubs, and especially if the established lawn grass is fairly thin, you could simply interplant among the grasses and let the resulting shade keep the grass in check, with the aid of thick mulch. See Chapter 14 for a more detailed discussion of mulch. This method will be less successful in dense, lush lawn.

Design Tip: Use No-mow or Low-grow Seed Mixes

Some seed companies offer a blend of grasses that naturally grow to a relatively low height and form a dense turf. These mixes consist primarily of fescues, which are cool season grasses that thrive in the northern third of the continental US. Since their maximum height is generally just 6 to 8 inches, they can be mown just once or twice a year, saving a lot of gas, time and your own energy. Specific seeding instructions are provided by the seed suppliers. One company that has led the way in developing these mixes is Prairie Nursery in Wisconsin (prairienursery.com). Your own local garden center may offer a comparable product.

Design Tip: Wildflower Meadows

If you want to preserve the open feeling that a lawn provides but avoid the work, energy consumption and environmental problems of lawn, planting a wildflower meadow may be right for you. Creating a meadow, however, requires thoughtful seed selection, to match the physical conditions of the site. The soil must be carefully prepared. The seeded ground will require attention to weeds in the first stages of growth. If you already have a lawn (as opposed to the bare ground of new construction), the process of eliminating lawn grass can consume quite a lot of energy — either in the equipment that mechanically removes lawn or in the herbicides that chemically remove it.

Despite these drawbacks, meadows offer several distinct advantages over lawn. Once established, they directly save energy by requiring infrequent mowing (generally just once every year or two) and no fertilizer, pesticides or herbicides. They make the most of the sun's energy and recycle their own waste while improving the soil. The soft soil and intertwined root systems of a meadow help hold rainfall, reducing runoff and erosion and keeping water out of storm drains. And, quite soon after they start growing, they'll be discovered by birds, bugs and butterflies. All of these great benefits, and they're beautiful too!

Where's the best place for a meadow? If you're starting from scratch and no lawn has yet been planted, a wildflower meadow should be designed as one component of the overall landscape. It should serve various needs: year-round beauty, wildlife habitat, sunny open space, play space for kids, a place to stroll, etc.

Fig. 8.6:
Every meadow is unique: here daisies and clover thrive in a meadow that's too remote to be watered or weeded. (This low-maintenance approach may not work in every situation.)

If you already have lawn, your choice of a meadow location might depend on the same factors as choosing a place to stop mowing: where the lawn isn't thriving (too damp, too dry) or where you don't need lawn. Perhaps one of the best places for a wildflower meadow is in our front yards, which may stand empty and unused most of the time. This is a great opportunity to show off our present-day values about energy and the environment, and to be a leader in the movement toward healthier landscapes.

What about sunlight? Some meadow plants will thrive in partial sun, such as might be found in the dappled shade of a woodland edge, but since grasses are the major component of successful meadows, and most grasses need a lot of sun, meadows should be located where they'll receive at least a half day of full sun. If you're interested in planting a meadow or converting some (or all) of your lawn to meadow, see the detailed instructions provided in Chapter 14.

Design Tip:
Different Ground-surface Materials

Paths and patios made of pea stone, flat stones, brick and other hard materials can occupy some of the lawn-free landscape. Of course, these materials shouldn't be used cavalierly and without thought to the shape, location and function of the resulting spaces. But they may

Fig. 8.7: *This landscape uses pea-stone instead of lawn to create open spaces and paths that meander between the gardens.*

serve just as well as (or even better than) lawn as a place to congregate, play, sunbathe and show off the beauty of your home and gardens. Initially, they might be somewhat more expensive than lawn to install, but in the long run, these low-maintenance surfaces will save a lot of time and energy. Remember that porous surfaces (cobble, brick, mulch, gravel, even a deck) will let rainwater percolate into the ground, helping to keep it cool.

Design Tip: Vegetable Gardens and Fruit Orchards

In this time of growing concern about the health (and energy) costs of imported and manufactured foods, doesn't it make sense to grow for ourselves at least a little of the food we eat? Of course, many people already do this, but not so long ago almost everyone did, even city dwellers.

As a society, we may have lost some of our common knowledge about how to grow food, but lots of information is available at garden centers, in catalogues and in the amazing world of the Internet. The best way to learn about gardens and orchards is to talk directly with someone — a neighbor, teacher or, best of all, an actual farmer — about the things that work best in your region. Remember, it's perfectly okay to put a vegetable garden in your front yard, if that's the part of your landscape that receives the most sunlight. It'll inspire other people!

ACTION:
Design a Lawn-free Landscape

This idea makes sense for those among us who don't need any lawn — not as a play area or gathering place, nor for picnicking, sunbathing

Permaculture

Permaculture is a school of thought that promotes the idea of growing food in every part of our landscapes, even in forests. Derived from the words "permanent" and "agriculture," this philosophy first gained widespread exposure in the 1970s through the work of Australians Bill Mollison and David Holmgren. Since then it has become a popular approach to ecological design, based on the goal of maximizing yield from every piece of land.

and kite-flying, nor as ball fields or athletic space. It's for people who either don't engage in these sorts of activities at all or who can find other places to do them. And it's for people who don't need lawn to make a social statement, or rather, who prefer their landscape to make a different sort of statement.

The best way to design a lawn-free landscape is right at the start, when you're planning or building a new house, before any grass has been planted, before your contractor automatically seeds the ground because he or she thinks that's what you'll want. Lawn can be removed after it's established, but grasses are persistent and don't surrender easily, so getting rid of them takes a bit of work. Eliminating unwanted lawn also wastes any energy already invested at the start.

If the idea of a lawn-free landscape appeals to you, however, don't hesitate to take on the task of removing old lawn. The point here is to avoid this extra step, if possible. In either case, designing a lawn-free landscape can involve some or all of the following techniques.

Design Tip: Minimize the Extent of Managed Landscape

If your house is in a wooded area, keep the cleared zone as small as possible. Ideally, in temperate climates, this means deciding just where the house will be built, then removing trees primarily to the south of the house but keeping healthy trees fairly close to the other three sides of the house. The goal here is to minimize the amount of space that ultimately needs to be repaired and revegetated after construction is done. Chapter 16 presents a detailed descrip-

Fig. 8.8: *A grove of mature semi-dwarf apple trees fills the front yard of this otherwise traditional home.*

Fig. 8.9: *Large swaths of moss, creeping vines and low perennials carpet this lawn-free landscape, tolerating occasional foot traffic of the strolling homeowner.*

Shared Lawn Space

To help minimize or reduce your need for lawn, consider using other established lawns for your outdoor activities. These might include public parks, a schoolyard, town or city athletic fields, a recently mown hayfield or even a neighbor's lawn (with permission, of course).

tion of energy-efficient methods for creating new home sites.

Design Tip: Maximize the Extent of Semi-wild or Wild Areas

Trees, shrubs and other plants that are already established are likely to be healthier, and grow faster, than any plants we bring into a landscape. If natural areas already exist anywhere on your property, design the landscape to include and incorporate them, even if this might later require some selective removal and pruning to make them suit your tastes.

Design Tip: Use Plants that Spread

Instead of keeping strictly delineated edges between different parts of the landscape, choose plants that will naturally creep beyond their original location. These can be low-growing plants such as ferns, vines, wildflowers and native grasses or taller shrubs and even trees. Most nurseries and plant catalogues designate which plants will spread. Keep in mind, however, that many plants called "spreading ground covers" can be quite aggressive and may take over parts of the garden where they're not wanted.

CHAPTER SUMMARY

One of the main things most of us can do to save energy right now is simply to have less mown grass in our landscapes. This chapter presents several ways to achieve this goal. We can simply stop mowing some portion of existing lawn by: choosing grassy areas that are either unimportant or not thriving anyway and just letting that grass get long; and mowing paths through or strips around these places, to indicate a new kind of landscape maintenance and personal preference. We can also replace some amount of lawn with other sorts of plants or landscape elements, such as wildflower meadows, low-mow grass mixes, shrubs and trees, conservation patches (discussed in the previous chapter), vegetable gardens or even patios and terraces.

A third option, which is becoming increasingly popular, is to design a landscape to contain no lawn at all. This involves incorporating some or all of the design tips just mentioned. It also requires choosing a lifestyle that needs no lawn and being willing to provide a different kind of care and attention when it comes to maintaining the landscape.

Regardless of what sort of plants you choose to occupy your gardens and grounds, a substantial amount of energy will be conserved if you design the entire landscape specifically to need minimal supplemental water. Chapter 9 explains why, and describes how to achieve this goal.

Using Water Efficiently

It's a simple fact: watering a landscape uses energy. This is true whether you live in the country and have your own well, with its single pump that pulls water up one gallon at a time, or in a city where water comes from municipal wells and treatment plants in thousands of gallons a minute. The process of getting water from where it is (in streams, lakes, reservoirs and below the ground) to where we want it (our homes, businesses, farms and landscapes) requires effort, and most of that effort is provided by electricity.

Until recently, most of us have been a bit careless about the way we've used water. And the relevant word here is "careless," as in, we just haven't cared all that much. Not about where water comes from, nor where it goes, nor how much we use, nor for what. We've just turned on the tap or the spigot and expected that voila! nice clean water will come rushing out. And it has.

But in recent days, we've been coming to our senses. Water shortages, restrictions and bans, droughts, lower water tables, salinization, shrinking aquifers — we've heard all about them, and many of us have experienced them first-hand. It's a new realization for most Americans: water is not, after all, unlimited. Shocking! Plus we're wondering about global warming. How will it affect regional rainfall and temperature, and what about the weather in our own town, our own yard? These issues, coupled with our desire to save energy, all point directly to the advice in this chapter: we should design our landscapes so they need and consume less water.

Fig. 9.1:
*Several plants
growing together
in one location
helps shade the
ground, reducing
the need for
watering.*

Using less water will immediately lower electricity bills. Perhaps even more important, it will also produce long-term energy savings: the equipment and facilities that treat, store and pump our water will last longer and need less frequent repair. When water is used wisely, so that it's fully absorbed and doesn't run off the land, this reduces both pollution and erosion, and prevents the cost of later repairs. And by designing property so it needs less water, we'll also save energy on landscape maintenance. We'll spend less time hauling a hose around, turning sprinklers on and off, fiddling with timers, monitoring everything and replacing plants that have perished from lapses in their watering regimen.

The following Actions show how to water landscapes wisely:

- Design gardens for least water demand.
- Manage runoff with topography.
- Collect rainwater.

ACTION: Design Gardens for Least Water Demand

The best way to save water in your landscape is simply to garden with plants that need only the water that's naturally bestowed by rain and held in your soil. Of course, if you grow vegetables, fruit or any kind of food, you'll have to water these plants to keep them productive. This is only reasonable. But the rest of the landscape — shrubs, trees, flowers, ferns and lawn (if you have any) — can consist of plants that don't depend on an extra supply of water.

Design Tip: Select Plants Suited to Local Water Conditions

To achieve this goal, pay attention to rainfall amounts and the moisture in your soil. You don't need actual measurements, just common sense. If your soil is dry and/or rain is very rare, choose plants that can handle this situation, that are drought-tolerant. In temperate regions, choose plants that are capable of tolerating a range of moisture conditions. (Many plants will simply slow down or wilt a bit when resources are scarce and then perk up again when things get better.) Most garden centers and nurseries provide basic information about a plant's moisture requirements.

The ideal plants, especially in situations where the soil is extremely wet or dry, may be native species. As stated earlier (see page 77 for a fuller discussion), native plants have evolved over thousands of years under a particular set of conditions. They've "figured out" how to thrive with just the resources that nature provides. (Please note: this is not to imply that they've *thought* about it, but rather that the species that could take advantage of the situation survived, and others didn't.) Plants that evolved in regions that experience extended dry periods may be perfectly suited to your landscape, their roots, stems and leaves already capable of living without extra water.

Design Tip:
Design a Water-conserving Lawn

The best way to reduce lawn watering is simply to get rid of some (or all) of the lawn. Alternatives to lawn are discussed in Chapter 8. If you need to have some lawn in your landscape, there are a few simple things you can do to cut down on how much water it needs.

First, make sure the soil itself is loose and full of tiny pores that let water trickle in and be absorbed. If your soil is hard and dry, you can create these pores by aerating the soil with a tool designed for that purpose (on small lawns, this can be done with a hand tool; otherwise you might need a power aerator). Even better, although slower, will be to add compost to your soil. On existing lawns, you can simply scatter a thin layer of loose compost over the surface, and micro-organisms will help incorporate it into the earth below, gradually making the soil more porous. For more details about preparing soil for a lawn, and for creating healthy lawns, see Chapter 14.

Next, assuming you've reduced your lawn to a size that just meets your needs, and assuming your soil is in good shape, you can save water by choosing grass species or varieties that will thrive without it. The turf industry has produced endless varieties of grass suited to every possible condition. If you're aiming to create a golf course or a deep luscious lawn, you may need the advice of an expert. Otherwise, a local garden center can guide you to the most

Fig. 9.2:

This yucca plant, native to the eastern half of the US, produces a large taproot that stores water, enabling it to stay alive even during extended drought.

drought-tolerant grasses that are suited to your climate and weather conditions.

An even better choice, in the larger scheme of things, is to select a native grass. In the US, two native species are becoming more common as lawn grass: blue grama grass (which can tolerate fairly cold winters) and buffalo grass (which won't thrive in cold or humid regions). Unlike most native grasses, which form clumps rather than the carpet we expect of conventional turf grasses, these two will create a fairly dense, uniform cover.

Design Tip: Mulch All Bare Ground

The water that you use in your gardens will do the most work for you and your plants if your soil is capable of holding onto it and making it available over a long stretch of time. The best way to accomplish this is to protect the surface of the ground with some sort of mulch material. Keep in mind that mulch does more than suppress weeds and (if organic) gradually break down to add its nutrients to the soil. It also can act like a spongy blanket, holding water and releasing moisture gradually downward and then keeping that moisture from evaporating.

You can choose between many different kinds of mulch to suit your own taste and budget; several options are discussed in more detail in Chapters 4 and F14. From the per-

Fig. 9.3: *A small mulch ring around a tree trunk may help prevent damage from mowers and trimmers, but that's all it does.*

spective of design, however, one thing is most important: the larger the area of mulch, the more good it will do. Remember that plants extract food from the soil only when their roots can absorb nutrients that are dissolved there. So if a plant is surrounded by a tiny ring of mulch, that circle is nourishing only a small portion of the entire root zone.

For a tree, whose roots extend outward in all directions farther than most of us imagine (not downward in a mirror image of the tree), the area of mulched soil should extend at least all the way out to the edge of the tree's canopy overhead. Even better is to group trees so that the mulch for each single tree overlaps and blends with neighboring mulch, creating one large zone of moist, rich, fertile soil. (Picture a forest, where the trees grow within a few feet of each other, with their roots all tangled up and taking nourishment from the same soil, with a rich layer of fallen leaves covering the ground.) When you're designing or laying out garden beds, remember to think about the way that mulch will cover the soil, the shape of the resulting mulched area as well as the location of individual plants. Position plants and beds so that you can merge mulched areas and create a larger area of moist soil.

Design Tip: Establish Watering Zones

Ideally, your property will be designed to need little supplemental water. In this scenario, only the place where food is grown would have to be watered, and the rest would be self-supporting. The reality, however, is that most of us haven't reached that goal yet, and may never reach it. To make the most of the water you do

Newly Planted and Baby Plants

Whenever a plant is transplanted, especially if its roots have been cut, moved or disturbed in any way, it will experience a kind of shock. The exact chemistry of this reaction is complex and hard to fully understand, but we do know that a shocked plant will recover most quickly if water is provided immediately after the move, and for at least a few weeks more. This is a little like feeding your baby food that's mashed up: it's easier for her little stomach to take in and make use of the nutrients. When soil is moist, more of its nutrients stay dissolved, so there are more of them available, in more places, for plant roots to absorb. Your infant may arch her back when she's hungry; your plants will just silently wilt.

provide, arrange your landscape so that plants that need similar amounts of water are grouped together in one general location, in *watering zones*. Plants in each zone will get moistened by a single watering episode, so you won't have to spend time and energy providing water to several different spots in your landscape, and so the water will be used most efficiently.

The zone that requires the most watering should probably also be the smallest zone, containing your vegetable garden (unless your garden is huge and takes up a lot of your property, in which case, congratulations!) and any delicate or fragile plants you just can't live without. A zone of moderate watering should also be relatively small: orchards, berry bushes, ornamental plants near the house. This last category might include plants that need some water during the driest part of the year, but if your plants are properly selected and the ground is well mulched, even these may not need much water. Finally, in an energy-efficient landscape, the zone of least (or no) watering should occupy a significant majority of the whole.

ACTION:
Manage Runoff with Topography

Anything that makes the most of the water you *do* supply to your landscape will decrease the total amount that's needed. In addition to making sure your soil itself is as absorptive as possible, here are a few more things you can do.

Design Tip:
Build Level Terraces in Hillsides

Sloped land can be shaped into a series of level plateaus, or terraces, separated by bands of steeper land, which may be self-supporting or held by retaining walls. These level places will slow the speed of water that's running off a hill, allowing it to stop for a moment and be absorbed.

Fig. 9.4: *A larger zone of mulch will make more nutrients available to a tree, greatly improving its health.*

Desiccation

Wind can remove moisture from a plant. Leaves (and needles) have holes, called stomata, on their surfaces. These open to tiny air spaces inside the leaf, where gas is exchanged with the environment. When stomata are open and the air is still, a boundary layer of saturated air helps hold humidity inside these air spaces. Moving air, however, removes this protective layer. As a result, more moisture is lost from the leaf, and the plant works to replace this by drawing moisture up from the soil. If there's not enough in the soil, the plant dries out, or desiccates. Basically, it wilts. And if no water is provided, eventually the plant will die.

This effect is easy to see in winter. When the ground is either very dry or frozen, water is not available for uptake. Evergreens in particular suffer in the winter, as their foliage continues to transpire and lose moisture even in the absence of any moisture to replace what's lost. By late winter and early spring, evergreens with brown needles or leaves are a common sight.

Retaining Walls

To save the most energy, build retaining walls out of local or recycled materials. These may be any sort of stone, locally made brick, bamboo, rot-resistant wood, rubber tires, etc. See Chapter 15 for a more detailed discussion of landscape construction materials.

Fig 9.5: *While no residential landscape can duplicate these extensive Balinese rice paddy terraces, this image does illustrate spectacular rainwater management.*

Fig. 9.6: *This lush garden of fruit and vegetables receives abundant runoff from the gently-sloping yard behind it.*

Of course, the greatest benefit will come from making the soil on these terraces as spongy and absorptive as possible. The best way is to let it contain a lot of interwoven plant roots and a nice rich layer of mulch (either supplied by you or, even better, provided by natural processes). If your land is steep or hilly, be sure to preserve any existing vegetation or let these slopes be gradually revegetated in semi-wild or wild growth, or as managed conservation patches (as discussed in Chapter 7).

Lawn, even if it's growing in the best porous soil, is the least absorptive type of ground surface except for packed earth or pavement, so if your goal is to let water sink into the ground, consider replacing or not having any lawn on steep slopes. This will also prevent having to mow on awkward, slippery and sometimes dangerous slopes. No matter what you decide to grow on your hillside land, creating terraces will help keep water in place. A further benefit of these terraces will be to diminish or eliminate soil erosion, so you won't have to spend energy replacing or repairing what's been washed away.

Design Tip: Position Gardens Appropriately in Relation to Slopes

When you're laying out all the various components of your landscape, keep in mind that the top of a hill is always drier than the bottom, the place where most surface water ends up, unless you've diverted or held it elsewhere. Placing a planted area at the foot of a hill will have two advantages: most plants will benefit from the extra water, unless the soil is too wet; and the whole garden will help absorb runoff, preventing it from continuing on across the landscape.

Your final decision about the location and shape of gardens will, of course, depend on the quality of your soil and the amount of rainfall in your region, along with the steepness of the slope and the size of the whole watershed that extends above it. But keep in mind that higher is almost always drier.

Design Tip:
Direct Water on the Ground

The ground can be shaped to help direct water where you want it to go. Rather than shunting surface water away from your landscape into ditches and storm drains that carry it somewhere else, consider treating water as a valuable resource that you want to use, and maybe not share with anyone else. Besides collecting rainwater in barrels or cisterns (discussed below), you can help move surface water directly to the place it will be used.

Swales are shallow ditches that catch water and move it slowly along, in a direction that's generally sideways to the direction of runoff. Some swales are so shallow and wide that they're hardly visible, and you'd only notice them through the soles of your feet, by walking across them. Some swales run more steeply downhill than others, depending on the terrain and the placement of other elements of a landscape.

Swales may be seeded with turf grass integrated into a lawn area, where the flow of water will hardly be slowed at all. They may be surfaced with pebbles or other rough, non-degradable material, which both slows the water movement somewhat and prevents erosion. In both cases, the swale will shed more water than it absorbs. Another option is to plant a swale

with grasses, ferns or shrubs that will benefit from the extra water. This sort of swale, sometimes termed a bio-swale, absorbs more water than it sheds.

In any case, you can purposely shape the earth of your landscape to carry runoff to a place where it will serve your needs, either to a holding area or to gardens that can absorb it. The trick is to make sure the bottom of the

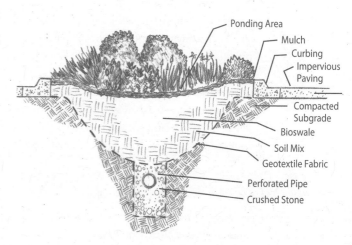

Fig. 9.7: *In addition to containing plants that thrive in moisture, many bioswales are constructed over a base of crushed stone that absorbs runoff and lets it percolate in the surrounding soil. In some cases, excess water is then carried in a pipe to the storm drain system.*

Watersheds

A watershed is the entire area of land that drains runoff toward a particular body of water. Also sometimes called *drainage basins* or *catchment areas*, watersheds are separated from each other by *divides*, which are ridges, mountaintops or any high point of land where water is diverted in two or more different directions, each direction leading to its own watershed. Little streams are supplied by little watersheds. The Mississippi River Watershed covers more than a million square miles and includes all or part of 31 states and two Canadian provinces.

swale slopes continuously in the direction you want it to go, regardless of how steep or gentle the sides may be.

Design Tip: Use Subsurface Drainage When Necessary

Some swales can be made so their center, the bottom of the swale, contains a trench filled with porous material, such as sand, small pebbles or gravel, where water can more easily percolate downward into the lower levels of the soil. Such a trench might also hold a perforated pipe (containing small holes) that will carry water along the base of the trench to an outlet somewhere else. Sometimes this outlet drains water into a buried bed of porous material, where it will continue percolating into the surrounding sub-grade. If the pipe is daylighted,

Keep Water Onsite

Increasingly, many cities and towns require that landowners keep all runoff within the boundaries of their own property. This is a good idea for two reasons: it cuts down on the amount of stormwater in public storm drains, thereby reducing wear and tear and later repair; and it prevents harm to other people's land, thereby improving neighbor relations (and potentially decreasing lawsuits).

Sharing Rainwater with Nature

Whenever you collect any of nature's resources for your own use, keep in mind the effect your actions can have on other creatures that share your landscape, both plants and animals. By directing rainwater into storage tanks or gardens, you might also be removing it from surrounding plants that have come to depend on it.

this outlet must be located within the property, rather than on someone else's property, and it should be in a place that allows the collected water to be useful.

ACTION: Collect Rainwater

Rainwater has been collected for centuries in the tropics and arid regions of the world. In recent decades, this activity has become increasingly popular in the American southwest, where new homes are popping up like weeds, and water to support all the people in those homes is dwindling. The subject of collecting rainwater is extensively covered in many books and websites. What follows is a basic overview of the options, along with a brief discussion of their various advantages and drawbacks.

Using collected rainwater in your landscape is essentially free, once your system is set up. It places no demand on groundwater or the public water supply system. And, even better, rainwater is naturally soft and contains no chlorine, minerals or salts.

Design Tip: Collect Rainwater Actively

Active rainwater collection involves collecting and storing water in some sort of container or structure for later use in the house or landscape. It generally entails capturing rain that falls on a flat surface, usually a roof, and directing it via gutters, downspouts and pipes to storage vessels, which may be *rain barrels* or *cisterns*.

All active rainwater collection systems include these basic components:

- the storage vessel itself
- pipes that deliver the water

- an outlet valve (or two) that can connect to either a spigot or hose
- a method for excluding debris and insects, a roof or a screen to cover the openings, or tightly fitted pipes

Rain barrels are water-storage containers that usually hold about 50 gallons or less and stand directly on the ground or on an elevated platform. They may be made of clean (unused) garbage cans, plastic bins manufactured to look like old-fashioned wine barrels, actual wine barrels or any other type of water-tight container. A particularly energy-efficient solution is to use recycled 55-gallon drums from the juice/soft-drink industry (easy to find via the Internet).

Many rain barrels are designed to receive water from standard gutter downspouts (also called leaders). Several manufacturers provide diverters for this purpose, which are sections of downspout that split into two pipes, one that's bent to feed water into the rain barrel and the other to continue down to (or into) the ground for overflow. Diverters are easy to install by simply removing the lower section of an existing downspout with a hacksaw.

Two additional advantages of rain barrels are: once they're set up, watering plants from them can be easier than hauling out a hose; and if you use a water-soluble fertilizer or compost tea in your gardens, these can be mixed directly into the stored water.

The main disadvantage of using a rain barrel is its relatively small size, compared to the amount of water needed for sustaining a large garden or landscape. Of course, the total water ultimately stored in any barrel depends on the size of the catchment area and the actual amount of rainfall. Most manufacturers claim that about a quarter inch of rain on a 500-square-foot roof will completely fill a 55-gallon drum. This amount of water might maintain a 50-square-foot vegetable garden for about a week, which may be more than enough for you. Or it could be not nearly enough in extended dry periods or if your gardens are bigger than that. To overcome this problem, rain barrels can be connected in a series of two or more, depending on your own unique situation and needs.

Cisterns make sense in regions where rain falls in great quantities but only during a partic-

Rainwater Harvested from Roof Runoff
Rainwater intended for drinking or growing food should not be harvested from roofs made of asphalt shingles or treated wood. The same is true for roofs that are color-coated or contain solder or galvanized metal, materials that can contaminate the water.

Roof Gutters in the Winter
Gutters work perfectly fine in snow-free regions of the world, but if you live in temperate and northern regions, keep in mind that gutters can be bent or ripped loose by the action of snow and ice sliding off a roof.

Compost Tea
Compost tea is a liquid fertilizer made from steeping compost in water. It can be sprayed directly on foliage or spread on the soil. In both methods, it provides nutrients to plants, increases beneficial organisms and helps suppress disease.

ular season, and then not again for a long time. Historically, cisterns were underground storage vessels, completely sealed (except for the inflow and outflow pipes) to prevent contamination and evaporation. Now, cisterns are also common above-ground. They may be concrete, metal or wood lined with waterproof material, big enough to hold a couple of hundred gallons or thousands. They may be integrated into a building's structure or free-standing in the landscape, as beautiful objects in their own right: a little stucco house, a short round silo with a conical roof, an upended section of large-diameter galvanized culvert, etc.

If your cistern is to be buried, you'll need some way to pump the water out, unless the cistern is located uphill from where the water will be used, allowing gravity to transport the water. Whether above or below-ground, cisterns are usually designed to be permanent structures with a long lifespan and little need for maintenance.

Fig. 9.8: *In New Mexico, as across much of the American southwest, cisterns and water storage tanks are the norm rather than the exception in many home landscapes.*

Design Tip:
Collect Rainwater Passively

Unlike active rainwater collection, which stores water for later use, passive collection involves creating ways for surface runoff to be concentrated and absorbed directly in the ground. It requires just two basic components:

- an area filled with material that allows water to infiltrate downward and
- terrain that's shaped to direct water toward that area

Passive rainwater collection systems may include infiltration basins, berms, swales and rain gardens. Infiltration basins are holes in the ground filled with loose material, often crushed rock, that contain a high proportion of air spaces where water can be temporarily stored. Sometimes, when a large amount of water needs to be held, these basins might also contain a concrete *dry well*, an empty container with perforated walls, surrounded by a wall of crushed rock. In most cases, the aim is to help water percolate downward into the earth below and there to return to the water table, though some basins have outflow pipes that feed water to plants in the landscape.

Another form of infiltration basin is a *sponge*, essentially a dense bundle of organic material, such as a straw bale or hay bale, buried near the place you want to capture moisture. Water gradually seeps out of this sponge to moisten the adjacent soil.

Berms and swales help water slow down in its flow. *Berms*, mounds of earth that interrupt the passage of water, are usually arranged across the slope, sometimes in broad curves that resemble boomerangs. *Contour swales* are shallow ditches that run almost parallel to the contour of the land, following a nearly level line. These are intentionally designed to pitch so slightly that surface water moves very slowly, giving it a chance to soak in; whatever water doesn't get absorbed will be directed to some sort of storage basin or area.

Rain gardens are like shallow bowls in the landscape filled with growing plants. They're often positioned specifically to capture the outflow from a building's downspouts. Most rain gardens have at their base a layer of crushed stone for good drainage, then a layer of porous but nutrient-rich soil as a growing medium. Select plants for their ability to survive (and even thrive) in wildly fluctuating moisture levels. A rain garden must be carefully built, with a provision for overflow, and its size carefully calculated to handle the amount of water it will receive, or it will simply become a big mushy puddle in the landscape.

CHAPTER SUMMARY

The basic fact underlying all the Actions in this chapter is that using less water saves energy. It will immediately lower electricity bills, and over time it will reduce the amount of energy needed for maintaining and repairing the systems that provide water.

To accomplish these benefits, this chapter explains how to design our landscapes to need little or no supplemental watering, and to make sure that whatever water is used is either put to immediate use, or stored for later use or allowed to soak into the earth where it will

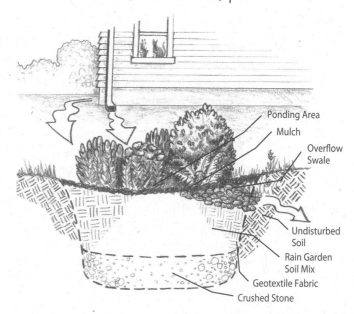

Ponding Area
Mulch
Overflow Swale
Undisturbed Soil
Rain Garden Soil Mix
Geotextile Fabric
Crushed Stone

Fig. 9.9:
Rain gardens are especially helpful in areas where there are few other places for surface runoff to be absorbed — cities and regions of dense suburban development — but they may also appeal in rural landscapes.

eventually return to the water table and replenish the underground supply.

We can intentionally arrange our landscapes to contain: plants suited to natural rainfall amounts; watering zones, where plants are grouped according to their moisture requirements; mulch and absorptive soil to hold water and prevent evaporation; terraces on steep slopes, to slow runoff and encourage percolation; gardens situated to take advantage of natural drainage patterns; and various systems for collecting and storing rainwater.

This concludes the portion of the book that focuses on designing the *planted portions* of our property to reduce our energy consumption. The four chapters in the next section present ideas for saving energy through the thoughtful arrangement of *built* landscape elements, including structures, patios, paths, walls, driveways and parking areas.

Green Roofs

One way to use rainwater wisely is simply to put it to work right where it falls, including on the roofs of buildings. If a roof is flat or gently sloped, it can be a place to grow plants, even food. Such a *green roof* will capture and hold rainfall, reducing the amount of water that enters storm drains. It will also act as an insulating blanket that helps keep a building cool in summer and warm in winter.[1]

Green roofs are layered growing systems that cover roofs specifically built (or retrofitted) for this purpose. Their basic components, from the top down, include:

- the plants themselves

- the growing medium, a lightweight mixture of soil and other engineered materials

- a drainage layer that helps retain water in the growing medium and remove excess water from the system

- a root barrier that keeps plants' roots within the growing medium

- a waterproof membrane that covers the roof sheathing

- a roof that's built strong enough to carry the extra load

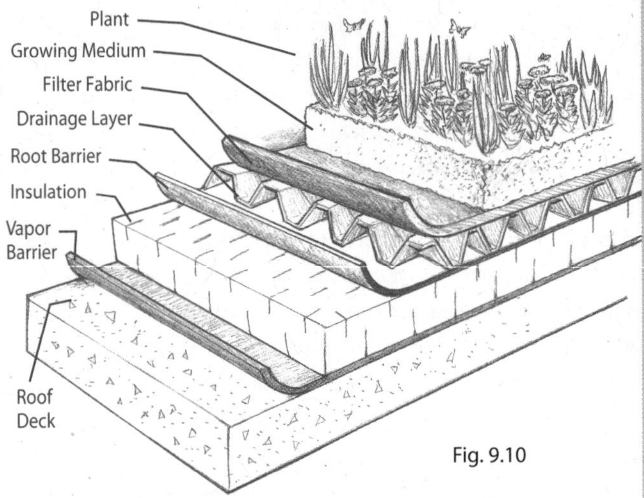

In practice, green roofs exist in two basic categories. Extensive systems are shallow (about 3 to 4 inches deep) and planted with drought-tolerant succulents or grasses that require minimal maintenance and no watering beyond natural rainfall. Intensive green roofs, by contrast, are deeper (6 to 12 inches or more, depending on what's intended to grow there) and planted with a wide range of plants, even trees and shrubs. This type of roof involves a much heavier load than extensive systems, and the plants generally require more maintenance and regular irrigation.

Additional benefits of green roofs include their ability to:

- reduce the heat-island effect in cities, because they remain cooler than a typical asphalt or coated roof, and because plant transpiration actively cools the air

- improve air quality by producing oxygen and absorbing CO_2

- protect roof membranes from UV breakdown, thereby reducing (or eliminating) the need to replace them

- provide citizens with a connection to the earth and growing things that's often missing in cities

For more resources on the topic of green roofs, see Appendix C.

Plant
Growing Medium
Filter Fabric
Drainage Layer
Root Barrier
Insulation
Vapor Barrier
Roof Deck

Fig. 9.10

Designing the Whole Property

THE SIZE, SHAPE AND ARRANGEMENT of every component of your property will determine how much energy you spend both in building the landscape and in living there. Not just your gardens and yard, but also paths, steps and walls, your driveway and parking places, the patio or deck that you use for outdoor living, even the house and garage — your whole landscape can be designed for energy efficiency, and this chapter shows how.

You will save energy at the very start, during the construction process, if you:

• Design your landscape to sit comfortably on the land, so the gardens and grounds conform to the shape of the land, rather than requiring that the terrain itself be dramatically altered.

• Preserve and make the most of what already exists on your property, such as trees and other established plants, exposed bedrock or boulders, old stone walls or fences and intriguing views.

You'll save energy in the process of living in and with your landscape if you:

• Arrange the major pieces of the property — the house, driveway and open spaces — to take advantage of sun and wind patterns.

• Design all the components so they work well together and meet your needs, so your everyday experiences — arriving, parking, entering, relaxing, entertaining, strolling, gardening, etc. — feel comfortable and convenient, and cause no strain.

• Shape the property so it's easy to take care of and requires little outside input.

By designing the entire property with these goals in mind, you'll spend less time, effort, money and fuel on bringing in new material, building more than is needed, compensating for awkward situations, replacing what's lost, repairing damage and keeping the landscape intact. The following four chapters discuss how to design and arrange the major landscape elements for energy conservation.

CHAPTER 10

Fitting the Landscape to the Land

THE WAY THAT A LANDSCAPE IS SITUATED on a property can have a tremendous impact on the amount of energy consumed in the process of building it. This is especially true for landscapes on sloped sites, where creating level places can involve a lot of earthmoving. Shaping the ground, transporting fill to or from the property, trucking in loam to replace what's lost or provide what's needed to repair damaged land: all of these activities consume tremendous amounts of fuel. And all of them can be limited — some even eliminated entirely — by thoughtful planning and design.

This chapter discusses the following Actions to help design landscapes so they fit well with the existing site:

- Revise your ideas to fit the terrain.
- Use the gentlest terrain for the things that need it.
- Use steeper slopes for things that don't need level land.

These actions aren't hard, but they do require care and a willingness to slow down and pay attention to the details of your property's terrain. Some people may be able to work

Earth-grading and Trees

Moving earth and reshaping the ground surface can be very harmful to trees. Their roots need moisture, nutrients and air in the soil, and they suffer when the ground gets disturbed or compacted. For a more detailed discussion of taking proper care of trees during construction, see Chapter 16.

out good solutions simply by looking at what's there and visualizing the final arrangement. In reality though, the average person (and even many who are trained in this field) generally tends to underestimate the steepness of a slope and the extent of earthmoving that will be involved in making land level.

As in the previous chapter, many of the suggestions here apply to larger lots more than to smaller ones, to rural or suburban areas more than to areas that are densely developed and to sloped sites more than to level ones. But all of these ideas contain information that's valuable in understanding how to design landscapes to fit their sites harmoniously.

HOW CAN YOU GET A BETTER UNDERSTANDING OF YOUR LAND?

In addition to simply exploring on foot, a good way to *see* the steep and gentle portions of your property is to examine a *topographic map* of the land. On these maps, contour lines depict the shape of the ground, with each contour line representing an (invisible) plane of uniform elevation. Since lines that are close together represent land that's steeper than lines spaced

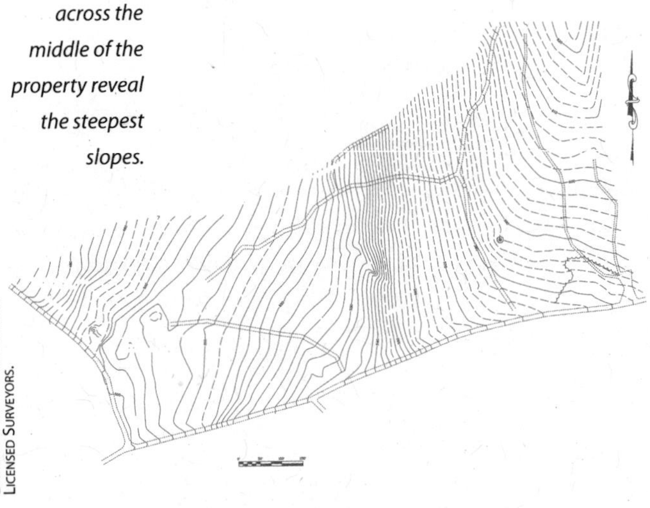

farther apart, it's easy to see at a glance the different sorts of slope.

Your local bookstore may sell topographic maps created by the United States Geological Survey (USGS); each covers a particular area, or quadrant, and is named for a town or city within that region. If not, order these maps online (topomaps.usgs.gov). Additional topographic information can be gleaned from Geographic Information Systems (GIS) maps or aerial photos available in various software programs. All of these methods work best on large pieces of property; if your property is smaller than two acres or so, these maps may not contain enough information to help in your design process. To get the greatest amount of detail about your land, the best option is to hire a surveyor or landscape architect to measure the property and accurately map its features.

A civil engineer or experienced local excavator can also help you understand your land and its potential. Be careful, however, about making large-scale decisions based *only* on their advice because, while many of these people have great knowledge and understanding of the land, they may not be fully tuned into the larger issues of how a landscape will look, function and feel in the overall scheme of things and the long run.

If your site is very steep or complicated, or if your plans are complex, a better option is to consult with a landscape architect or landscape designer who specializes in site planning. These professionals understand the tangible realities of working with land and the physical requirements of creating livable landscapes, as well as the more esoteric issues of form and beauty, and they know how to integrate all of these issues with your

Fig. 10.1: *While the contour lines in this map are somewhat evenly spaced, the lower left corner contains widely-spaced lines that indicate gentler slopes. Closely-spaced lines across the middle of the property reveal the steepest slopes.*

own unique needs and desires. (Appendix A provides instructions for measuring or determining slope on contour (topographic) maps.)

ACTION:
Revise Your Ideas to Fit the Terrain

Many of us carry in our mind's eye some sort of image of how we think our home landscape should look. For some of us, this picture may be clear and very detailed, while for others, it's just a vague notion, a feeling from childhood or a partial scene recalled from a photo or magazine. Whatever your own image, if a landscape is to be energy efficient, it has to be arranged to fit the physical reality of your actual property.

Design Tip: Work with What You Have

Whether the land is flat or sloped, rocky or smooth, damp or dry, wooded or open, *you will save energy* — both your own and the Earth's — if you modify your ideas to fit what's there rather than modifying what's there to accommodate your preconceived desires.

This simple shift in attitude may feel unfamiliar or uncomfortable to those of us raised in a society that places few limits on our expectations. It is, however, one of the most important steps you can take in creating an energy-efficient (and environmentally friendly) landscape. The following Actions describe in more detail how this new attitude can be applied.

Fig. 10.2: *To build a stairway without changing the shape of this steep slope, stone slabs are set directly into the ground (on a prepared base of crushed stone), with a few landings positioned as needed.*

Basic Explanation of Slope Percentages

The land's *slope* is the amount that land rises vertically within a certain horizontal distance. This relationship between *rise* and *run* is often expressed in two different ways. Some people describe slope as a ratio, as 10:1, or ten to one; others describe the very same slope as 1:10, or one in ten. But which is rise and which is run? To be absolutely clear about what is meant, it's a good idea to indicate which side of the ratio refers to the rise, and which to the run, as in 1v:10h (one vertical to ten horizontal). Or simply use percentages (10 percent), which eliminate any confusion.

Here are some sample slope percentages.

- 1 percent slopes tilt 1 foot of rise in 100 feet of distance (6" in 50'). This is the ideal minimum slope needed for rainwater to drain off a hard or paved surface.

- 2 percent slopes tilt 1 foot of rise in 50 feet of distance, (12" in 50'). This slightly greater slope allows rainwater to drain off lawn or a rough surface.

- 5 percent slopes tilt 1 foot of rise in 20 feet of distance. This is the ideal maximum slope for parking spaces and for any cross pitch on a driving surface.

- 10 percent slopes tilt 1 foot of rise in 10 feet of distance. This is the ideal maximum slope for driveways in regions that receive snow and ice.

- 25 percent slopes tilt 2.5 feet of rise in 10 feet of distance. This is ideally the steepest slope to use for lawns, for ease and safety in mowing.

ACTION: Use the Gentlest Terrain for Things That Need It

Every landscape contains elements that really must be flat or nearly flat. If a house is to be built on slab rather than with a basement, the slab must be perfectly level and the land around it must slope gently away from the building on all sides. The area where cars park and turn around should tilt a little bit for drainage, but ideally no more than 5 percent in any direction, for safety (see box on previous page).

A stone patio must also slope a tiny bit for drainage, usually no more than 1 to 2 percent (a pitch that's imperceptible to both our eye and our feet). Outdoor play spaces should provide

Fig. 10.3: This little terrace occupies a level portion of the property's back yard; the surface's very slight pitch helps rainwater shed away from the house to be absorbed in the surrounding gardens.

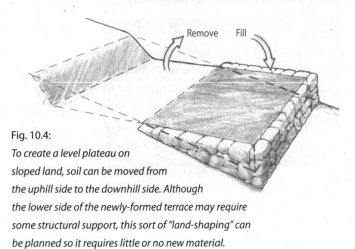

Fig. 10.4:

To create a level plateau on sloped land, soil can be moved from the uphill side to the downhill side. Although the lower side of the newly-formed terrace may require some structural support, this sort of "land-shaping" can be planned so it requires little or no new material.

at least some amount of level land, and yards intended for athletic games should be nearly level as well. Also, on rural and suburban property, a subsurface septic system will probably need to be constructed on land that's at most only gently sloped, and its upper surface will usually end up being level.

Design Tip: Move the Least Amount of Soil Necessary

What's so hard about moving soil? Here's one simple example. Say you want to create a level plateau that's 40 feet x 100 feet on land that slopes at 5 percent. This would involve either moving 1,000 cubic feet (37 cubic yards) of earth from the uphill side of the space to the downhill side (then providing support on the low side for the loose soil that's now piled up), or removing 4,000 cubic feet (148 cubic yards) of material from the site altogether (and then somehow supporting or healing the 2-foot-high cut into the uphill slope). Could you move this much soil by hand? How long would it take a diesel-gulping (pollution-spewing) backhoe to dig out and move that earth? What would happen if the land turned out to be very rocky, or solid bedrock? Where would the leftover soil be moved *to* and how would it get there?

The best way to save energy in the construction of a landscape is to identify the portions of the terrain that are already as close to level as possible, and then to arrange the overall layout of the landscape so patios, play areas, the septic system and the car zone can be positioned on that land. In this way, the steeper terrain will be left alone or used for the parts of your landscape that don't need flat land.

ACTION: Use Steeper Slopes for Things That Don't Need Level Land

A good landscape component to place on the sloped portion of a site is the house itself. If the building is constructed with a basement or crawl space foundation rather than on a slab, the land can drop away from front to back of the house or from one side to the other, or both. Retaining walls can support the descending slope and create level plateaus that partly conceal the exposed foundation. If the slope is steep enough, the basement of the house may have a door that gives access to the lower level of ground.

This needs to be done with care, so the first floor and basement floor are set in a proper relationship to the ground level, with the first floor being far enough above the ground to protect the sill and floor from moisture, and with the basement floor being close enough to the ground for comfortable access. In every case, the bottom of a foundation needs to extend below grade enough (or be covered enough) to protect it from frost action. Every region has an established frost level below which builders know they must extend the bottom of any building's foundation.

Design Tip: Design Decks Thoughtfully

An elevated deck that extends out from the house also makes sense on sloped land. This is especially true on steep slopes, where building a patio or raised terrace might be quite expensive. A common practice is to build a deck along the entire length of a house wall, and extend it out over the entire basement wall. Unfortunately, this often prevents sunlight from entering basement windows and makes access to the basement door somewhat difficult. It also often results in a deck that's long and skinny, often with a door in the center, effectively producing two small spaces on either side of the door that are uninviting and awkward to use.

A better choice in deck design is to build the structure so it extends over only part of the basement wall and perhaps wraps around one corner of the house. If properly positioned, this arrangement lets light into some basement windows, makes the basement door more accessible and creates a spacious corner area of the deck that can more comfortably hold a table and chairs or seating area.

Fig. 10.5:
This house is built deeply into the slope, with a lower-level deck that allows maximum sunlight to enter the basement windows. Here, in Katywil Eco-Village (in Colrain, Massachusetts), this arrangement preserves precious level land for car spaces, outdoor play and growing food.

Fig. 10.6:
Wrapping the southwest corner of the house, this deck provides a comfortable corner gathering space and allows plenty of light into basement window along the house's back wall.

ARCHITECTURAL CREDIT: AUSTIN DESIGN, INC.

Design Tip: Use Slopes for Terraces and Patios

Another type of landscape feature that works well on sloped land is terraced patios or gardens. This idea can be especially effective on gentle or moderate slopes, because it allows supporting or retaining walls to be fairly short. Retaining walls that are taller than three feet generally require special care in both design and construction, to make sure they're safe and capable of supporting the weight of earth behind them. On very high or steep slopes, the safest choice may be to build a series of short retaining walls that *step down* the slope, creating tiered or layered terraces in the spaces between the walls.

Wildflower meadows and/or mown lawn can occupy the sloping portions of your property. In general, both of these elements work best on slopes gentler than about 30 percent (one foot of vertical rise in 3 feet of horizontal distance), which allows them to be mowed or maintained without difficulty. Steeper slopes may be slippery and dangerous to mow.

Finally, the best way to use the steepest land on any property may be simply to leave it alone. This is especially true for steep land that already contains established trees, shrubs or other vegetation. Removing the plants from steep land exposes it to the risk of erosion, and revegetating steep slopes is far more complex and difficult than planting gentle or level land. (See Chapter 14 for more guidance about plants, gardens and planting techniques.)

CHAPTER SUMMARY

The reasons for designing landscape so they fit the land well are to minimize earthmoving and to keep the area of disturbance as small as possible. Both of these actions save energy by limiting the amount of fuel used in the process of construction, and by making the final repair and revegetation as easy as possible.

This chapter provides guidance about getting a good understanding of the slopes and terrain of your property, then using this knowledge to position the major elements of your landscape in ways that will require the least change in the shape of the land. In essence, this involves designing the size, shape and arrangement of things *in response to* the physical conditions of the site. It also can involve letting go of certain preconceptions and absolute requirements about how you thought things *should* look and function, and instead being open to new possibilities about how they *can* look and function, for the sake of great savings, both immediate and future.

The major landscape components that should be positioned on level or gentle land include outdoor living space, play areas and parking spaces. Elements that don't need level land include the house itself, garden terraces, decks and driveways. Of course, all of these latter elements can be built perfectly well on level land, if that's all the site contains, but if much of the site is sloped, it's preferable to use the gentlest land for the things that need it.

Fig. 10.7:
Two dry-laid stone retaining walls, one slightly taller than the other, "step up" the slope between this house's basement entrance and its back yard. The upper wall supports a level lawn/play area.

CHAPTER 11

Designing the Car Zone

Take a quick glance around and you'll probably notice that vehicles occupy a lot of space in the landscape. In cities and the commercial parts of any town, vast amounts of pavement are devoted to roads and parking areas. Even in our home landscapes, the amount of space occupied by the *car zone* — a driveway and off-street parking — may often be 10, 20 or as much as 50 times larger than the vehicles themselves.

Of course, driveways need to be *built* right, so they're durable and hardy, but we can also make *design* choices that will reduce the energy consumed in our car zones, in the following three ways.

Construction. Because most land is naturally too soft to support vehicles, nearly every square foot of space that we drive and park on has to be created with an immense input of effort, almost always by heavy equipment. The relentless activity of earthmoving and paving machinery, oceans of asphalt, tons of concrete and mountains of stone use a staggering amount of petroleum. And every one of our driveways, every single parking space, no matter how small and innocent, adds to the cost. By paying attention to the size, shape and location of our car zones, we will save energy.

Fig. 11.1: *This country driveway stays narrow as it passes through woodland and only widens where cars need to park and turn.*

119

Maintenance and Repair. If a driveway is paved, it will have to be resurfaced someday. If unpaved, ruts and puddles will inevitably appear, and if it's steep the surface will likely erode in a heavy rain. The edges of driveways break down, tree roots burrow below and lift the surface, a snowplow may catch an edge or tear the pavement. Without exception, every driveway eventually requires repair, almost always involving the input of carbon-based fuels. Well-designed driveways, however, need minimum repair.

Normal Use. If the shape of the space easily accommodates vehicle turning, backing and parking, and if a snowplow can maneuver easily, we'll use less gas every day. If a driveway gets warmed by the sun in winter and shaded in summer, we'll spend less energy on snow removal and air conditioning our cars.

The following Actions describe several ways to design car zones to minimize energy consumption during the construction, repair and the everyday use of these essential spaces within our landscapes.

+ Put the driveway in the right place.
+ Make the car zone big enough, but not too big.
+ Choose suitable paving material.

(Please note: this discussion does not address roads and public ways, which are designed by civil engineers, highway departments and zoning laws.)

ACTION:
Put the Driveway in the Right Place

Your driveway may already be built and finished. Maybe it's totally fine and in a perfectly good place. Or maybe not. Many driveways don't function quite as well as we'd like. Yours might be too steep, so it's a little scary to use or dangerous when slippery. Perhaps it catches too much runoff and erodes easily, or it gets rutted in rainy seasons because it was built without adequate support. Or maybe your driveway doesn't work for reasons that are less tangible. Is yours in an odd relationship to the house, so the arrival experience is unattractive or uncomfortable? Are visitors confused about where to park or enter? Does pavement dominate an important view, or do cars seem to crowd the house? For these and a host of other possible reasons, you might consider moving your driveway.

But wait, wouldn't this consume a lot of energy, and isn't that what we're trying to avoid? The answer is yes, and not only that, this step is likely to be quite expensive. Moving or reshaping a driveway is a big deal, a job that should only be done if it's really essential.

Overview of Driveway Construction

To make a driveway that's stable and strong enough for vehicles, builders follow these general steps, with local variations depending on soil conditions:

- Remove existing topsoil; store for use elsewhere on site or truck away.
- Grade the ground into the appropriate shape; this often involves excavating several inches, sometimes a foot or more.
- Install drainage (ditches, swales, culverts, etc.) if necessary.
- Truck in, spread and compact suitable base materials for support and drainage.
- Place the surface layer: asphalt, macadam, concrete, crushed stone or other locally available loose material.
- Smooth and finish the surface so water drains off.

This is why it's so important to put a driveway in the right place to begin with. If it's safe, durable and easy to use, if it just feels right and natural, it won't ever need to be moved. The goal is to create a driveway that you basically never notice, because it's just quietly doing its job: moving cars and people comfortably and conveniently between the road and the house. And the most important step in creating a comfortable driveway is to put it in the right location.

Of course, in many landscapes, there's only one logical place for the driveway (although it should still be designed in the right shape and size, as described in the next Action). This is particularly true on small lots or when a garage is close to the road.

Far more often, though, and especially in suburban and rural areas, a house's driveway is an accidental by-product of the construction process. Here's what usually happens. The building contractor chooses a place for an access drive with one purpose in mind: keeping immediate project costs to a minimum. This makes sense, as far as it goes. But rarely do builders consider the complex mixture of physical and psychological tasks that a driveway should perform for the people who will eventually *live* in the house. And then, just because a driveway is already in place, and money has been spent on creating it, too frequently what served for the builder's access drive gets paved (literally set in stone) and by default becomes the permanent driveway.

Living with a poorly designed driveway is like getting a bad cold: you suddenly realize how much you miss feeling fine. The big difference with a driveway is that you won't naturally recover in a week, a month or in any number of years. The only solution will be to relocate and reshape the driveway. This wastes the time and energy you already spent, and then uses more of both to build the new driveway that you want.

The following Design Tips will help you to figure out the best location for your driveway and to evaluate your current driveway and decide whether you ought to move it. If you're lucky enough to be in the early stages of building a house, before the construction drive has been created, think carefully about its position and take charge of this decision. If the builder has already laid in a rough drive, consider whether this is the best place for the permanent one. And if your property is steep or the landscape is complex, hire a landscape architect or designer to help you. In the long run, it will be cheaper by far to position the driveway well at the start than to replace it later.

Design Tip: Design a Comfortable Driveway Slope

A driveway that's too steep can be a problem for both the cars and the people using it and for the driveway surface itself. The surface of a steep driveway can get rutted by tires spinning too hard, or it can wash out in heavy rain. Driveways that get icy in winter, especially if they're paved, may need to be sanded to keep

Fig. 11.2: *After allowing the construction process to determine the shape and location of their driveway, will these new homeowners now go to the trouble (and expense) of creating a landscape less dominated by pavement?*

Fig. 11.3:
This extremely steep driveway may be perfectly navigable in summer, but imagine driving it when it's covered in snow or ice!

them passable, and the sand will later accumulate along the edges, looking ugly, smothering plants or needing to be removed. In everyday use, an overly steep driveway may be the cause of accidents that range from merely inconvenient to actually dangerous. These accidents can waste your time, ruin your day, upset everybody and make your friends reluctant to visit. And worst of all, dealing with all of these situations — the cars, the people and the driveway itself — consumes energy, your own and the Earth's.

How steep is too steep? There's no absolute formula, and the answer depends on many things. Most important is your local climate conditions, because snow and ice make everything more difficult. Other factors include whether or not the driveway is paved, the steepness of the land itself and what other choices are available, a driver's ability and attitude, the type of car using the driveway and the condition of its tires. If you and most of your friends have four-wheel-drive cars, your driveway can safely be steeper than the norm. But for delivery trucks, emergency vehicles and at least a few of your friends or relatives, your steep driveway will be a problem.

So, *what's a general rule that will work for in most situations?* The maximum slope, the steepest a driveway should be, is 12 percent, 12 feet of vertical rise in 100 feet of horizontal run, or 1 foot of rise in about 8.5 feet of run. To be safer, especially in locations where a driveway may even occasionally be covered with snow or ice, a better maximum is 10 percent (1 foot of rise in 10 feet of run), and 8 percent would be best. In mountainous terrain, where most people are accustomed to driving on steep slopes, or in regions that receive no snow, it's not unusual to find driveways as steep as 15 to 20 percent, but to avoid accidents and ensure drivers' comfort, this should be an exception rather than the rule.

No matter how steep your driveway has to be, there are two parts of it that must slope as gently as possible. The start of the drive (where it intersects the public road) and the end of the drive (where cars park and people walk toward the house) should have a gradient no steeper than 5 percent. This is especially important in wintry climates, but it also applies in hotter regions. Having a nearly level pad — ideally as least as long as one car length — at the driveway's entrance will help keep cars from accidentally sliding out into the road in slippery conditions (some local zoning ordinances actually require this). A nearly level space near the house will make parking and walking safer and more comfortable for everyone.

To figure out the slope of an existing or proposed driveway, follow instructions provided in Appendix A. And again, if your site is complex, you will benefit from getting the help of a landscape architect or designer.

If you discover that your driveway is or will be too steep, what should you do? You have three choices (actually four, if you include just living with it). You can raise the bottom, perhaps by choosing a different point of entrance from the road, or, if you're building a house, by choosing a different location for the building. You can lower the top, in the same way. Both of these options reduce the vertical rise of the driveway while keeping the distance the same. Or you can keep the top and bottom elevations the same and make the whole driveway longer, thereby reducing the overall slope. This might be accomplished by realigning the drive, adding a curve or orienting the drive in a completely different direction than you started out imagining. Or you might work out a solution that combines these choices. Keep in mind that angling diagonally up a slope will make a driveway less steep than going straight up that slope.

Two Final Notes about Slope

It's okay if short sections of a driveway are steeper than 10 to 12 percent, especially if there are gentler runs on either side of the steep portions, and especially if these are all on a straight section of the drive. Having a steep slope on a curve doesn't work well because cars naturally need to *slow down* a bit to make the turn while they also need to *speed up* a bit to get up the steeper slope. And curves are where ice, snow and soft mud (so common in rural New England, during mud season) present the worst problems.

Steep driveways that are unpaved can wash out in heavy or extended rainfalls. This is especially true if they're not graded in a way that allows water to shed sideways off the driving surface. When water runs straight down an unpaved driveway, it will pick up bits of loose soil, which will soon erode little gullies that can eventually become deep ruts or worse. If your driveway has to be steeper than 10 to 12 percent, make sure the surface drains well.

Design Tip:
Three Problem Areas to Avoid

There are several aspects of the landscape that will automatically either add to the cost of constructing a driveway or hasten its demise, or both. First among these is **wet soil**. Ground that contains a lot of water, either because this spot collects runoff from higher ground or it holds seepage from below, is never strong enough to support vehicles. In addition, if a driveway that's been built in wet soil doesn't have a way to shed runoff, the resulting standing water can cause erosion or lead to freeze-thaw damage. The only way to build a driveway in wet soil is to excavate and remove the soft earth, and replace it with material that's more stable (and raising the surface a bit, so it stands above the neighboring ground level, may also be a good idea). Usually this requires some form of sand and gravel, or whatever's locally available. These materials themselves are generally not expensive; their real drawback is the energy needed to extract them from their source and truck them to your location.

Wetlands
Be sure to check with your local environmental regulatory board (conservation committee, department of environment, etc.) about whether your wet soil is actually part of a regulated wetland where construction may be limited or prohibited.

Solid bedrock presents an opposite sort of challenge from wet soil. While it may provide a perfectly stable and non-eroding driving surface, bedrock rarely comes in exactly the right shape and slope for a driveway. In some cases you might be able to work around it. You could skirt the bedrock area, or keep a strange bump in one section of the driveway or figure out some other creative solution.

More often, however, bedrock will have to be removed from a driveway, and this process can be a huge energy sink. If the rock is loose enough, it could be excavated by heavy equipment nibbling away at it. If it's completely solid, it'll have to be blasted with dynamite or cracked by chemical action. In any case, the final step in all of these actions will be to move the excess rock away from the driveway bed, either by shoving it to some other part of the site or by loading it into a truck and hauling it away. Every step equals energy, energy, energy. A better choice, if the site allows, is to find a different location for the driveway, away from any bedrock.

A final landscape feature to be avoided when locating your driveway is the ground immediately beneath very **large, mature trees.** Shade trees are a treasure in virtually any landscape. Branches arching overhead, a tunnel of foliage, pools of deep shade, dappled shadows

Fig. 11.4:
To build this new driveway so close to valuable trees, arborists prepared the site, first by cutting tree roots cleanly and then by nourishing the entire root zone.

dancing over the ground — who doesn't delight in these? But when it comes to choosing a position for your driveway, be very careful about trying to achieve these effects instantly.

Positioning your driveway too near the trunk of a large tree is a problem for two reasons. First, building a driveway almost always involves excavating the top several inches of earth. This is where most tree roots live, and excavating this layer will inevitably mean that tree roots have to be cut. Also for large trees, the roots near the trunk provide support that keeps the tree from toppling over in wind or storms. When its roots are cut, the tree may eventually fall, leading to an expensive repair and the loss of the tree's beauty, shade and vital wildlife function. The second reason is that the weight of vehicles compacts the earth, which both crushes the tree's roots and eliminates pores in the soil that absorb air, water and nutrients, all of which are vital to a tree's survival.

It's okay to build a driveway within a few feet of very small trees, but with large trees it's best to stay at least as far from the trunk as the length of the branches overhead, and farther is better. If your driveway must pass close to large trees, Chapter 16 provides guidance about how to cause the least harm during the construction process.

ACTION: Design the Car Zone Big Enough, but Not Too Big

No matter what kind of driveway you have, whether it's surfaced with sand, stone, asphalt, concrete or a nice new batch of crushed oyster shells, every cubic yard of excavation, every truckload of fill, every ton of pavement and every square inch of area equals energy spent. If efficiency is your aim, an essential first step is to keep the car zone to its minimum workable size.

How big is a car, and how much space does it need? The cars and trucks we use in our everyday lives rarely exceed 20 feet in length, and many are shorter. Luxury sedans, station wagons, SUVs, vans and even pickup trucks are usually no more than 17 or 18 feet long; compact and medium-size cars are typically only about 14 to 16 feet long. In the face of public demand for greater fuel efficiency, automakers are working to design cars that are shorter still.

The same pattern holds true for the width of vehicles, though this dimension is limited by the width of our existing roads. While big trucks and even fire engines are rarely wider than about 8 feet, our own personal vehicles are usually between 5 and 6 feet wide. Even large pickups never exceed 7 feet in width. So, what does this mean for the design of driveways?

Design Tip:
Design the Driveway's Width Properly

For starters, driveways can be narrower than you might think. As little as 8 or 9 feet of pavement will be wide enough for most normal use, especially if the driveway is straight. Driveways that are long and curved can be this narrow for most of their length, if a few widened places are provided for two cars to pass.

For most people, though, a driving surface that's 10 to 12 feet wide will be more comfortable. This is especially true if the driveway is very winding or often used by larger cars, or if it receives frequent visits from delivery trucks,

needs extra space for snowbanks or abuts a slope or steep bank. With the exception of short drives that lead directly to a two-car garage (and often serve as a parking space for two cars), there's no reason for the driving portion of a driveway ever to be more than 12 feet wide.

Design Tip:
Design Parking Spaces Properly

A general rule of thumb is that each car needs a space about 9 to 10 feet wide. Most public parking lots observe this guideline, and you've probably noticed the places where this wasn't true, because you had a hard time turning in and backing out. A 10-foot-wide parking space

Fig. 11.5: *This twelve-foot wide drive provides plenty of space for cars while also causing least harm to the adjacent woodland. When the driveway was originally built, the nearby trees were quite small, hence barely affected by the construction.*

Plants Beside a Driveway
Be careful about placing shrubs right beside a driveway, where they'll get damaged by car doors opening, people walking or snow being piled. Keep in mind the mature size of any plant, not just its cute little starting size. Trees can be planted near a driveway if there's plenty of adjacent space where their roots can find nourishment. Perhaps the best kind of plants to place alongside a driveway are low herbaceous plants such as meadow grasses, ferns and woodland ground plants, all of which can survive under snowbanks, won't interfere with car doors and can handle a bit of accidental foot traffic.

Fig. 11.6: *When space is limited, it's amazing how narrow a driveway can be!*

lets people open car doors and walk comfortably. Wider parking spaces are rarely necessary (unless you drive a camper), but a narrower width can work just fine in some situations. If you have a very small car, or a very small property, you could probably manage quite well with a parking space that's only 8 feet wide, though walking around a car in this tight space might sometimes be a bit awkward. Just remember, many people regularly park in urban garages no bigger than 10 feet wide.

As far as the length of a parking space is concerned, this depends on the cars being stored there. In most public parking lots, spaces are 18 to 20 feet long. This length is also probably a good idea in your home car zone, even if your own car is short, to accommodate any visitors' larger vehicles, delivery trucks, etc. and to protect parked cars from any errant driving on the adjacent pavement (some people don't back out of their garage quite as straight as they'd

like). However, every situation is unique, and your own may not allow a 20-foot-long parking space. Just keep in mind that anything longer than this is probably unnecessary, unless you anticipate needing to pile a lot of snow at the end of the space.

So, what about the curved space that leads into the parking space, the place where cars turn in and back out? This gets a little trickier, because the turning radius of different vehicles can vary widely. Some cars, even relatively large ones, have a short wheel base that allows the car to make a very tight turn, while some smaller vehicles require a wider turning area. Even though any particular parking space itself may be modest in size, maneuvering a car into and out of it can require a generous curve.

Our aim here is to find the right balance between minimizing the driveway's size, to save energy in construction and materials, and making it big enough for safety and comfort. While there's a tendency to make driveways and parking spaces wider than necessary, the turning curve is where most people underestimate how much space is needed.

The curve that will work best in most situations has a radius of at least 15 feet. A radius of about 18 to 20 feet will do a better job of protecting adjacent ground and structures from damage, but unless your driveway is regularly used by large vehicles, this more generous size is probably not needed. A curve with a radius smaller than 15 feet should be avoided, because in this situation, most cars, simply by the limits of their own wheel base, will be forced to drive off the pavement when turning in or backing out of a parking space. This will damage both the driveway pavement itself and the adjacent ground, and both will eventually need repair. Where a driveway intersects a public road, the turning curve should have radius of at least 20 feet, to accommodate emergency vehicles.

In this country, a magnificent driveway has come to stand for wealth, social status and the power to create anything we want. Many people with average means yearn to have a wide driveway and generous expanses of parking, no matter how modest their home. But gradually, oh so gradually, we're all coming to understand that good things don't have to be grand in scale. If our driveways are to proclaim anything about us and our values, it should be that being big enough is just fine, and more is too much.

ACTION:
Choose Suitable Paving Material

What is the most energy-efficient material to use for the surface of your driveway? Your best choice will depend on climate, site conditions, driveway size, expected use of the driveway and your own lifestyle. The following discussion compares the energy used to produce, install and repair different driveway materials.

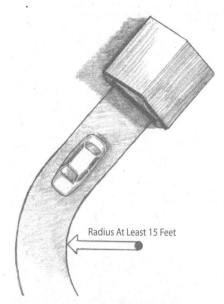

Fig. 11.7:
Driveways must be designed to allow for a turning radius of at least 15 feet. Tighter curves will simply be driven over. And note: the point where a driveway's curve begins must be well outside the garage (or parking space), by at least half a car length, so a turning car doesn't bump into walls (or other parked cars).

Radius At Least 15 Feet

Fig. 11.8:
Same place, same size, same purpose… both of these driveways do their essential job while also expressing the personal preferences of their owners.

Porous Concrete

Also known as *permeable* concrete, porous concrete is made without sand or fine particles, and with a specific ratio of cement to water, so the resulting cured material contains about 15 to 25 percent voids. These tiny air pockets in the concrete let rainfall (as much as 3 to 8 gallons of water per minute) pass through to seep into the ground below.

Porous concrete holds less heat than regular concrete, and the absorbed water helps to cool the ground. This kind of paving can reduce the need for detention basins, drainage swales and other stormwater management structures, thereby cutting down on the amount of land that gets developed in a big project (and, yes, this saves energy).

Design Tip: Solid Materials

Concrete is one of the most widely used driveway surfaces in this country. It's especially popular in the south, where it holds up well in hot weather. The light color of concrete reflects sunlight so the ground stays cooler, helping to reduce the heat-island effect in cities. In frost-prone regions, its easy snow removal is somewhat offset by its vulnerability to salt damage.

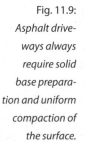

Fig. 11.9:
Asphalt driveways always require solid base preparation and uniform compaction of the surface.

While site preparation and installation costs are higher for concrete than for other materials, well-made concrete driveways may last 50 years or more. Poor construction, however, can lead to cracks and deterioration of the surface, especially in frost-prone regions, and the results may be difficult to repair. Because of its high initial cost, concrete may be a better choice for relatively small driveways than for large ones.

The energy used in producing concrete, which involves heating limestone or other calcium source to 2700°F (1480°C), is higher than for any other type of driveway surface. This drawback may be partly offset by the fact that recycled material may be used to make some kinds of concrete, and almost all old concrete can be ground up and reused (often as the sub-base for other paving, stonework or drainage trenches; see Chapter 15).

Asphalt driveway surfaces are made of a thick liquid petroleum product, sometimes

Pavement and Stormwater Management

In densely developed areas, buildings' roofs and large amounts of pavement limit the amount of land available to absorb rain and snowmelt. The resulting runoff, historically, has been channeled into ditches and pipes, then disposed into streams, rivers and the ocean. The cost for this "management" method has been high, both in harm to the environment and in money to maintain and repair these disposal systems.

To solve this problem, many cities are now working to eliminate the old methods of concentrating runoff. Instead, they're implementing landscape-based ideas for diffusing or spreading out runoff, with the goal of letting more water be absorbed right where it falls, or very nearby.

Some of the most common new strategies involve using pervious pavement — including concrete, asphalt and unit pavers — specifically designed to let water percolate through the surface, either directly into the ground or to a temporary storage basin for gradual infiltration. These pervious pavements reduce tax dollars spent on stormwater management, while also lowering air temperatures and reducing the heat-island effect in cities. (See Chapter 4 for more about cool pavement).

called tar, mixed with crushed stone, spread hot on a prepared, firm base and allowed to cool. This surface softens again when exposed to hot sunlight, plus its dark color absorbs daytime heat, so asphalt driveways are more suitable in northern climates than in the south.

Both asphalt and concrete driveways require a solid base, but installation costs for asphalt are initially cheaper. However, asphalt generally lasts only 25 to 30 years and may require frequent repairing of small cracks and resealing of its surface, an easy job but one that regularly uses more material. In general, asphalt is not as strong as concrete under heavy loads. Snow removal from an asphalt driveway is easy, and its dark color helps melt both snow and ice. As an added bonus, nearly all old asphalt can be taken up, reground and used in making new asphalt.

Design Tip: Aggregate Materials

Although precast concrete **pavers** and similar manufactured paving products can provide a flexible and durable surface for driveways, their manufacture consumes large quantities of energy. Many of these products are made in foreign countries with low employment costs (and lax environmental standards), and the resulting transports costs further diminish their benefit. Somewhat less energy consuming are locally made stone **cobbles** and other natural stone, including **brick.** These materials make a driveway durable, and using local sources will save the energy of long-distance transport that's associated with imported materials.

All of these aggregate materials are likely to be more expensive to install than either concrete or asphalt, partly because they have to be

laid by hand rather than spread by machine. They're also potentially problematic in regions that experience winter frost, as individual stones may be lifted out of level, which can make snow shoveling and plowing difficult. However, repairing surfaces made of pavers, bricks and other flat stone is relatively easy.

The least expensive driveway material is **loose stone.** Called by many names such as gravel, pea stone, crushed stone or chips, this is simply stone that has been crushed and graded to a uniform size. Crushed seashells or other local material also falls into this category. An alternative type of loose stone is a blend of very small sharp chips mixed with stone dust, both usually a by-product of larger crushing operations, which compact tightly together and form a firm surface. All loose stone pavement requires minimal energy to produce and transport from local sources. Site preparation and installation are easy. The main energy drawback of a driveway surfaced with loose material is replacing stones that have been scattered beyond the driveway's edges during snow removal.

Fig. 11.10:
Pre-cast concrete pavers, manufactured in a wide variety of colors and sizes, are becoming increasingly popular as a substitute for poured concrete or asphalt pavement.

Design Tip: A Hybrid Solution

In some situations, the ideal solution will be to combine the best qualities of both asphalt and loose stone in a surface called *oil and stone, tar and chip* or some other similar term. Basically this is a surface made by spreading hot liquid asphalt over the area to be paved, then covering it with a thin coating of loose stone that's then partly compressed or pushed down into the tar. Excess loose stone remains on the surface, where repeated traffic gradually embeds much of this, too, into the tar.

Like asphalt, oil-and-stone paving gets soft when heated, so it won't work very well on surfaces that receive a lot of direct summer sunlight. But it's less expensive, in both energy and money, than just asphalt, and its surface doesn't need to be regularly sealed or repaired. A new layer of stones will rejuvenate the surface if needed.

Also like asphalt, this type of paving provides a flexible and durable driving surface that's reasonably strong (though not as strong as concrete). It's especially appropriate on rural driveways that are paved with loose stone but have some steep sections that might wash out; the oil and stone can be spread just in the areas where it's needed. As is the case with other loose stone paving, snow plowing usually pushes some stones to the edges of the pavement and into the landscape with snow piles.

The main drawback of oil-and-stone paving has nothing to do with energy efficiency: it's simply that finding a contractor to lay this kind of pavement can be difficult. Many country roads are paved with this system, so highway departments are prepared to do the job, but they won't necessarily take on a small driveway job, and not all driveway paving companies have the right equipment or experience. However, if this sort of driveway surface can be built, it's often an ideal solution.

CHAPTER SUMMARY

This chapter covers the complex and little-understood subject of driveway design. Few people might even consider this a design issue, yet as the above discussion shows, the way a driveway is positioned and shaped in relation to its surroundings can have a major impact. A thoughtfully designed driveway makes everyday activities easier and more comfortable, but more important for the message of this book, it also saves energy, during construction, maintenance and normal use.

The first step to consider in this process is the actual location of the driveway, particularly in relation to slope. Overly steep driving surfaces can be uncomfortable or impossible to use at certain times of the year. This chapter outlines rules of thumb that prevent these problems. It also covers the ideal size of a driveway and its associated parking spaces and explains the cost of making them too big or too small. Finally, the chapter evaluates various paving materials, their advantages and disadvantages in terms of cost, care, lifetime and everyday living.

The next chapter in this section on designing the whole property presents several ideas for getting the most out of every component of a landscape, arranging things for multi-purpose and using materials efficiently.

CHAPTER 12

Making the Most of Every Element

Your landscape can be designed so that it comfortably supports the activities of your everyday life while also satisfying your aesthetic tastes. You will save energy if you consider both purpose and appearance at the start of every landscape project. This is true whether you're adding a patio, revitalizing an old garden, fixing your entry path, building a garage (yes, that's a landscape project!), siting a new home or just planting a single tree.

How is this true? Everything we do to create and shape our landscapes uses energy. When we move earth around, the tractors, backhoes, loaders and other equipment needed to do this heavy work consume carbon-based fuels. When we plant trees, shrubs and gardens, we may use extra soil, soil amendments and mulch. When we build paths, walls and decks, we need a supply of stone, brick or wood. The energy used to produce and transport all of these materials is the embedded energy cost of our projects. If we plan carefully to maximize the usefulness of everything in our landscapes, we can reduce both direct and embedded fuel consumption.

This chapter presents Actions for saving energy in the following ways:

+ Design for function as well as appearance.
+ Design for multi-purpose.
+ Use materials efficiently.

ACTION: Design for Function as Well as Appearance

By designing your landscape so that it satisfies your actual living needs and helps make your daily experiences go smoothly, you won't need to change things around later to make them work better or feel good. You'll avoid the need to take out old stuff and bring in new things. And if your landscape functions well, you won't feel that urge to adjust things two, three or four times, to finally create something that feels right.

So, how can you accomplish this? Here's how: before you start working on any landscape project, simply ask yourself one question. In addition to making this (whatever it is) look good, what is the real job (or jobs) it needs to do? Just think for a moment about purpose, apart from appearance. In your considerations, you can always add the aesthetic component later, but removing it at the start will help clear

Fig. 12.1: *On this slender site, where the house's front door is not visible from the driveway, a gracious stone path clearly invites visitors to their intended destination.*

Fig. 12.2: *This rustic patio embodies several important design principles: provide outdoor living spaces that are useful, convenient and inviting; fit the site well; perform several jobs safely and simultaneously; and please all the senses.*

your brain and let you focus on the harder question. This is a moment to set aside emotion, to temporarily ignore all those nostalgic feelings, dreamy images and magazine pictures. It's a time to be just practical.

Design Tip: Identify All the Functions of Every Landscape Element

Below is a list of jobs that various elements in your landscape can perform (and you can probably think of more), along with a few suggestions about how to accomplish them.

Front Walkways

- Provide a safe, comfortable surface. This generally means a maximum slope of 5 to 8 percent; anything steeper will probably be slippery in ice or rain and should have steps somewhere.
- Should be wide enough for two people to walk side by side, at least 3 feet wide in a small landscape, 4 feet wide if the space is big enough and the path won't look out of scale with its surroundings.
- Clearly invite people to the door you want them to use. From the beginning of the path, they should see either the door or a landing that indicates destination.
- Complement the style or materials of the house itself.

Main Outdoor Gathering Places

- Provide enough total area to hold the people who will normally use the patio, deck or any hard-surfaced area plus some amount of extra people, depending on how you like to entertain. Lay out on the ground somewhere your chairs, grill and other items, leaving room for people to easily walk around, and see how much space they need. Try to find the best balance between too small to be useful and so large that it feels uninviting.

+ Contain at least one space that's large enough for your table and chairs. A minimum size, for a 4-foot table and four chairs is about 12 feet in diameter.

+ Offer a sense of partial enclosure. Design it so at least one part of the space has some sort of back.

+ Should be safe and easy to get into and out of, both from the house and out toward the landscape. This might mean having just a few steps between inside and out rather than a long flight of stairs, or a generous landing at the door — anything to increase safety while carrying food or loaded trays from the house.

+ Should be shaped so chairs can be oriented toward at least one or two interesting features, perhaps one scene nearby and another view farther away.

Garden Paths

+ Invite, beckon and lead people to, and through, a variety of views and experiences. Let the shape of both path and garden complement each other or weave together.

+ Provide access to any part of the garden that will require care and attention.

+ Leave some space for a wheelbarrow or garden cart.

+ Shed runoff into adjacent growing areas, or let rainwater percolate through to the ground below.

Pool Decks

+ Provide a space, wood, concrete, stone, etc, large enough for people to congregate. This may mean an enlarged area at one end or side of the pool, or a raised platform, a multi-level space, or anything that clearly says "gather here." It should not be a narrow runway beside the pool.

Fig. 12.4: *Even a simple rectangular pool surround can be thoughtfully designed to contain a widened space for sunbathing and an even bigger space that's partly shaded, for larger gatherings. (Notice the pool cover, closed at the end of each day, which is not only a good idea for safety but which also helps the pool water stay warm on cool nights, saving energy.)*

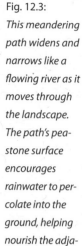

Fig. 12.3: *This meandering path widens and narrows like a flowing river as it moves through the landscape. The path's pea-stone surface encourages rainwater to percolate into the ground, helping nourish the adjacent gardens.*

- Offer seating areas in both sun and shade, for people's different needs and moods, at the all times of day the pool will be used.

- Have non-slip surfaces made of light-colored material, so the walking surface doesn't get too hot for bare feet.

Fig. 12.5: *Tucked cleverly into an embankment, this wall and its steps create a comfortable, inviting and whimsical transition between the upper and lower yards.*

DESIGN CREDIT: MARDERS BRIDGEHAMPTON NURSERY, INC.

Fig. 12.6: *If you have enough space, why not let your front walk widen out a bit and create a landing area near your door? A few chairs here would make it even more inviting and give you another place to sit, perhaps in a ray of morning sunshine or basking in cool afternoon shade.*

- Conceal pool equipment.
- Support a photovoltaic array?

Stone walls

- Enclose a space.
- Define an edge.
- Hold a slope, if a retaining wall.
- Give a feeling of solidity and permanence.
- Provide a sitting place.
- Hold rock from elsewhere on the property.
- Display treasures.
- Grow plants, in nooks that contain soil.
- Support wildlife, in nooks that don't contain soil.

ACTION: Design for Multipurpose

Now that you're comfortable thinking about your landscape in terms of the jobs it can do for you (in addition to looking beautiful), the next step toward increasing your property's energy efficiency is to design elements so they can perform several functions simultaneously. By loading up on the roles being performed by any one component in the landscape, you can cut down on the total number of different *things* you need. In the previous discussion you may have already started imagining how this might be accomplished in your own landscape. Here are some examples to inspire you further.

Design Tip:
Front Walks, Landings and Gardens

Your front walkway could widen out into a generous landing near the door, creating space for a chair and little table, so on a spring day you can sit outside for a moment before going to

Clotheslines

One of the easiest energy-saving actions we all can take, and certainly the oldest, is simply to dry our clothes outdoors. Electric clothes dryers consume more energy than any other home appliance except clothes washers and refrigerators. Every landscape design should include the location for a clothesline, preferably out of direct sun and away from any important views.

work, soaking up the sun. Maybe on this same landing, a visitor rests for moment, enjoying your view, waiting for you to answer the doorbell. Perhaps a small tree or group of shrubs wraps around the end of the landing, which provides a beautiful sight for people walking up the path. These same plants might also create privacy from a neighboring lot and offer a hiding place for birds that come to your feeder or birdbath.

Design Tip: Patios and Walls

Your patio can have two different kinds of spaces, a larger one for entertaining and a smaller intimate nook for quieter times. Perhaps these spaces are on two different levels, or maybe the nook is a little distance away but still connected to the larger area, so you take some time getting to it, strolling under a tree that cools the seating area as it also shades your southwest windows. And around the perimeter, a swath of garden plants hides and ornaments the patio's hard edges, while the soft soil below these plants soaks up the rainwater that sheets off the invisibly, slightly tilted surface.

If your house floor is a couple of feet higher than the surrounding ground, perhaps instead of building a deck that will inevitably have to be replaced, and will require lifelong regular maintenance, you can build a patio on a raised terrace that's supported by a low retaining wall. And, if there's enough space in the landscape, you can make the terrace large enough to incorporate some garden beds along the outer edges of the upper level. With a little forethought, these beds could be designed to tilt gradually away, so the top of the retaining wall is a bit lower than the level of the patio, saving

both stone and energy. They might also contain space for growing herbs or a few vegetables, right beside your table!

Design Tip: Decks and Fences

A small deck between your house and a lower patio eliminates the need for steps directly outside the door, providing a safe transition between inside and out. This small landing area can also be big enough to hold a couple of chairs and some potted herbs, making it a nice place to sit for a moment, perhaps taking a break from life or maybe watching over children and activities taking place below.

The new fence you're planning to install can *simultaneously* define the edge of your property, provide privacy, make a statement about your style, enclose a useful outdoor living space, provide a backdrop for flowers and support vines or trellises for growing food.

Design Tip: Other Ideas

Even if there's no way to accomplish any of these many-layered designs on your property,

Fig. 12.7:
Designing a terrace to have a sloped garden at its outer edge can eliminate the need for a safety railing while also reducing the labor and materials needed for construction. Plus, it's beautiful!

Fig. 12.8: *In this manicured landscape, the formal bluestone walkway defines a tidy, crisp edge between the garden bed and lawn.*

some landscape elements can certainly perform at least two roles at the same time.

- A retaining wall can also serve as a seating area if it's intentionally made to be just 18 to 24 inches tall (if your slope is higher than this, consider building two short walls

- A walkway can lead where it has to lead, but at the same time it can define an edge between two different kinds of spaces. As an example, rather than bisecting your front lawn with the entry path and having garden beds somewhere nearby, consider designing all three components together, so the path follows the edge of the garden beds, with lawn on its other side.

- A hedge can give you privacy from the street or a neighbor, and it can also provide food for birds, if you include native shrubs and trees that bear fruit or nuts (see Chapter 7 for a more detailed discussion about native plants). And if evergreen, it can serve as habitat for birds, in both urban and subur-

ban landscapes, which is especially important in winter.

- If you plan to build a house on a wooded lot, the open south-facing yard where your children will play might also be the right location for your below-ground septic drain field, reducing the amount of land that needs to be cleared.

- A grove of trees near the house that provides shade in the morning or afternoon can simultaneously be a place that absorbs rainfall and drainage from the house or surrounding land, if the earth around the trees is soft and mulched and shaped to serve this purpose.

- The part of your property that doesn't need to be covered with lawn can be a meadow or semi-wild zone, which will reduce mowing and maintenance chores while also providing habitat for birds and butterflies.

ACTION: Use Materials Efficiently

One final way to save energy is to know the capabilities and limitations of the materials we use in building our landscapes and to design with those qualities in mind. This will make the most of the energy consumed in producing those materials, and it will ultimately save on the amount of those materials that get consumed in our projects. For ideas about efficient building techniques, see Chapter 15.

Design Tip:
Landscape Elements Made of Wood

All the wood products that we use in our landscapes — to build decks, boardwalks, ramps, fences — are produced in standard sizes, each with a specific width, height and length: two-by-four, two-by-six, two-by-ten, four-by-six and countless other combinations. They refer to the *nominal* size (in inches, in the US and Canada) of a particular piece of lumber, with each size being able to carry a particular maximum load.

This is not the place for detailed instruction about exactly how to design the structures you need in your landscape. Determining the right width, thickness and spacing of construction members is best done on a case-by-case basis, with the advice of an experienced builder. Rather, the goal here is to remind you to design the size and shape of outdoor structures in a way that uses wood products most efficiently, so you create the least waste.

How can you do this? One way is to design the size and shape of wood structures so they can make the most of the common standard lengths of lumber: 8, 12 and 16 feet. A deck that's 13 feet wide might need to use a lot of 16-foot members, with the extra 3 feet being cut off and wasted. And how about a wheelchair ramp or boardwalk that's 4 feet 8 inches wide? There's no standard length that will neatly provide that length of board without wasting a long section. Of course, some of this excess is unavoidable, but you can keep standard dimensions in mind when making design decisions.

Another way to be efficient with wood is to understand that it's inherently rectilinear, and to design accordingly. Lumber works best in construction that has angles, which can be cut easily with standard tools. This isn't to suggest that wood can't be made into organic shapes, but rather that this may not be the best use for

this material. If you really need a structure to be round or curvy, consider using a different material, like stone, adobe or metal.

Design Tip:
Landscape Elements Made of Stone

Different kinds of stone also have their inherent qualities that make them best suited to various jobs. If you want a formal, straight-

Fig. 12.9: *An elegant boardwalk in New York City's Hudson River Park uses standard-length lumber, minimizing waste.*

Fig. 12.10: *This semi-formal patio is paved with standard-size, 3-foot square bluestone slabs, laid diagonally to the house. For perfect economy, the triangular pieces along the patio's edge are exactly half of one square.*

edged patio or path design, avoid using stone that has to be cut and fitted into the straight edges you desire. Instead use stone that comes from the quarry in rectilinear shapes, like bluestone or granite. Or use small stone products like cobble or brick that can easily be laid in a straight line.

For curved shapes, or spaces that you want to have an informal, softer edge, consider using stone that's naturally irregular, with unpredictable shapes and sizes that can be arranged in interesting combinations. Brick can also work well in curvy designs, although this may involve some amount of custom fitting and the associated waste. Or use loose aggregate, like pea stone or other small, smooth, uniformly graded rock product, with some sort of flexible edging (again, brick can work in this situation).

Although large pieces of flat stone may be heavy and difficult to work with, they might reduce the amount of cutting and fitting required by smaller stones occupying the same area. Also keep in mind the importance of using whatever is locally available in order to reduce the energy cost of transport.

Fig. 12.11:
In Costa Rica, the makers of this elegant path created a level surface from the tiniest building blocks.

ROLF BRIGGS

Design Tip:
Recycled/Salvaged/Onsite Materials

One of the best ways to use materials efficiently is to reuse them in new forms and applications, so the energy that was consumed to produce them the first time goes twice as far. You've probably already seen this idea in action, maybe without consciously noticing it. How about that retaining wall made out of old truck tires? The Madonna in an old bathtub? Chapter 15 presents several practical ideas for creatively incorporating a variety of recycled or salvaged materials in home landscape construction.

CHAPTER SUMMARY

When we design our landscapes so they work well, we'll save energy. It's just that simple. This chapter shows how to make every landscape element as versatile as possible, plan ahead so each feature satisfies many needs, and work toward multi-use design, to reduce the number of different elements needed for everyday comfort and pleasure. Designing with these goals in mind will reduce backtracking and undoing. It will also eliminate the need to completely overhaul major landscape projects later, when it has become clear that they don't really work.

This chapter covers the design of patios, decks, walkways, walls and gardens. It suggests many ways to design these elements so they satisfy basic physical requirements as well as subtle psychological and aesthetic ones, so they meet personal needs as well as perform larger environmental jobs and support wildlife. All of these ideas, along with specific recommendations about using materials efficiently, add up to immediate and long-term savings.

Situating New Homes with Energy in Mind

IF YOU'RE PLANNING TO BUILD a new home and you have the opportunity to choose its location and orientation, the advice in this chapter will help you achieve the best results. In urban settings or tight suburban developments, you may be able to implement only a few of these recommendations. But making good choices at the very beginning, and positioning your house well in relation to the sun and surrounding conditions, will generate tremendous savings and prevent later regrets.

Many buildings are specifically designed for energy efficiency. Some of the most ambitious even aim to consume no carbon-based resources at all. Whatever type of house you plan to build, the amount of energy needed to heat and cool its interior spaces will depend in large part on the house being positioned appropriately in

Fig. 13.1: *Sheltered from cold winds by a wooded hillside on the northwest, and open to a large hay field on the south, this house is well positioned for maximum winter comfort.*

Green Building

The US Green Building Council (usgbc.org) offers a certification program, Leadership in Energy and Environmental Design (LEED), that lists specific goals to be accomplished in designing buildings for efficiency and minimal impact on the environment. The program then rates buildings depending on how many of these goals are achieved. The Sustainable Sites Initiative (sustainablesites.org) works to create voluntary guidelines and standards for sustainable land design, construction and maintenance.

Swimming Pools

In temperate or cool regions, where the water in swimming pools is usually heated to extend their season of usefulness, it makes sense to position a pool so it can capture the sun's warmth and reduce the energy input needed. This will usually be in a south- or west-facing yard. If the arrangement of the landscape dictates that the pool must be located in a north- or east-facing yard, place it far enough away from the building that most of the pool is outside the building's shadow for at least 6 to 8 hours a day.

relation to the sun, the wind and prevailing weather conditions of your region.

The Actions in this chapter apply primarily to temperate or cold regions. If you live in hotter regions of the country, these Actions may not only be unhelpful, they may actually work against energy efficiency. As throughout the book, Regional Notes provide appropriate advice.

In addition, many people live in dense suburban or outer-urban regions. Here, because of small lot size, zoning restrictions or accepted custom, most houses are built to face the street, regardless of sun and wind direction. Many of this chapter's suggestions might not apply in such cases. But a few small nuggets of truth may be useful in urban situations, and the whole chapter could come in handy either as advice for friends or in your own future.

This chapter explains the following Actions for positioning a new building with energy in mind:

+ Position the house for maximum solar gain.
+ Situate buildings in accord with the wind.
+ Plan first, cut later.
+ Buy the right land for your needs.

ACTION: Position the House for Maximum Solar Gain

While the design of a building — its shape, windows, insulation, operating systems and countless other details — strongly affects how efficient it *can* be, the orientation of a building relative to the sun ultimately determines how efficient it *will* be.

Design Tip:
Orient the Building Toward South

In the northern hemisphere, orient the house so the largest expanse(s) of its walls or roof face within about 30° of due south. This will expose the maximum area to the sun for winter heating, and it will also enable roof-mounted solar modules to work effectively if you decide to install them, either now or in the future (see Chapter 14). Also consider designing the building to be L-shaped, with its inside corner — and plenty of windows — oriented generally toward the south. This arrangement will bring the most light and warmth into different rooms throughout the year. It will also provide space for a protected outdoor sitting area, which can be especially valuable during spring and fall, in the transition time between the long, warm days of summer and the shorter, cooler days of winter. (See Chapter 2 for guidance about shading west-facing windows in summer.)

If your land slopes downhill toward the south, orienting the house for solar gain will be relatively easy. If your land slopes steeply downhill in a northerly direction, however, your house will feel cool in summer but winter sunlight may be extremely limited. In this case, strive to find a place on the site where the most sunlight is available, to passively warm the house in winter. This might be either near the top of the hill, or perhaps in a place where the hillside curves around toward either the east or west, where more morning or afternoon sunlight will be available.

Design Tip: Avoid the Center

If your property is flat or gently sloped, the best place for the house is on the north side of the lot. This position leaves the greatest amount of south yard open for exposure to the sun at all times of the year. In rural and suburban property, this arrangement might also create a south-facing yard for play and outdoor activity that, if soil conditions allow, could do double duty as the location for the septic system.

Hot-Arid and Hot-Humid Regions

In regions of the country where more energy is needed to cool a house in summer than to warm it in winter, a south-facing yard may contribute to over-heating the house. To avoid this

Fig. 13.2: *On this wooded property, a window-filled south-facing wall and an open south yard allow abundant sunshine into the house in winter while trees that were intentionally saved during construction help cool the house in summer.*

Fig. 13.3: *Positioning the house on the north side of a lot, to maximize the south-facing yard, is not a new idea, as evidenced by this older home. (Could it be time to remove that overgrown spruce tree in the front yard?)*

situation, positioning your house on the south side of a lot will create a north-facing yard that's naturally shaded (at least partly) by the house itself.

ACTION: Situate Buildings in Accord with the Wind

Slopes that face north or northwest are fully exposed to cold winter winds. Because the ground falls away toward the wind, trees or fences established on the north will need to be very tall to blunt the wind's effect. In such situations, the best solution is to limit the number of doors and windows on the north side of the house or to place a secondary structure, such as the garage, between the house and the incoming wind (both of which might be difficult choices, if this is also the direction of the best views). In general, it's best to avoid building on steep north-facing slopes.

Hot-Arid Regions

In regions where the air is hot and dry, it may be more important to deflect summer breezes than to capture them, to minimize their drying effect. Positioning your house on a north-facing slope will help accomplish this.

Fig. 13.4: In summer, the same house pictured in figure 13.1 is shaded by trees to the southeast and southwest, and cooled by thermal breezes rising up the slope.

Design Tip: The Ideal Arrangement

Land with a southerly slope offers the best combination of protection from winter wind and exposure to summer breezes. In these situations, the optimal location for a house is partway between the top and bottom of the slope. This places the house directly in the path of summer thermal breezes that flow uphill in the morning and descend downhill in the evening, which can cool a house both outside and inside.

Whether located on level or sloping land, if a house is exposed to strong winds in either the winter or summer, consider positioning new additions or outbuildings purposely to deflect the wind. Of course some additions will probably need to meet other requirements, such as connecting to an existing door, giving access to an established yard, facing a desirable view or providing parking and storage for vehicles. But, if possible, keep the wind in mind when designing additions or new buildings in the landscape.

Design Tip: Things to Avoid

If possible, resist the temptation to build directly on the top of a hill, for two reasons: to get the best protection from north winds and to preserve the view from below of uninterrupted ridgeline, a valuable community asset. A third reason to avoid hilltops is the likelihood that they're made almost entirely of bedrock (the reason they haven't eroded away), which can make construction more difficult.

It's also best to avoid building at the very bottom of a slope or in a pocket of low-lying land. This is where cold air collects at night, in both summer and winter. More important, it's also the place toward which surface runoff and underground water flow. Large areas of terrain sloping toward the house can cause problems that include

+ a basement that's always wet, with moisture seeping through the concrete and into every crack, whenever it rains;

+ water pressure actually causing cracks;

+ soggy lawn that your kids can't use and you can't mow;

+ gardens that wash out every spring; and

+ early spring rain collecting in shallow puddles on top of frozen snow.

The point here is simply to remind you, when preparing to build a new home (or even when buying an existing home), to think about the generally unseen and easily overlooked reality of land that drains toward your house. If you have any questions about a particular property and the extent of the drainage area, buy a USGS topographic map that includes your property and look carefully at the amount of terrain that slopes toward your land. If you suspect there might be a problem but you can't figure out just how big a problem it is, consult with a landscape architect or engineer. As with all the advice in this book, avoiding and preventing problems at the start is a significant way to save the energy needed for repair and reconstruction later.

ACTION: Plan First, Cut Later

On land that contains trees — whether they're young saplings dotting a meadow, a grove of mixed young and old species, a few solitary

Fig. 13.5: *Make sure that the cooling benefits of building on a slope are not overwhelmed by the negative consequences of too much runoff flowing toward your foundation.*

specimens or a whole healthy forest — do not start the planning process by eliminating the plants! If you want to see better, to find where the best views are or just to get a sense of the larger property, bring a ladder to the site, climb a tree, or wait until winter when the foliage has fallen. Walk around the site many times, discovering its treasures. If you need to get a better sense of the terrain, check a topographic map or consult with a landscape architect.

The vegetation that exists on a site is part of your investment. It has the potential to save you vast amounts of time and money later, when construction is complete and it's time to repair and revegetate naked land. Trees that are already established in the landscape, which by themselves found the best place to grow and thrive, are far, far ahead of any trees you might buy or transplant. They'll grow faster and stay healthier and will give you shade and protection more quickly than any import. Their vital role within an established ecosystem, the habitat they provide for local wildlife and their appearance of belonging there, all these added benefits have little to do with energy efficiency yet make a positive difference, for your own enjoyment and for the health of the world.

ACTION:
Buy the Right Land for Your Needs

Buying land is a surprisingly complex decision. You and your family might wish to live in a particular city or town, or even a certain part of that town, e.g., near good schools, family or your church. For many of us, the decision also involves making several other choices, about issues that may or may not overlap: an urban, suburban or rural location; a lot that's small, medium or large; a cleared, open lot or a wooded

Fig. 13.6:
By saving this walnut tree when the house was built, a farsighted builder contributed greatly to the comfort (and beauty) of the home.

and wild one; terrain that's flat, rolling or steeply sloping. The list goes on and on.

Design Tip: What's Right for You?

Whatever type of property suits your own preferences, certain characteristics of the land itself will help make your home more energy efficient. Below are six qualities to keep in mind when evaluating a potential purchase. These qualities make the most sense in cold and temperate parts of the world; in hotter climates, it may be preferable to reverse the suggestions about north and south.

Southerly orientation: Whether the land is level, gentle or sloping, a site that allows the house to be oriented within 30° of due south offers the potential for greatest solar gain. Sloped land should tilt downhill in a southerly direction; north-facing slopes limit the amount of sun that can reach a house in winter. Avoid buying land where objects south of your house — a hill, other buildings or a neighbor's mature trees — will block summer sun in winter.

Not too steep: While a house can be built on very steep land, cars require level or gently sloping space to park and maneuver safely. Level land for outdoor activity is also generally desirable, though not in every situation. A maximum slope of 10 percent allows these spaces to be created without excessive earthmoving. Land steeper than 15 percent slope can be difficult to shape and build on, and it often involves importing materials from elsewhere, which consumes both energy and a project's budget.

Protection from cold winds: A sheltering slope or grove of trees located to the north or northwest of the house will deflect winter winds. Even neighboring homes and other buildings near your house may have a similar effect. Avoid land where the terrain or nearby buildings will funnel and intensify northerly winds blowing toward your house.

Good substrate: Land that's easy to work will save vast amounts of time, energy and materials (as well as trouble and tribulations) in the construction of your house, driveway, utilities, septic system and outdoor living spaces.

Avoid building on land that is extremely rocky, or wet and unstable. Check with the USDA's Natural Resources Conservation Service (nrcs.usda.gov), a local agricultural extension service, an engineer or a landscape architect to find out more about the soil conditions of any land before buying it.

Trees in the right place: Land that is forested or contains mature trees offers the potential to help cool your house in the summer, if the trees are suitably positioned. This is especially true

That Special Spot

If you've purchased property that is undeveloped, you may have fallen in love with one particular place on the land, one spot that feels just perfectly wonderful, one place that might even have been the whole reason you bought the property. This could be a gorgeous grove of trees, a dramatic bedrock ridge, an overlook or little plateau with breathtaking views, or any combination of these and many other elements that inspire us all. If so, do not build your house on that spot!

The construction process is extremely destructive, and except in very rare cases, it generally consumes at least twice as much space as planned. Earthmoving, stockpiling, storing equipment and material storage, maneuvering vehicles all disturb a much larger area than most of us can ever imagine ahead of time. Construction workers are generally focused on getting their work done on time and within budget; they really can't be as attentive as we'd wish to the particular plants or site features that we care about. No matter how hard you try, placing your house on

the most special part of your land will likely destroy the very qualities about that place that you love (see Chapter 16 for guidance about minimizing construction damage).

A better choice is to save that special spot, perhaps even turn it into a place to visit. Instead, build your house somewhere nearby, or even quite far away, so that, in the process of going to that cherished destination, you'll also pass through other parts of your land and experience their undiscovered treasures. And the special place you cherish will keep its glorious nature intact.

Fig. 13.7: *Who wouldn't want to live near this powerful tree? Building here, however, would only destroy the marvelous feeling of this spot, and quite likely harm the tree itself.*

if the trees are deciduous rather than evergreen. Before clearing any wooded site, check Chapter 2 for more detailed guidance about the location of shade trees relative to your house, so you can preserve the trees that will help you later.

Legal issues: The land you hope to build on must be located outside any regulated wetland buffer zones, resource protection areas, river floodplains or other regulated zones. Check with your local zoning committee, conservation board, building inspector or other regulatory departments to make sure that the home you wish to build is legally permissible on the land you plan to buy.

CHAPTER SUMMARY

The process of designing and building a new home is full of completely new decisions and compromises and fraught with pressure. It's also an experience that few of us have the chance to learn from and do better the next time. If you're lucky enough to be involved in creating a new home, and if you have the opportunity to choose its position and orientation, the ideas in this chapter will help. By following this advice, you'll maximize the energy efficiency of any house style you choose.

This is not to suggest that the house design itself doesn't matter. It does. But every house will experience greater savings if the building is oriented properly in relation to the sun, wind and surrounding environment. In addition, this chapter describes the process of evaluating all the assets of any site and deciding what is most important to save, before removing anything, to get the greatest value from your investment. Finally, it provides an overview of qualities to seek in new land before purchasing any property.

This concludes the section of the book that focuses on *designing* landscapes for energy efficiency. The next section presents detailed guidance about *building and caring for* our landscapes in ways that specifically save energy. The topics covered include planting and maintaining planted areas; building structures with wood, stone and alternative materials; and constructing new homesites in ways that minimize harm and maximize efficiency.

Construction and Care

TREES PLANTED SO THEY THRIVE, stone walls built to stand for generations, slopes that are stable and resist erosion ... when everything in our landscapes is constructed for durability, stability and a long life, we save energy. How? By building things just once and not again. By using the resources needed for the job, and then not using more later. By reducing the need for repairs and maintenance. In the long run, these efficiencies mean we use less fuel to run equipment and less electricity to power the job (direct costs), and we decrease the energy consumed to produce and transport the materials needed for our landscape projects (embedded costs).

This section discusses how to plant things and build things so they last as long as possible. It also includes tips for maintaining and caring for our landscapes in the most effective, efficient ways. And, because the use of recycled and local materials is a fundamental principle of energy efficiency, each chapter in this section also includes ideas for achieving this goal.

Rather than giving detailed building instructions, these three chapters provide rules of thumb, along with some facts and ideas to keep in mind, so that the major components of your landscape rarely need to be fixed or replaced, and the entire property holds up well over time. The subjects covered in this section include plants and planting, structures in the landscape and new homesites.

CHAPTER 14

Installing and Maintaining Planted Areas

THIS CHAPTER COVERS the several interrelated steps involved in most landscape *planting* projects: preparing soil and plants, and then installing and caring for growing things. With energy efficiency as the goal, our discussion focuses on three common components of many American landscapes: trees, shrubs and lawn. It also includes the less common but increasingly appealing new idea of wildflower meadows. The subject of gardening with herbaceous plants is not covered here, because countless other references cover this issue in great detail and there's little unique energy-saving advice to add to the topic. However, many of the recommendations here will apply to every sort of gardening.

This chapter contains the following Actions to guide your planting process:

- Limit topsoil imported from off-site.
- Amend soil only when necessary, and with a light touch.
- Plant trees and shrubs properly.
- Mulch bare soil.
- Plant wildflower meadows so they thrive.
- Create healthy low-maintenance lawns.
- Water efficiently.
- Acquire plants appropriately.

ACTION:
Limit Importing Topsoil from Off-site

As noted in Chapter 7, the most energy-efficient approach to planting our landscapes is to select plants best suited to the conditions of the site. In many cases, it may not make sense to have all of our planting choices be

Fig. 14.1: *A common sight, this traditionally "cleared" lot leaves vast amounts of raw land in need of re-vegetation. The bare, spindly tree trunks stand as evidence of recent forest cutting. (Note the carelessly positioned construction drive, dividing the lot in half... will this become the final driveway? Is it an inviting or appealing arrangement? See Chapter 11 for more thoughts about driveway design.)*

Fig. 14.2: *Full of lowbush blueberry, wintergreen, Canada mayflower, princess pine and one baby mountain laurel, these sods were rescued from an abandoned field slated for development. They'll fit perfectly in a new garden with acidic soil and full sun exposure.*

determined by the quality of the soil on our property. Still, to save energy, we should aim to let at least some portion of the soil remain in its natural condition, and ideally, except on very small lots, this portion ought to be the majority of the site.

One complicating factor here is that many new home landscapes contain no soil in its natural condition, all of it having been removed or compacted beyond recognition during the construction process. These sites have often then been blanketed with a few inches of material generally labeled *topsoil*. Sometimes this might be a layer of soil that was stripped and stockpiled from the site itself, before construction started, but it's not uncommon for new landscapes to need more soil than is available in that pile.

Construction Tip: Storing Topsoil

Soil stored in piles for any length of time becomes less healthy with every passing week. The weight of the pile presses down on interior soils, squeezing out the oxygen that was there to begin with, killing the soil microbes that depended on that oxygen. A better way to store topsoil is to place it in rows or smaller piles, with enough organic matter (leaves, etc) mixed in to preserve the soil's pores.

In woodland settings where the topsoil is full of microbes and plant life, the best way to preserve topsoil is to sharply cut and lift entire mats of it from the ground, intact. These patches can be just four to six inches thick, depending on what's growing in them, or they might even be thinner if bedrock is near the surface. In any case, gently set each patch aside (ideally in a place that doesn't contain other plants) and mulch around its edges to keep the soil moist. These patches can then (preferably within a few weeks) be set back into the new landscape, level with the surrounding ground.

Construction Tip: Using Less

Whatever its origin, topsoil imported to your property carries a heavy load of costs, in harm to the environment or in consumption of energy and natural resources, or both. It just makes

What Is Topsoil?

The term "topsoil" refers to the upper layer of the Earth's crust. It usually implies a rich soil that contains a mixture of minerals and decomposed organic matter, with the resulting material being dark brown, moist and crumbly. In arid environments, what little topsoil exists might be mostly sand.

Topsoil is the layer of soil that supports plant growth, via the interaction of plant roots, water, air, nutrients and soil microorganisms. The depth of topsoil varies and is generally considered to be the distance between the surface of the ground and the top of the first densely packed layer below, called subsoil.

In the construction business, material that's labeled and sold as topsoil must consist of particles of a certain size, with the majority falling in the range of 0.002 mm to 0.05 mm. Such soil is technically termed "silt." Soil made of particles smaller than 0.002 mm is considered to be clay, and particles larger than 0.05 mm, up to about 2.00 mm, are termed "sand."

Topsoil also must contain some amount of decomposed biologic material, but no specific rules regulate this amount. Quite often the topsoil that's delivered to unsuspecting customers contains precious little that could be called organic matter.

Some topsoil is actually a human-made concoction. Various ingredients — sand, gravel, clay, roots, leaves, twigs, excess material from other construction sites — are poured into a processor, a huge machine that crushes everything into a certain size (and of course is powered by fuel). The resulting mixture contains particles the right size to be labeled topsoil, along with some unspecified amount of organic material. But it rarely contains enough nutrients and microbes, in the right proportions, to be useful as a growing medium, and it virtually always lacks healthy soil structure.

Topsoil that's brought into a new landscape has to have come from somewhere else, perhaps from within the property, another site just down the road or farmland being stripped for development in a neighboring town. Depending on where you live, it could have been transported a very long distance. No matter where it comes from, though, moving topsoil from one location to another is undesirable for several reasons. It diminishes the life and vitality of its original location and then usually creates a lesser amount of vitality in its new home because the soil's structure, microbial activity and overall health have been reduced in the process. And this unsatisfactory outcome is accomplished at great expense, by burning untold gallons of fuel to power the equipment and vehicles that excavate, transport and spread the soil.

sense to use as little of this precious material as possible. To limit the amount of soil you import to your property, consider reducing the size of your lawn, expanding the unimproved or semi-wild portions of your property and following several of the other design suggestions in Chapter 7.

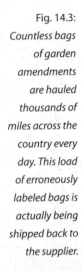

Fig. 14.3: *Countless bags of garden amendments are hauled thousands of miles across the country every day. This load of erroneously labeled bags is actually being shipped back to the supplier.*

Construction Tip: Other Soil Issues

If you need to modify the shape of the ground itself — to ensure drainage, provide useful outdoor spaces, make a safer driveway, or for any other landscape purpose — this reshaping should happen at the level of the subsoil, not the topsoil. Any extra material that's required for the job should be some sort of fill, usually a mixture of sand and gravel that's easy to work and inorganic in nature.

While it's a good idea, during construction or earth grading, to salvage the top layer of fertile soil and save it for later use, it's important to set it aside for as short a time as possible, to

minimize compaction and maximize the soil's health. If possible, you should also cover the exposed soil, to prevent weed seeds from blowing onto the surface and germinating there.

If your project does require more topsoil than you have onsite, be sure that whatever you import is as high-quality as possible. Ideally it should be dark brown and crumbly, with some of the soil in small clumps or clods held together by organic matter. It should feel neither gritty nor slippery, but, like Goldilocks' just-right porridge, its texture should be midway between those two extremes.

ACTION: Amend Soil Only When Necessary, and with a Light Touch

Soil chemistry is a vast subject. We don't fully understand the complex mechanisms of nutrient breakdown and absorption by plants, nor the many unseen interactions between soil organisms and plant roots. We don't really know the types of soil structure and particle size that work best for different species. It's so difficult to know exactly what's ideal for a single plants, let alone a whole garden, and it's so easy to harm plants by adding either the wrong thing, or too much or too little of the right thing. (Chapter 7 presents a more detailed discussion about the nature of soil.)

In addition to the question of their effect on plants, the substances we add to garden soil also require great amounts of energy to be manufactured. Minerals extracted from the earth; chemicals heated, treated, blended and boxed; bags of product heaped to the ceiling in warehouses and garden centers; vast quantities of natural gas, electricity and diesel fuel

consumed to create and transport these materials ... we can save energy at every step and in countless ways simply by buying and using soil amendments *in moderation*.

Construction Tip: Some Situations Require No Improvement

Not all plants require improved soil. Many native plant species are perfectly well adapted to growing in soil that conventional gardeners might consider poor. As Leslie Sauer says in *The Once and Future Forest*, referring to working and gardening in woodlands: "Creating less hospitable conditions in the conventional sense can actually enhance the performance of native species."[1]

This is also true for wildflower meadows, which can thrive in soils that are degraded, dry, sandy, clayey, or otherwise unsuited to growing lawn grass. All that's required is selecting the species of grasses and flowers that evolved and can thrive in conditions that match yours, where these plants actually have a competitive advantage over other fussier species. (See the Action on creating wildflower meadows, below, for more advice.)

Construction Tip: Amend Soil with Compost

In nearly every garden situation, the ideal way to repair and enhance soil is to add compost. The one exception is completely natural woodland gardens, which will prefer the nutrients of their own leaf litter. Compost is made by combining organic wastes in suitable ratios (in piles, rows or containers), then letting that mixture age in the presence of oxygen, which usually generates high heat that kills weed seeds, and finally letting the substance mature to a stable condition.

Compost is very nearly a miracle substance. The US Environmental Protection Agency Resource Conservation website says:

> Compost can: suppress plant diseases and pests; reduce or eliminate the need for chemical fertilizers; promote higher yields of agricultural crops, facilitate forest restoration; remediate soils contaminated by hazardous waste; remove solids, oil, grease and heavy metals from stormwater runoff; and provide cost savings of at least 50 percent over conventional soil, water and air pollution remediation technologies.[2]

How does compost help your soil? When you mix compost into the top layer of your soil, or even just spread it over the surface and let busy little soil organisms mix it gradually downward, the minerals and nutrients that existed in the original materials get blended into the soil and become available to plants. Compost also improves the texture of most soils: it helps loosen and lighten heavy clay soil, and it builds structure in sandy soil, by promoting the growth of soil micro-organisms that bind soil particles together.

Many garden centers sell compost by the bagful. Increasing numbers of farmers and large-scale compost operations sell it by the truckload. One of the greatest advantages of using compost in our landscapes, however, is that most of us can make it ourselves. Compost is a way to use organic resources directly on the site where they were created. Whether these resources are grass clippings, fallen leaves, weeds and the cleanings from a vegetable garden, or the food waste from your kitchen, compost makes the most of free materials and involves

What to Compost	
Animal manure	Hay and straw
Cardboard	Houseplants
Clean paper	Leaves
Coffee grounds and filters	Nut shells
Cotton rags	Sawdust
Dryer and vacuum cleaner lint	Shredded newspaper
Eggshells	Tea bags
Fireplace ashes	Wood chips
Fruits and vegetables	Wool rag
Grass clippings	Yard trimmings
Hair and fur	

Fig. 14.4: *In many nature centers, fallen leaves are collected, chopped up and re-distributed in place, providing mulch that's perfectly suited to the needs of the plants growing there. These majestic red oaks are thriving in the native plant region of the Brooklyn Botanic Garden.*

no transportation or embedded energy costs. Plus it keeps yard and food waste out of landfills. To make your own compost, all that's required is a willingness to recycle unwanted organic matter in a way that helps it break down. Thousands of books, pamphlets and websites explain how.

An important factor to keep in mind, with compost or any type of soil amendment, is the soil's acidity, or pH (see Chapter 7 for a more detailed explanation of pH). Some composts can make soils more acidic, which may or may not be desirable. Remember to check pH levels with a simple soil test, either by using a kit from a garden center or, for more accuracy, by sending samples to a local agricultural extension service.

Construction Tip: Amend Soil with Leaf Litter

One of the best ways to repair soil — actually, it's the same method that nature uses — is to just let fallen leaves, twigs and dead wood remain on the ground and break down gradually in place. You can rake all this material up and chop or grind it into smaller bits, or you can compost and spread it later in a different place, but the most energy-efficient choice is just to leave this precious resource on the ground, right where it falls. Micro-organisms will have a picnic in it. And when you start to see networks of little white filaments twining here and there amidst the litter, you'll know you've succeeded: the soil is getting richer and more fertile without any help from you. Of course, this might require redesigning your landscape to include more space around trees for fallen leaves. Keep in mind, you can modify your soil in phases rather than all at once, making some spaces ready for plants right away while letting others develop over time.

Simply leaving litter on the ground works best in natural and semi-wild parts of the landscape, but the basic principle also applies to our more manicured gardens. From the total amount of stuff that nature drops on the ground, you can safely take about half and sprinkle it as a mulch wherever you want (and make sure to spread the remaining original litter out so it covers the ground). This will gradually transform the soil in your garden beds into rich crumbly earth. Grinding up the leaves before you spread them, with a mower or leaf chopper, will help speed their decomposition. This step, however, consumes energy and isn't necessary: nature doesn't bother to do it, but rather just waits for the decomposers to show up.

Many towns offer local or regional leaf composting services. While this seems like a good idea, and is somewhat preferable to buying manufactured compost, it does have its drawbacks. The practice of raking up fallen leaves and then carting them off to a local composting center, where they'll be processed and then transferred to some other homeowner who'll then carry them to yet another location, is a waste of energy. The leaves themselves are nature's gift to you and your landscape.

Construction Tip: Other Amendments

Green manure crops. For centuries, farmers have rejuvenated soil by growing certain plants and then tilling them into the soil before they go to seed. Once mixed into the earth, they break down, essentially providing a form of in-ground compost. Many green manure crops are leguminous plants that also add nitrogen to the soil. To find out what species are best in your region, and to avoid using species that could be invasive, get more information from local cooperative extension or agriculture agent.

Peat moss. Widely sold as a soil amendment to improve drainage, peat moss adds no useful nutrients to the soil, and it raises soil acidity significantly. Because peat moss is mined from just below the surface in the regions where it has accumulated over millennia (primarily Canada), its manufacture causes disastrous harm to the ecosystems

Fig. 14.5:
All peat moss operations depend on completely stripping surface vegetation to reach the treasure below. Here, gigantic vacuums suck up the compacted material before delivering it to a processing shed, where it will be dried, sorted, sieved and bagged.

Use the Right Stuff

When using leaf litter to condition your soil, try to match the type of leaves with the needs of the plants. Acid-loving plants such as blueberries and mountain laurels will thrive in the acidic leaves of oak and birch trees, while alkaline-loving plants such as dogwoods, hydrangea and junipers will do better with the more neutral litter of maples, basswood and cherry trees.

above ground, which then require energy to repair. It also involves a high embedded cost, in its harvesting, cleaning, processing, bagging and transport. Coir, a similar product made from coconut palms, also provides drainage but no nutrients. It offers the benefit of being a renewable resource, yet its production and transport also consume energy.

Fertilizer. Plants thrive when the soil contains small amounts of several different minerals. The most important among these (beyond the basic nitrogen, phosphorus and potassium in conventional fertilizer) are calcium, boron, copper, manganese and zinc. Healthy soil that's full of organic matter and active soil organisms usually supplies all these minerals. If your soil is poor, however, and if your plants appear to be ailing, consider applying small doses of *organic* fertilizer that contains these ingredients, in early summer or fall. Bear in mind the two good reasons for using fertilizer with restraint: excess or inappropriate use of fertilizers can do more harm than good, and the manufacture of fertilizer is an extremely energy-consuming process. Another product that a growing number of farmer and gardeners use to restore (or re-mineralize) depleted soils is fine rock dust.

The most suitable materials and amounts to use in various situations are still being researched, but the idea makes a lot of sense.

Construction Tip:
Loosen or Aerate the Soil

When soil gets compacted, all its particles are pressed together, eliminating the pores that would normally hold air and water. Different species require different amounts of air and moisture, and respond differently when faced with shortages, but these resources are essential to all plants except those that have evolved to survive without them, such as aquatic plants. While a small degree of soil compaction may be beneficial for seed germination and moisture retention, too much can be quite harmful.

In hard soil, rainwater can't soak in, so it either runs off or it puddles on the surface, smothering roots (and making it difficult to walk there). The absence of moisture in the soil means that nutrients don't dissolve and hence can't be absorbed by roots. Soil organisms suffer, roots work harder to penetrate the soil, and the result is that plants gradually either die or just limp along, failing to thrive. In compacted lawn soil, grass roots have a hard time growing, so the grass blades suffer, the lawn gets weak, and diseases and insects have an easier target.

What causes soil compaction? Soil compaction can be the result of a single heavy force or many repeated lighter ones. Trucks and earthmoving machinery, which compress soil during construction, are the main culprits, but even the repeated passes of a heavy lawn mower will compact soil. The effect is worse on soil that's wet. Stockpiling soil and repeated vibrations also cause soil particles to squeeze together. In lawns, soil compaction may be mostly due to the absence or depletion of nutrients by hungry grass roots, which eliminates the many wiggly soil organisms that would normally create millions of little pores.

How can you tell if your soil is compacted? Soil may be compacted just near the surface, or in an invisible hardpan several inches below. Agronomists might diagnose surface compaction with a tool called a penetrometer. The rest of us can figure it out simply by feeling the ground, with a hand or by walking on it, or by sight. If there's no spring in the feeling of the ground, if the sensation is the same as on well-used walking paths, the soil is compacted. If you dig up a patch of soil, from the lawn or elsewhere, you can see if plant roots are trapped in the top inch or two.

The solution for surface compaction is to loosen or aerate the soil, which can be done in two ways:

- The quicker, most energy-consuming way is to use an aeration tool that pokes holes in the ground or removes plugs of soil. This may be either a hand or power tool. Your choice will probably depend on how hard the soil is and how much work you want to expend.

- The slower, more energy-efficient way is to spread organic matter and let soil organisms gradually work this down into the hard layer beneath, blending the two together. This approach works well on lawns and gardens and is probably the best choice in natural or

semi-wild areas, where mechanical action might cause unintended and unnoticed harm.

Whichever approach works best for you, when you aerate compacted soil, the result will be increased movement of water, nutrients and oxygen between the soil and plants, improved plant rooting, greater activity of soil microorganisms and enhanced rainfall infiltration. Plants will grow better, and you'll spend less energy taking care of them and replacing them when they fail. (What's not to like about that?)

A more serious problem, one that's much harder to fix, occurs when the surface layer of soil seems fine and healthy, but a deeper, hidden layer of soil is compacted so solidly that it might just as well be concrete. This is usually the result of heavy machinery driving repeatedly over the ground, such as during new construction and major landscape installations (swimming pools, tennis courts, large stonework, etc.). Even

Fig. 14.6: *When the earth around tree roots is heavily compacted, extreme measures may be needed to save a tree. Here soil is being air-spaded, to fluff it up and eliminate any soil surrounding the trunk flare.*

TREE SPECIALISTS, INC.

when contractors, at the end of the job, spread new loose soil over the compacted areas, this thin layer is rarely adequate to support plant growth. Worse, the hardpan absorbs no rain. This can mean either that water remains on the surface on level ground or drains away too quickly on sloped ground. In both situations, trees, shrubs and even lawn grass will suffer and gradually fail, often for no apparent reason.

The only way to discover whether deep compaction is the problem is to dig down 8 to 12 inches and see if you hit an impenetrable layer. And the only way to fix hardpan is to mechanically fracture and loosen it. This requires major equipment, is shockingly expensive and a huge energy sink. It also undoes work and wastes plants already installed. *This is why it's so important to prevent deep compaction during construction.* Chapter 16 presents detailed site protection measures for this purpose.

ACTION:
Plant Trees and Shrubs Properly

When planting a tree or shrub, remember that most woody plants grow in the top 18 inches of the soil. Their *roots do not grow in a mirror image of the plant above.* While many trees and most shrubs have shallow roots systems, a few tree species, such as oak, hickory and cherry, put down taproots that may extend 15 feet deep or more, if soil conditions allow. Other

tree species, such as catalpa, magnolia and some birches, have deep lateral roots that take over the job of supporting the tree once the taproot gets to a certain length. Both taproots and deep laterals help the tree tolerate drought but make transplanting difficult.

All planting jobs will be most successful if you:

• keep roots moist during the planting process,
• avoid planting at the beginning of a hot day and
• make preparations ahead of time to water immediately after planting.

Good planting techniques help plants adjust quickly to their new environment. Trees, shrubs, flowers, meadows and lawn will need minimal care, stay healthy longer and fail less often than when they're planted poorly. They'll be more likely not only to survive the shock of being moved but also to thrive. Before starting to dig or plant, read the earlier discussion about soil amendments. And in established woodland gardens, use extreme restraint when adding anything or modifying soil.

The following basic steps for success apply to all woody plants, both trees and shrubs. Remember, taking care at the start of any planting project will save you trouble, time, money and energy in the long run.

Construction Tip: Preparing the Plant

• Carefully and completely remove whatever is holding the root ball, whether this is burlap and twine, a plastic pot or a wire basket. Reuse and recycle any containers or wrapping material.

Tree Protection
Many cities and towns have instituted *Tree Protection Ordinances* that specify best ways to work around large trees, along with penalties for causing harm. Be sure to check with local officials about whether such regulations exist and will affect your work.

- Examine the trunk where it meets the soil. It should show a distinct flare or widening at the bottom. Remove all soil that covers this flare. If any roots have wrapped themselves partway around the flare, snip them off with sharp pruners. If the tree lacks a flare, or if the trunk shows any cuts or splits, return the plant to your supplier.

- If the roots are extremely dense or circling the ball, remove or gently untangle the outer layer of root, or make some clean, shallow slices through the mass. Cut away dead or dried out roots.

- Trim off any dead or broken branches. Do not follow the now-outdated advice to reduce strain on the plant by removing a lot of top growth. Studies have found that plants need the maximum amount of foliage to photosynthesize and provide energy to help the roots adjust to their new home. Wait at least one year before pruning heavily.

Construction Tip: Digging the Hole

- Measure the distance between the bottom of the trunk flare and the bottom of the root ball. *Dig the hole no deeper than this measurement.* Lay a straight object (perhaps the handle of a shovel) across the hole and measure the depth precisely. For large trees, subtract one inch of depth for every inch of trunk caliper, because large trees will settle later.

- Do not dig a hole deeper than necessary. Any loose soil in the bottom of the hole will compress under the weight of a new plant, causing the plant to sink.

- The trunk's flare should always be completely above ground, never buried. Soil moisture and soil organisms will harm the bark and reduce its ability to protect the inner living layers of the tree. Placing the trunk a little too far out of the ground is always better than too deep, as more soil can be added later if needed. Trees planted too deep can only be repaired by complete replanting.

Fig. 14.7: *Even professional nurseries sometimes sell trees with root balls that are packed too high around a tree's trunk. With all new tree purchases, take care (or make sure your landscape professional takes care) to find the trunk's natural flare, then remove any excess soil and plant the tree so its flare is above ground.*

Wire Baskets

Some contractors and nurseries say it's okay to leave wire baskets on the root balls of plants. However, baskets can limit root growth. Imagine the tree getting old, with its thick, sturdy roots expanding outward every year; eventually the wire will cut right through the roots' tissue, killing them. Wire baskets in the soil also can harm soil wildlife and the fingers of future gardeners. All baskets should be removed, even if this requires snipping the individual wires.

* Make the hole two to three times wider than the root ball, with sides that slope gently inward. Remember to avoid digging so close to established trees that their roots are significantly cut, compacted or disturbed.

* Save all parent soil, beside or surrounding the hole.

Construction Tip: Placing the Tree or Shrub

* Slide or roll the tree into the hole. If you need to pick up a plant, hold it by the root ball. Do not hoist plants by their trunks, as the weight of soil in the root ball can tear the roots or cause the ball to fall apart. Do not add water to root balls before planting. If the soil in a root ball is very dry and loose, some moisture may help hold it together, but the best solution is to leave the burlap on the ball as you lower it into the hole, and then gently slide the burlap out.

* Keep the ball in the center of the hole and fill in around the edges with the saved parent or native soil. If the soil is poor, mix compost or aged leaf litter in with the original soil before replacing it. Use *no more than 5 to 10 percent compost*, to keep from creating a potted effect.

* Lightly water the soil once or twice while placing it in the hole, to help it settle and remove any air pockets. Do not saturate the soil at this time. Firmly press the soil into place but don't compact it heavily.

Construction Tip: Last Steps

* **Berming:** Build up low earthen berms around the perimeter of the planting basin to help contain water. These are especially important in dry soil but may not be needed in rich absorbent soil with plenty of mulch all around. Berms should be removed after six to eight months to encourage roots to extend their growing tips beyond the original hole.

* **Staking:** If a root ball is small relative to the height of the tree, or if the soil is loose or if a tree is likely to be affected by wind, stake the tree to stabilize the roots as they get established. Use straps or webbing, not wire or twine, and attach at a point that's below half the tree's height. Woody plants are actually strengthened when their upper trunk and branches are allowed to bend in response to breeze.

* **Mulching:** Cover the soil with 2 to 4 inches of rotted wood chips or leaf litter. *Keep all mulch at least 2 to 3 inches away from the bark of the trunk* (See Action: Mulch Bare Soil, below.)

* **Watering:** Water the planting hole, letting the basin fill up completely at least once. If

Treat the Forest Well

When digging in established woodlands, take great care to minimize soil compaction in the planting area. Use a sharp spade to make sure all roots from surrounding trees are cut cleanly, to give them the best chance for recovery. Remember that many forest tree roots grow near the surface and can extend for hundreds of feet in any direction. Never cut more than 30 percent of another tree's feeder root zone, and never cut major supporting roots. Instead, change the location of the new hole, or dig around the root.

water drains through very quickly, fill the basin again. Keep the new plant well watered for the first 3 to 6 months; plants adapted to dry soil need less water. About one inch of rain per week is adequate for most plants throughout the growing season, so don't add more than this. If possible, use a sprinkler, rather than a hose, to simulate rainfall. Also, watering beyond the plant's drip line will encourage root growth.

Other Planting Issues
Bare-root Planting

Many plants will tolerate being planted without any ball of soil around their roots. This planting method, which used to be the norm, fell from favor in the last half century, but it's gaining popularity again, as a way to save money and effort but also as experiments prove that it works as well as or better than root-ball planting, in some situations.

Bare-root planting should be done when the plant is dormant (late fall or early spring), before any foliage appears, and it works better with younger plants than older ones. After

Fig. 14.8: *Proper tree staking for small trees like these involves using low straps that let the top of the tree sway a bit in the wind, which strengthens its wood, without letting the ball move in the planting hole.*

How to Prune a Branch

Never cut a branch flush with the trunk of the tree. This outdated method has been proven to harm trees, by removing the branch collar where cells create healing scar tissue. Every branch has such a collar, a slight bulge that angles out below the branch.

The best way to prune a branch is to identify the edge of this collar, then make your first cut several inches out from it, in a small notch on the underside of the branch. The second cut should come down from above, just slightly beyond the notch, to let the branch fall away cleanly, without tearing. Your final cut should remove the remaining stub, coming from below at an angle perpendicular to the branch's original angle, not necessarily parallel to the trunk. It should follow the edge of the branch collar, with the top of the cut ending fairly close to the trunk. In all cases, avoid cutting into the bark of the trunk.

Bonnie Appleton, Professor of Horticulture, Virginia Tech University

Fig. 14.9:
An increasingly popular choice, bare-root planting works well if a tree's roots are kept moist and given plenty of suitable soil to settle into.

gently digging the roots from the ground, clip away any broken or sharply bent sections, to give each root a clean growing tip for best water absorption and healing. All roots must be kept moist before planting (in a medium of loose damp soil, sawdust or shredded newspaper), but avoid leaving them in water or extreme moisture for a long time, to avoid causing mold or rot.

· Place the plant on a shallow cone of firm soil and spread the roots out in a hole large enough for their full length. Do not circle them around within the hole. Fill the hole one-third deep with soil, then water generously, creating a slurry. Wiggle the plant slightly in place, to ensure good contact between the roots and soil, and help them settle together. Beyond this advice, observe the same guidelines as above regarding the depth of the hole, the trunk flare, the use of parent soil, staking and mulching.

New Construction Sites

Be sure there's water available to irrigate new plants. If water hasn't been hooked up yet or if no one is available to provide it as needed, postpone the installation. Without adequate water, new plants will simply fail and need to be replaced.

Transplanting

Moving woody plants from the wild is never recommended, because these plants often have very unpredictable root zones, plus they're involved in complex interactions with their native soil that no gardener can duplicate. However, there may be times when you need to move a plant that's already established in your landscape. To ensure the greatest success, follow all the advice listed above, along with these extra tips:

· Dig the new hole first, before digging up the plant.

· When digging the plant, make the root ball wide enough to contain as much of the root zone as possible. On any plants installed within the last year, the root zone probably won't extend much beyond the original pot size. This is the currently accepted rule of thumb for root ball size: for deciduous trees, make the root ball at least 12 inches in diameter for every 1 inch of stem thickness (caliper), and for evergreen trees, make the root ball at least 10 inches wide for every 1 inch of stem caliper.[3] Many shrubs have very shallow but wide-spreading roots, so digging a *pancake* type of root ball (as thin as 6 to 8 inches) will work best for them.

- Never hoist the plant out of its hole by pulling up on the trunk! This will break roots and dislodge soil. Instead, reach down into the hole and lift the entire root ball.

- Immediately put the exposed root ball in burlap or some kind of material to hold the soil together and keep the roots moist.

- As above, water the newly planted tree or shrub regularly and deeply for the first 3 to 6 months, making sure the soil stays at least slightly moist.

Much of the information above is derived from instructions provided by the expert arborists and horticulturists at Tree Specialists, Inc., in Holliston, Massachusetts. Visit their website (treespecialists.com) for more advice.

ACTION: Mulch Bare Garden Soil

In nature, many plants grow in soil that's carpeted with a thick, spongy layer of fallen leaves and woodland debris. This debris gradually decomposes, and its essential nutrients are returned to the soil. For plants that evolved in these conditions, soil covered by an absorptive blanket of mulch is still the best sort of environment for their roots. In arid environments, smaller amounts of organic matter fall to the ground and decompose, so this blanket is thinner, but still it exists.

Kinds of Mulch

The best type of mulch for your landscape and gardens depends on what purpose it will serve, your geographic location, your personal aesthetics and budget. The relative merits of some mulches are summarized below.

Organic or Biologic Mulches That Will Gradually Decompose

Chopped leaves: Attractive, may be made at home, best if from a local source

Compost: Attractive, may make your own, select with care to avoid weed seeds

Straw: Suitable for vegetable gardens, avoid any with seed heads

Salt-marsh hay: Suitable for new lawn seeding or vegetable garden; avoid long transport

Fresh wood chips: Easily available, not good in perennial gardens; deplete nitrogen

Seasoned wood chips: Preferable; won't deplete nitrogen in soil

Cocoa shells: Attractive, expensive, high potassium content may cause problems

Fig. 14.10: *A wide circle of mulch helps keep this mature sugar maple thriving. In the layer of chopped (and seasoned) leaves and twigs, a variety of ferns and low woodland plants will soon create a textured carpet here to enliven the brown mulch.*

Inorganic Mulches That Will Persist in the Landscape

Pebbles: Will gradually sink into soil unless a sheet barrier is spread below

Crushed rock: Available in many colors; avoid crushed limestone

Crushed shells: May alter pH of soil

Black plastic: High manufacture cost, weeds grow through holes made for plants

Whether organic or inorganic, all mulch will:

+ curtail the growth of weeds,
+ keep soil moist and reduce the need for supplemental water,
+ keep soil warmer in winter and cooler in summer and
+ maintain a safety buffer around trees, to prevent mower damage.

Organic mulches offer these added benefits over inorganic mulch:

+ improved soil fertility, soil structure and aeration

Seasoned Organic Mulch

In most cases, because raw mulch robs nitrogen from the soil at the start of its decomposition process, it's a good idea to let all organic mulches age or season for a few months or more before spreading them in your garden.

When Should You Apply Mulch?

The insulating effects of mulch will moderate soil temperatures. Since the goal of this guideline is to help keep the ground cool, the best time to apply landscape mulch is in late spring, after the ground has warmed up enough to support vigorous plant growth, but before daytime temperatures get hot.

+ greater numbers of soil organisms
+ better plant health and resistance to diseases and insects
+ more symbiotic interactions in the soil

For the greatest soil regeneration, the best type of organic mulch is *ramial* wood chips made from small branches, twigs and leaves. This sort of mulch has the ideal carbon-to-nitrogen ratio for quick breakdown without causing nitrogen deficiency in the soil. The brush and branches leftover from logging and tree-pruning operations are a great source of ramial wood chips.[4]

Care Tip: Depth and Width of Mulch Area

Mulch should be spread in a layer that's 1 to 4 inches deep. In general, inorganic mulches can be deeper than organic ones, as they're less likely to become waterlogged and matted, which can be more harmful than helpful. See below for additional precautions.

Spread mulch to cover as much root zone as possible. In the case of trees, this means it should extend at least to the edge of the branch canopy. Tree roots may grow outward, if nutrients are available, for hundreds of feet. Conventional landscape aesthetics and attitudes may inhibit spreading mulch as far as would be ideal, but we should all begin to make mulched areas at least a little wider than usual.

Care Tip: Some Important Measures to Take, and What to Avoid

+ *Mulch should never be more than 4 inches deep, and 2 to 3 inches is probably best in most situations. Plants' roots need oxygen and* water. Mulch that's too thick, matted or waterlogged can actually smother the roots below.

- Placing mulch in contact with the bark of trees and shrubs can create problems with mold, mildew, insects and disease. The bark of a plant is its protective coat. Excess mulch against a tree creates a perfect habitat for rodents, who will nibble through bark to reach the living (yummy and nutritious) cambium layer below, reducing nutrient uptake and potentially girdling the tree. *Never create mulch volcanoes around tree trunks!*

- Avoid using mulch that's so fine-textured that it simply mats together when wet, which can actually prevent further infiltration.

- When replenishing or rejuvenating an old mulch area, be sure to scratch or loosen the surface of the existing layer, to assure infiltration.

- Established weeds, especially grasses, won't be smothered by organic mulch alone. Remember that just removing top growth is rarely sufficient to kill weeds, which usually have hardy and aggressive roots. Take steps to remove or inhibit existing weeds before spreading the mulch.

- Landscape fabrics, which allow water and air to penetrate into the ground, may effectively suppress weed growth, but the organic mulch layer that's usually spread on top of these fabrics, for aesthetic reasons, will eventually support weeds of its own (and these fabrics nearly always end up being visible anyway). Plus, being synthetic, their production consumes energy, and they're not biodegradable.

Avoid these products if possible.

Care Tip: Mulches to Avoid

- Despite its aesthetic appeal to some people, dyed mulch has several drawbacks. It's generally made from the shredded chips of discarded wood and old pallets, and may even contain pressure-treated wood, which is toxic to plants, insects, animals and humans.

- Fresh animal manure, newly chipped wood or bark, or any unseasoned mulch will also deplete the soil before it breaks down and begins to replenish the soil.

- Grass clippings should be used only thinly and allowed to dry out before adding more.

- Straw works well, but it blows around easily and may be better used in a compost pile.

- Hay usually contains weed seeds that have the potential to do more harm than good. Many people recommend using salt-marsh hay, because it's free of weed seeds, but this only makes sense as an energy saver if you live near a salt marsh.

ACTION: Plant Wildflower Meadows So They Thrive

Wildflower meadows can serve many of the same purposes as lawn: complementing the house, keeping space open, letting sunlight into the landscape, providing a foreground for distant views. And they are a great energy-efficient alternative to turf grass. While their preparation and installation is somewhat more complex than simply seeding an expanse of grass, meadows offer many additional benefits over conventional lawn:

Fig. 14.11: *This meadow is simply a field left unmowed throughout the summer. Each fall, the tall grasses and flowers are trimmed to just a few inches tall (in this case with a tractor-pulled mower, but string trimmers work equally well in smaller meadows).*

Fig. 14.12: *A single pass of the mower maintains a strip of tidy lawn between this soft meadow edge and the domesticated portion of the landscape.*

- They require little or no mowing during the growing season and only minimal maintenance after being established.

- They help keep soil moist and cool; if large enough, they help cool the air and nearby living spaces.

- They provide essential habitat for many birds that can't live elsewhere.

- They make our landscapes beautiful in every season.

As noted earlier, many species of grasses and wildflowers are adapted to growing in poor soil, so meadows make a lot of sense in new house sites, where they can reduce or eliminate the need for imported topsoil.

The Construction Tips below apply to creating a wildflower meadow on bare soil. If you already have established lawn in your landscape, an even more energy-wise method for creating a meadow is simply to stop mowing the grass. The result may not be as immediately beautiful as seeding a whole new meadow, nor will it contain purely native species, but this approach takes no energy and resources to prepare the soil, and it causes the least disturbance. Chapter 8 presents a more detailed discussion of this option.

To accomplish a conversion from lawn to meadow, whether it's a new meadow or a liberated lawn, you may also need to make a slight conversion in attitude — in yourself, your family, your neighbors. As discussed in Chapter 8, the result of not mowing will be a shaggy appearance that may be foreign or off-putting to some people. This negative reaction can be assuaged somewhat if you take three steps:

1. Keep a mown *tidiness strip* along one or more edges of the unmown grass.

2. Educate people about your intentions; maybe put up a sign identifying this as a conservation area.

3. Insert noticeable flowering plants, alone or in groups or drifts, to add color and variety and immediately give the meadow an appearance of intention and validity.

Construction Tip:
Step One — Make Decisions

• Decide what part of the landscape to seed as a meadow. The site should be sunny and open, and receive good air circulation. Southwest- and east-facing sites are better than north-facing. If the site is surrounded by weedy areas or fields of agricultural grasses, site preparation will be more complex, and controlling future weed invasions may be difficult.

• Consider whether to create the meadow by spreading seed or transplanting plugs (tiny seedlings) or established plants. Seeding costs less but takes longer to mature. Seeding in spring or early summer will produce growth in the first year. Fall seeding will germinate the following spring; if done on a slope, this will require a nurse crop to hold the soil.

• Decide which grasses and flower species to grow, depending on the quality of your soil and the amount of direct sun it receives. All seed suppliers provide guidance about individual plants' needs. Keep in mind that some plants can be seeded in poor or unimproved soil.

Construction Tip:
Step Two — Prepare the Site

• Evaluate the soil. Sandy soil contains particles that are large, light and easy to work. This soil drains very quickly and tends to be acidic. Clay soil contains tiny particles tightly packed together. It holds water easily and may be rich in nutrients, but is hard to work. Loam soil — a blend of sand, clay and intermediate particles called silt — drains well, holds moisture and nutrients well and makes good growing medium for most plants.

• If your soil is extremely sandy or clayey, and you don't want to use only the plants that will tolerate those conditions, consider augmenting the soil with compost or chopped leaves. Or seed with a green manure (buckwheat or winter wheat) and till this crop into the soil before it goes to seed. *Avoid using sawdust, bark mulch and wood chips, which rob nitrogen from the soil as they decompose.*

• Eliminate existing vegetation. There are four possible ways to do this; each has its own advantages and drawbacks:

  • Smother a weed-free lawn with layers of cardboard or newspaper under a layer of mulch, or with thick black plastic or rubber sheeting (pond liner or roofing liner). Leave in place for 2 to 3 months. If the lawn contains lots of weeds, they may need more time to be killed.

  • If using herbicide on the lawn, remember that none are proven completely safe, but organic products are the least toxic.

Fig. 14.13: *For seeding the new hillside meadow behind this house, native grass seeds are mixed with damp sawdust (foreground) as a carrier to facilitate spreading. Flowers will be planted in drifts rather than broadcast with the seed.*

- Use a sod cutter or other machinery to strip away the top layer of soil. This will remove many, but probably not all, weed seeds. The remaining soil may be mixed with compost or new topsoil, or planted directly with seeds of plants that thrive in infertile soil.

- Till the soil to a depth of 4 to 5 inches every 2 to 3 weeks for a whole growing season. This brings weed seeds to the surface and lets them grow there until killed by the next tilling. If rhizomatous weed grasses (quack grass) exist, do this for a whole year. If the field is old agricultural grasses, till it for at least two years.

Construction Tip:
Step Three — Seed the Site

- Order the correct seeds for the soil conditions. In any meadow mix, include grass seeds to produce about 70 to 80 percent grass coverage.

- Hand-broadcasting is effective for small areas. Mix the seed with damp sawdust or other inert material (2 bushels per 1,000 square feet of seeding area). Spread half the resulting material evenly across the whole area. Take extra seed from the second half if necessary. Scatter the remaining seed mix by walking perpendicular to your first pass, adjusting the amount so it covers the whole area.

- Mechanical broadcasting makes sense for large areas. Don't mix the seed with inert materials. Consider instead using a special double-seed box seeder that separates the larger grass seeds from the smaller (actually tiny) flower seeds. No-till drills are available to rent for very large areas that have not been tilled, which causes the least germination of weed seeds. Consult an expert for further information.

- Seed nurse crops if desired to help minimize weed germination. *Never use winter wheat, winter rye (their roots suppress other seeds' germination) or perennial rye (it out-competes other seedlings) as a nurse crop.*

- Roll the seeded area after planting to ensure good seed-to-soil contact.

- Cover the seeded area with 1 to 2 inches of straw or marsh hay. *Do not use field hay, which contains weed seeds.* On sloped sites, hold the mulch in place with jute or plastic netting.

- For spring seedings, water regularly for 6 to 8 weeks, just enough to keep the soil moist, every other day for 15 to 30 minutes. Water early in the morning, and don't overwater.

After 8 weeks, water only if it doesn't rain for a week.

+ For fall seedings, do not water.

Construction Tip:
Step Four — Control Weeds

In first year of a meadow seeding, expect to see some weeds germinate and grow more quickly than the meadow grasses and flowers, which spend their early life developing their roots.

+ When new plants reach 12 inches high, mow the entire area to 6 inches to suppress weeds and prevent their going to seed. This also keeps them from shading the new seedlings, which are slower to develop than weeds and are generally not even 6 inches tall at this time.

+ Mow regularly throughout the first season whenever growth reaches 12 inches, usually about once a month, depending on rain and weed height. A flail-type mower is best, since it chops up the clippings, as is a string-trimmer mower. Rotary mower clippings may smother the seedlings; in addition, most can't be raised to a 6-inch cutting height. Some string mowers can be set to 6 inches.

+ Don't pull weeds unless you're sure what they are and pulling them out won't disturb nearby seedlings. Instead, if necessary, cut them off at their base when they're in bloom and hence at their weakest point.

+ At the end of the season, don't mow but rather leave the tall growth to protect the young plants during winter.

+ In the second spring, mow the entire planting close to the ground and rake off the cuttings to expose the soil to the sun's warmth. Do not burn the meadow in its second season. If weeds continue as a problem in the second year, mow in mid to late June, to a height of one foot.

Care Tip: Long-term Care

+ In mid-spring of the third year and beyond (in both seeded meadows and lawn grass left to grow tall), either mow the meadow to within an inch of the ground and remove the cuttings or burn the meadow, just when sugar maples begin to leaf out.

+ Burning is the preferred method for maintaining a meadow, as it sets back the cool-season grasses and weeds without harming the later-growing warm-season native grasses. Burning also removes the previous year's growth and plant litter, and exposes the soil to the sun. Be sure to check

Fig. 14.14: *This meadow gets burned once in early spring (note the hose and water buckets for safety). In mid-summer, after ground- nesting birds have departed, alternating halves of the meadow are mowed each year, to a height of six inches, to remove any woody plants that have sprouted up. (See figure 8.3 for a summer view of the results.)*

with your town for a permit to burn, as many towns will not allow this. Do not burn the meadow after plants have reached one foot in height. Whether mowing or burning, it's a good idea to do only half of the area each year, to help preserve habitat for wildlife, while still preventing the invasion of woody plants overall.

- Mow paths through the meadow to link destinations. Make paths as wide as your mower for simplicity of maintenance, or as wide as two passes of the mower, for more protection from ticks that may perch on overhanging grasses.
- Never spray herbicides in a meadow planting.

The Original Lawn Mowers

Consider the possibility of using sheep, goats or other small grazers to keep your lawn short. They add nutrients to the soil, consume no gas and produce no pollution (well, except perhaps a little methane…). Keeping sheep may not be an option for most homeowners, but in some fantasy future, green landscape companies may offer the services of a mobile flock.

Fig. 14.15

The information above is derived in part from the *Catalog & Growing Guide* of Prairie Nursery, a native plant and seed nursery located in Westfield, Wisconsin. Visit their website (prairienursery.com) for more advice.

ACTION: Create Healthy, Low-maintenance Lawns

Many grass species evolved in ecosystems that included grazers, who periodically nipped off the top of every plant within reach of their non-stop munching. In response, grasses developed the ability to regrow easily, and sometimes quite vigorously, provided not too much of each blade was removed. Also, in extremes of climate and weather, all grasses naturally take care of themselves by going temporarily dormant, withdrawing nutrients from their tops to stop photosynthesis while keeping their roots alive.

When we mow grass, we're acting a bit like the original grazers. Trouble is, we tend to cut our grass too short and too often, and unlike meandering buffalo, we rarely return any nutrients to the soil, to help the grass grow. Conventional lawn treatments supply substances that feed the grass rather than the soil. Even worse, these chemicals often actually kill soil organisms that would help restore soil health if nutrients *were* provided.

One further problem: instead of accepting dormant (tan) lawn as a natural part of grass's survival strategy, we strive to keep grass green all summer long. This consumes huge amounts of water and energy. And, when watering is done in combination with standard lawn treatments, on soil that often can't absorb the water, the resulting runoff is laden with chemicals that pollute soil, streams, lakes and humans.

Healthy lawn is an assemblage of grass plants that can grow vigorously year after year with little help from us, very limited maintenance and virtually no input of energy. The best way to keep our lawns healthy is to choose the right grass for the conditions of the site, then to nourish it by providing healthy soil in which to grow, and to avoid the addition of all conventional fertilizers, herbicides and pesticides. The following construction tips detail how to accomplish these goals with new lawn. Suggestions for modifying existing lawn are noted in the appropriate places.

Construction Tip: Provide Healthy Soil

As stated repeatedly, healthy soil is a springy sponge that contains air, water, minerals and organic nutrients that decompose slowly and support millions of invisible micro-organisms, which break down the nutrients into elements the plants can use. These micro-organisms also help break down fallen grass clippings and thatch.

While other sections of this book have recommended using a very light touch when amending soil, a successful lawn depends to a great extent on providing good soil. Ideally, soil intended for growing lawn grass should:

- be at least 6 inches deep; 10 or 12 inches would be better,
- contain a balanced mixture of clay, silt and sand and about 5 percent organic matter,
- have a structure that's crumbly and loose, and
- have a nearly neutral acidity/alkalinity level (ideally between pH 6 and pH 7. See page 85 for explanation of pH).

The Five Problems with Conventional Lawn Treatment

1. We fertilize grass with chemicals that don't give the grass all the food it needs. These are the 15 elements necessary for grass growth: oxygen, carbon, hydrogen, nitrogen, potassium, phosphorous, calcium, magnesium, sulfur, boron, chlorine, copper, manganese, molybdenum and zinc. Without *all* of these (some in tiny amounts), the few elements that are provided in traditional fertilizer can't be used.[5]

2. We feed the grass, not the soil. Grass doesn't distinguish between synthetic and natural chemicals; it will take up either type. But without all the elements they need, grass roots don't develop healthy and strong, but instead depend on a constant supply of more fertilizer.

3. Soil can't hold the excess chemicals, especially compacted soil that hasn't been otherwise nourished. Whatever doesn't get absorbed very quickly by plants gets washed away, vaporized or leached down into the lower soil layer, there to pollute the ground water.

4. Conventional lawn treatment kills beneficial organisms that can help break down nutrients and aerate the soil.

5. Synthetic fertilizers are produced by blending hydrogen and nitrogen at temperatures between 750° and 1200° F, consuming huge amounts of energy in the process.[6]

Fig. 14.16: *On steep hillsides that are planted as lawn, water runs off too quickly and mowing can be difficult and dangerous. Consider instead creating usable terraces or planting the slope with low-maintenance, self-sustaining vegetation, as in the upper slope shown here.*

Adjusting the pH Level of Soil

After assessing your soil with a pH testing kit, add substances as necessary, in the recommended proportions. Calcitic limestone will reduce acidity (raise the pH); sulphur will reduce alkalinity (lower the pH). Remember that soil test kits sold at garden centers provide only approximate results, and a better choice is to send soil samples to an agricultural extension service or private testing lab. This advice is especially important for landscape professionals to heed.

Improving the Soil of Existing Lawns

Add organic matter by spreading a half inch of compost over the whole surface, in spring and fall, after mowing the grass (remove excessive clippings, if necessary). Test the soil pH and correct as needed by distributing amendments on the surface rather than mixing them into the soil.

The time to establish these ideal conditions is before the soil is spread, by mixing all the ingredients together in a pile or truck bed. *The challenge of satisfying all of these requirements is yet another reason to limit lawn to only those places where it's really needed.*

Construction Tip: Grade the Soil

Shape the ground so water drains off the lawn rather than collecting in low spots. Ideally any major earth-grading should be done primarily with subsoil, not with precious topsoil. Avoid adding extra soil depth around existing trees or over their roots (tree roots need air and water). Lightly compact the new soil by rolling it with a drum (only half-full with water), to eliminate air pockets and reveal low spots.

Avoid planting lawn on steep slopes, which will either need some sort of erosion control during the germination period or may erode before the roots get established. Also, mowing steep slopes is difficult and dangerous. If the site is sloped, consider creating level or gentle grade terraces, supported by stone/boulder walls or steep planted banks.

Construction Tip: Seed the Lawn

Choose the right grass species for the soil and climate conditions. Countless varieties are produced by the turf industry, so find out as much as possible about what works best in your region. Remember, in cool temperate regions, you might consider using low-mow or no-mow seed mixes in as much of the landscape as possible, to save energy on mowing. See Chapter 8 for more information.

Fall seeding is preferable to spring seeding, as there are fewer weed seeds blowing around at that time, plus the grass can get established before having to handle the stress of summer heat. Avoid seeding during extremely dry periods and immediately after a rain. The ideal time to seed a lawn is just before a light rain.

Maintenance Tip: After-seeding Care

Water frequently and shallowly at first, just to keep the soil surface constantly moist. Avoid drowning or washing away the seed. After the seed has germinated, water every other day, for several weeks, depending on weather. By three months after seeding, cut back watering to the same amount used for an established lawn, about an inch a week, depending on soil type, sun exposure, grass types, etc. *It's especially important to provide enough water that it can soak deep into the soil, even if this means watering less frequently.* This is far preferable to watering often but shallowly, which only serves to keep grass roots growing near the surface instead of reaching downward. If the roots of the lawn don't extend down two inches within a few weeks, add phosphorus.

Mow the lawn whenever the grass is tall enough that mowing will remove *only* the top third. Make sure mower blades are sharp, to avoid tugging the grass from the soil. To save the most energy, use the lightest lawn mower feasible for the size and condition of your lawn. Avoid riding mowers whenever possible. For a small lawn, consider an electric mower, which will have a battery or require an extension cord. Many excellent push mowers are now available, and think of the great exercise using one will give you!

And remember, even if you already have a large lawn, you can simply stop mowing parts of it, perhaps a little more each year, and let a wild meadow take its place. This will save the most energy of all.

ACTION: Water Wisely

The most important thing to remember about watering efficiently is to purposely design your landscape to need little water beyond what's provided by natural rainfall and snow. Chapter 9 presents several design ideas for accomplishing this basic goal, including: choosing plants suited to your climate and soil; keeping the ground as absorptive as possible by using mulch and creating healthy, spongy soil in your lawn; establishing watering zones; managing runoff with topography and collecting rainwater for use on your gardens and grounds. Assuming you've implemented some or all of these suggestions, your need for extra water will be minimal and easily satisfied by following the two tips below. Together all these Actions will save energy.

Maintenance Tip:
Schedule Irrigation Wisely

The invention of the sprinkler, in the late 1800s, is a main reason that the North American lawn became so widely possible in the early 1900s, despite the fact that much of this continent receives insufficient rainfall to support lush grass. Now, since lawn grass seems to have become an essential component of almost every residential landscape (except perhaps yours, if follow the advice in Chapter 8), we all must decide how much water to add to our lawns,

Fig. 14.17: *Shaded lawn needs less water that sunny lawn, and much of the water used to irrigate a sloped lawn merely runs downhill to pool at the bottom or drain off site. Is this irrigation really necessary? Wouldn't a nice woodsy carpet of pine needles and ferns be more appropriate (and more beautiful) here?*

the lawn, when the wind is still or humidity is high. The conventional approach to lawn watering is to *increase* watering during hotter seasons, during times of high wind, dry air and drought. However, as explained earlier, grass is capable of going dormant for long stretches of time, letting its top growth stop photosynthesizing, storing nutrients in its roots and then springing back to life when better conditions return. So it's equally appropriate to simply adjust a watering regime downward during hot times and to adjust our aesthetic expectations accordingly.

How much should you water? Sandy soil soaks up water quickly and releases it downward quickly too, so it's a good idea to water this very porous soil in smaller quantities more frequently. In contrast, clayey soil absorbs water slowly and then holds onto it for a long time, so it's better to water such dense soil with smaller amounts of water, for more extended stretches of time, but less frequently.

How can you know what's enough? The simplest method is, after watering for a while, to just push a screwdriver down into the soil. If it can penetrate at least six inches, the soil is adequately moist, assuming your goal is to keep the lawn lush. If not, then you need to water for longer periods or more often, so water can percolate more deeply. By paying attention to your lawn's needs over a period of time, you'll get a sense of what works best. A rain gauge will help you know how much water has recently fallen. The ideal, of course, in this whole process is to keep the soil so loose and full of organic material and micro-organisms that a little bit of water goes a long way.

throughout the growing season, to keep them alive. The following discussion is not a complete treatise on lawn-watering techniques, but rather a review of relevant issues to keep in mind.

Most important, every situation is unique, and there are no absolute rules. The basic goal is to keep the soil deeply moist, so grass roots can extract the necessary nutrients. The amount of water needed to accomplish this goal depends on several factors, including soil quality, type of grass, time of year and time of day, and weather conditions.

A rule of thumb is that lawns need about one inch of water per week. Lesser amounts are appropriate during cooler seasons, or when there are lots of clouds in the sky or shade on

Watering Other Parts of the Landscape

Increasingly, as we move away from our devotion to lush lawn, we'll need to use less water to keep grass green. For both survival and pleasure, though, we'll still need to water these other important part of our landscapes:

+ vegetable gardens, agricultural fields and other food-producing areas
+ any newly planted garden beds, trees or shrubs; they need regular and frequent watering while their roots adjust to the new environment
+ special or tender plants that are essential to a landscape composition but may not have been selected for low-water demand

In all these cases, take steps to use only the amount of water that is clearly required, to make sure the water soaks in and doesn't drain away and to use natural runoff and harvested rainwater whenever possible.

Maintenance Tip: Use the Right Watering System for the Job

The simplest watering systems consist of above-ground sprinklers attached to a hose or soaker hoses that let water seep steadily out along their entire length. At the other extreme are in-ground sprinklers supplied by buried pipes, or drip systems generally fed by fixed water spigots. To water our landscapes most efficiently, it's important to choose the most appropriate system for the job that needs to be done. Below is a more detailed description of each system, along with its main attributes.

Above-ground sprinklers are the simplest, least expensive choice. Because they're attached to a hose and can be moved to wherever they're needed, they allow full control over the area to be watered. Common types include:

+ Oscillators, which spray water from a perforated tube that rotates slightly on its own axis, back and forth to a degree that's determined by a setting on the mechanism. Oscillators cover up to almost 4,000 square feet on a rectangular patch of ground. Some contain a built-in timer for pre-setting the duration of watering.
+ Rotary sprinklers make sense for smaller areas. They contain two to four short arms that spin from a central axis, spraying water in a circular pattern.
+ Stationary sprinklers simply sit and spew water in a set pattern based on the shape of the fixture and the distribution of holes. These mechanisms are probably the least expensive choice.

Soaker hoses are perforated with a million tiny holes along their entire length, to emit water in a trickle or fine short spray directly onto the soil. This sort of system is ideal for watering vegetable gardens and linear beds, though the hose itself can be wound around randomly distributed plants in an infinite range of possibilities. Hoses can also be joined end to end to form an extremely long loop with only minor loss of water pressure. The main disadvantages of soaker hoses are that they may sometimes spring a leak that releases too much water, depriving the rest of the hose, and they're not easy to reposition after plants have started growing. Because they put water directly into the ground, however, much less water is lost to evaporation than is the case with sprinklers, making them perhaps the most efficient type of watering system for the investment.

In-ground sprinklers, usually called irrigation systems, include buried sprinkler heads that sit flush with the surface of the ground, then pop up on demand to spray water in a fixed circular pattern. These systems require a certain minimum water pressure to function well, along with careful design and installation to make sure the water is used most efficiently. This discussion is not the place for detailed explanation of sprinkler zones, valves, pipe sizes and routes, and the distribution of sprinkler heads. Rather, it's a reminder that this type of system requires electricity to function, needs to be regularly tuned up to keep it running efficiently, then winterized and restarted every spring and, finally, often involves pre-set watering schedules that spew water whether or not it's needed. The message here is to think carefully before investing in such a system when other options might be equally effective.

Drip systems are nearly as complex as in-ground irrigation. They include several interconnected components: valves, backflow preventers, pressure regulators, air vents, filters, tubings, fittings and emitters, which are small openings spaced at various intervals along the tubing. Commonly used in nurseries, large planting installations and for agricultural irrigation, drip irrigation provides direct contact between water and the ground, eliminating the evaporation of conventional sprinkler-type irrigation. But they too require a high level of water pressure and extensive knowledge to install.

ACTION: Acquire Plants Appropriately

To supply ourselves with the plants we want in the most energy-efficient way, consider taking one or more (or all!) of the following steps:

Buy Small Plants

Smaller plants actually grow faster than larger ones. They recover more easily from transplant shock, they're easier to move and handle, planting them requires less soil and resources, and they're less expensive than larger plants. They've also spent less time being grown in a nursery, which equals less energy spent on getting them to their current size. Large plants, especially large trees, have a high failure rate. They grow so slowly that in many cases a smaller tree planted at the same time will catch up to and even exceed the size of a larger tree in just a few years, depending, of course, on how different they were to begin with.

Buy Locally Grown Plants

To save energy on the transportation of plants, buy locally. Many nurseries import large quantities of plants from wholesale suppliers, but all nursery owners are business people who aim to make a profit, so the more their customers ask for locally grown products, the more they'll seek to offer such plants. Small-scale plant growing operations exist everywhere, and they're becoming more abundant all the time, as demand increases.

Another advantage of buying plants grown within your own region is that these plants are more likely to be hardy and suited to your climate zone. Many millions of plants are grown in the south and shipped to nurseries further north, where innocent buyers take home exciting treasures that will surely languish despite the best care, simply because they're in the wrong world.

Rescue Plants

As a general rule, plants should never be dug from the wild. When natural areas are about to be developed, however, one of the first steps is often the complete removal of vegetation. If you're aware that this is about to happen, it just makes sense to salvage any plants that would otherwise be killed. This rescue should be done with care, of course, to make sure the plants survive and your efforts are worthwhile, but since these plants would otherwise be completely lost, the need for extreme care is a bit lower.

One way to take advantage of this opportunity is actually to check with your local planning office to find out about proposed new construction. Be sure to get permission from any property owner before digging plants; many people will actually be grateful for your efforts, as it may assuage any regrets they might feel about harming the site.

Grow Plants from Seed

The absolutely most energy-efficient way to acquire plants is to grow them from seed. This approach lets nature do the entire job, with virtually no input from us beyond providing the initial soil and some attention to watering.

Many of us are already familiar with growing from seed in our lawns and all the steps: preparing the soil, spreading the seed, watering, watching, taking care of the new growth, celebrating the beautiful result. We can do the

same with many other plants. The main difference will be a matter of time, as few plants reach their maturity as quickly as grass, although many native grass species take two years to mature. It may not make sense to grow trees and large shrubs from seeds, but we can easily grow many kinds of flower and ferns in a single year, and many small shrubs will reach a good size in two to four years.

CHAPTER SUMMARY

This chapter presents advice about how to install and care for the planted portions of our landscapes. These ideas will help save energy immediately, in the process of construction, but even more important, they will lead to long-term success, producing even more savings in the future.

Most planting projects begin with some form of soil preparation. Ideally, for the sake of both energy and the environment, an important first step is to limit the amount of soil brought into

Fig. 14.18:
This small-scale plant nursery in western Massachusetts supplies high-quality and unusual woodland plants to dozens of mainstream retailers and garden centers.

the site from other places. It's preferable to use only what's there at the start. This may involve various methods for storing topsoil before construction begins or amending it lightly to make it more useful. Other suggestions include: using compost and leaf litter to nourish soil, loosening the soil to make it more absorbent and open to nutrients, and even adjusting the design goals of the project if necessary.

The chapter presents techniques for planting trees and shrubs, including: how to prepare plants, preparing planting holes, placing root balls properly, backfilling and taking final steps to ensure greatest success. This is followed by a discussion of mulching materials and methods, to keep soil moist and plants healthy.

Detailed advice is also provided for installing wildflower meadows and vigorous, low-maintenance lawn. Both of these topics include maintenance recommendations for the near and long term. The chapter ends with a discussion of efficient watering strategies and equipment and suggestions for how to save energy in the process of acquiring plants.

CHAPTER 15

Building Structures in the Landscape

Let's begin with the assumption that any landscape structure you're about to build — patio, path, wall, deck, etc. — has been designed in accord with at least some of the energy-efficient principles discussed in Section IV. Whatever the project, if it's not planned to fit the land, function well and satisfy multiple purposes, consider revisiting chapters 10 through 13.

This chapter does not give detailed instructions about *how* to build things, nor does it address every possible situation, every regional or local condition. Plenty of other books and references give advice about constructing landscape features. Rather, the goal here is to provide a basic understanding of *what* to do, and *why* to do it, so the structures you build are as sound and durable as possible, and won't

need to be repaired or replaced any time soon (or perhaps, ever).

The Actions in this chapter cover the following subjects:

+ Patios and paths
+ Stone walls
+ Structures made of wood
+ Alternative, energy-saving materials

ACTION:
Lay Patios and Paths to be Durable

Time-consuming and energy-intensive, all stonework involves several steps and requires great attention to detail. Stone surfaces on the ground, in particular, demand special care. Not only should this stonework look good, it also needs to withstand the wear and tear of regular

Fig. 15.1:
To get the most benefit from stone's extreme durability, make sure to build your patio with proper attention to detail, in both the base preparation and the surface itself.

use, and it must allow surface water to drain off, to prevent puddles, frost heaves and washouts. The following Construction Tips explain how to get the most satisfying and durable results from your work.

Construction Tip: Base Preparation

The first step in making long-lasting patios and paths is to establish a stable base. This may be the most time-consuming (and least fun) part of a stonework project, but if you skip it or skim over it, you'll only diminish the value of your efforts and energy. Below are the steps involved in preparing a base, along with the reasons they're important.

Excavation

+ Remove organic soil from the surface. Taking away any spongy material reduces the amount of water absorbed below the stone surface, which prevents both squishiness after a rain

and freeze-thaw damage in the winter. It also saves valuable fertile soil for use in other places where it's needed.

+ Excavate the top layers of loose earth down to the subsoil, or to where the soil is firmly compacted. This might be a few inches in some situations, or up to a foot in others. Particularly in wet soil, excavate enough to allow for placing substantial depth of drainage material below the surface.

+ Keep in mind that newly placed earth continues to settle for about a year, just from gravity and rain action. When laying stone on areas of new fill, compact the earth firmly, with a hand tamper on small jobs or a power compacter if the area is large. It's preferable to build on earth that's been in place for at least a year.

Tree Roots

+ If any tree roots extend into the construction area, pause for a moment before cutting them. Large roots may be essential for keeping a tree upright, especially on slopes. Small roots just below the surface absorb nutrients and send them up to feed the tree. Consider relocating the stonework or, if that's not possible, leave the roots in place and carefully dig out the soil around them. Avoid nicking their protective outer coating! The roots of a healthy tree can safely pass below stonework, especially if the path or patio is at least 10 to 20 feet from the trunk.

+ As a last choice, tree roots may be cut. Cut a large root with a sharp saw and a clean slicing action, so the raw end has the best chance to heal (like a cut in our own skin). Smaller roots can be cut with a sharp spade and a quick downward thrust. Never rip or twist roots loose. And never remove more that 25 percent of a tree's entire root zone. Ideally, if you need to cut roots, do this several weeks or months before construction begins, and water the injured ends well, to help them build scar tissue.

Filling the Base

• Fill the excavated area with crushed stone. The size of this stone will vary depending on soil and climate conditions. Larger stones mean larger air spaces between the stones, and these spaces can hold more water than the small spaces left between small stones. In very dry regions, where the ground never freezes, and where whatever rain does fall will percolate quickly, the stones may be smaller than in regions with a lot of rain, wet soils and/or ground that freezes in winter. In an extremely wet site (if this is the only place to build), consider laying perforated drain pipe in the base, to drain excess water.

• Some situations may call for laying a base in two different layers, with larger stones below for maximum drainage, and smaller material above, in direct contact with underside of the surface stone. If there's a significant difference between the stone size in the two layers, consider placing filter fabric on top of the lower layer before spreading the upper layer, to keep the smaller stones from sifting down into the base layer. In any case, the whole base should be firmly compacted before the path or patio stones are laid onto it.

Fig. 15.2: *Tree roots that have been cleanly cut, as shown here, heal faster than roots that are torn and shredded.*

Fig. 15.3: *This patio's compacted sub-base (note the power compactor on the right) is now receiving its top layer of smaller crushed stone.*

Where Not to Build

Avoid installing a patio at the bottom of any sort of drainage basin or bowl in the landscape, where water has no outlet and will simply stand there making your life miserable, especially if the soil is dense and easily saturated.

Construction Tip: Laying the Stone

Fig. 15.4: A string stretched from one side of this path to the other helps reveal the final surface level.

Once you've created the foundation for your stonework project, the work of actually laying stone can begin. This will probably be the most enjoyable part of the project, as you begin to see the final surface taking shape and you imagine how the new space will feel and function in your life. Keep in mind the following instructions when laying stones.

Fig. 15.5: An imperceptible "cross-pitch" makes surface water drain sideways across this patio, away from the house and toward the absorbent garden beds.

Putting Stone in Place

• Lay stones so the final surface is smooth and safe to walk on, with no edges or single pieces higher than the rest. This job is a bit fussy, especially if the stones that you're using have an irregular thickness. But to prevent accidents and increase your pleasure in the final product, attention to detail at this stage is essential. It's much harder to fix unevenness after the project is all done and cleaned up than to just do it right to begin with.

• Tight joints between the stones may be desirable for aesthetic reasons, but leaving joints wider will help water percolate to the ground below, reducing runoff. Some larger gaps can also support small plants.

• Make sure the perimeter of the stonework is well-supported, so stones won't crack or wiggle out of place, and base material can't wash away.

• Compact any loosened stuff beneath by tamping individual flat stones above (protected with a thick timber or plank to prevent cracking). Remove any large air spaces below the stone, where loose material might gradually slide around (especially in wet conditions) and possibly destabilize the surface.

Ensuring Good Drainage

• Set the stones so the final surface tilts just slightly, so water can sheet off. Also make sure that water draining off a hard surface has a place to end up, ideally where it will be harmlessly absorbed. A rule of thumb is that level surfaces should pitch at least one inch in eight feet (one percent), and at most one inch in four feet (two percent).

- Any patio near a house should pitch away from the building, to keep water from flowing toward the foundation. Paths should pitch slightly to one side or the other, ideally toward the downward side of any sloped land. Avoid having runoff flow along the course of a sloping path, by giving it a *cross-pitch* and creating places where water can run off to the side. If a path is laid on perfectly level land, place its surface at least level with, or even slightly above, the adjacent ground, and make sure it's never lower that the land on either side, to keep it from collecting water and perhaps getting icy in winter.

- Stonework (or concrete) surfaces surrounding a swimming pool must tilt slightly away from the pool, to keep dirt and debris from draining toward the pool water.

Construction Tip: Finishing the Surface

- Stones that are laid dry (without mortar) usually require some sort of granular material — sand or stone dust — in between them to help keep the individual components in place. It's essential with bricks, cobbles and other small stone. This is also a place where small steppable plants may thrive. With flat stones that are very large and heavy, filling the joints may not be necessary for stability, though it might still be desirable for appearances or to support small plants growing in between the stones. One advantage of leaving joints unfilled is that water and air can then penetrate into the ground, nourishing any tree roots that may exist below the stonework.

- Walk around and all over the entire surface, testing for wiggles and loose stones. Pay special attention to the corners and edges of individual stones. If necessary, lift out loose stones and repack the leveling material below.

Fig. 15.6: *Gaps left in the joints between stones may be filled either with stone dust or with soil that supports the growth of small plants (which will ultimately require somewhat more maintenance — weeding — than the stone dust).*

Fig. 15.7:
This lawn terrace, created as a place for kids to play on an otherwise sloped site, is supported by a wall made of irregular fieldstone that was harvested from old collapsed stone walls on the property itself: a perfect efficiency.

ACTION:
Build Stone Walls So They Hold Up Well

Base Preparation

Just as patios and paths need to be built on a stable foundation, so too do walls and steps, perhaps even more so because of their concentrated weight. Follow the base preparation advice above, with this additional consideration.

Tall walls and large steps require more support than shorter walls, narrower steps and short runs of stairs. If your wall is taller than 2 feet or your steps are wider than 3 to 4 feet, with runs of more than 3 or 4 steps, pay special attention to the solidity of the earth below and the depth of the base, which might range from 6 to 12 inches. This is especially true for any concrete or mortared structures, which are inflexible and will simply crack if the foundation shifts even a little bit. It's a good idea to check with local stonemasons for advice about base depths in your particular conditions.

Building the Wall

- In regions where the ground freezes in winter, and particularly in places that tend to be wet, dry-laid construction is preferable to using mortar, because dry stone structures are flexible and can move in response to any slight shifting in the base. This option only makes sense, of course, if rock suitable for dry stacking is available in your own region. Round and small rocks may not stay in place very well without some sort of "glue," but experienced stone masons can often build amazingly durable structures with whatever local stone exists.

- Over time, dry-stacked stones will naturally move very slightly in response to gravity and any small movement of the earth below. To make sure that the stones in a wall will shift *toward the interior* of a wall rather than toward the outside, walls should be built so their faces have a slight *batter* or slant toward the center. A general rule of thumb is 1 inch of slant for each 1 foot of wall height; this means that free-standing walls are wider at the base than at the top. Also, lay flat stones so they're slightly tilted inward rather than outward.

- Retaining walls, i.e., walls pressed against a slope, must be built so both rainwater and groundwater can seep through. If water pressure is not relieved, it can eventually cause a wall to crack or crumble. All retaining walls need to be backfilled with loose rubble, to let water sink downward more than forward toward the wall. In extremely wet conditions, pressure can be relieved by a pipe laid at the bottom of this rubble, along the length of the wall, to carry water sideways and away from the wall. Mortared walls must contain *weep holes*, pipes or tubes set into the wall at intervals to let water from behind the wall flow through to the front. Dry-laid walls inherently contain enough small gaps to relieve water pressure without weep holes.

+ In regions that freeze, stone walls will benefit from having a waterproof top layer. This will keep rain from penetrating to the interior, freezing (expanding) and pushing the stones out of place. Just mortaring the top layer of stones to prevent seepage, or to hold loose stones together, generally doesn't work in the long run: the movement of dry-laid stones below will eventually crack the mortar (witness the countless collapsed stone

walls all across old New England farms). A preferable solution is to cap the wall with large slabs of the same stone or different material.

Fig. 15.8:
This wall slants inward slightly; this "batter" increases the wall's ability to resist the pressure of the earth behind it, making the wall more durable. The capstone's overhang or "reveal" is an attractive but structurally optional detail.

RICHARD BURCK ASSOCIATES

Fig. 15.9: *Capstones may either match or contrast with the body of a wall.*

ACTION:
Build Wood Structures for Long Life

Wood is a sponge. It's very hard, to be sure, and you can't wring it out when it gets soggy, but wood contains millions of tiny pores that take in and release moisture just like a sponge. Whether indoors or out, wood shrinks and swells in accord with the amount of moisture in the air. Outdoor wood structures are particularly active: they shift in response to rain, sun, dampness rising from the ground and daily fluctuations in humidity. And this absorptive/moving quality is the main reason for nearly every problem with wood structures, including cracks, twists, cupping, warping, shrinkage and peeling paint.

Wood is also an ideal habitat for all sorts of tiny (sometimes invisible) creatures. After all, many insects flourish in living trees, and millions of microbes spend their time breaking down weakened or dead trees. These creatures are all perfectly happy to carry on as usual when they encounter anything made of wood, inhabiting or eating or decomposing our decks, arbors, furniture and fences. And, as an added twist of bad luck for us, wood fibers that have been softened by moisture are also easier for these pesky critters to burrow into, wiggle through and digest. The overall result of these activities is *decay*, when wood fibers weaken and break down, and the wood gradually falls apart.

All of these problems — moisture, wood movement and decay — shorten the lifetime of wooden structures. Careful construction techniques can moderate the effect of wood's movement, so that individual members of any structure are able to shift slightly without getting loose or putting stress on the whole. Beyond that, however, the best way to keep your structures intact is to minimize the amount of moisture and insect damage.

When you're about to build any landscape features out of wood, the following tips will help you prolong their life and postpone their repair and replacement as long as possible.

Construction Tip: Choose Moisture- and Decay-resistant Wood

Many trees are naturally resistant to either moisture or decay, or both. Some tree species have very dense wood: they either contain very tiny pores, or their pores are entirely plugged (with cellular bodies called tyloses). Moisture doesn't easily penetrate these tight-grained woods, which include black locust, white oak and many tropical species such as teak and mahogany.

Other wood contains chemical compounds (tannins) and oils that are naturally repellent to insects. These chemicals exist in many parts of plants, including bark and leaves, but their highest concentrations are in the heartwood or center of trees, which is often darkened in color by their presence. Sapwood, the lighter-colored, outer wood of tree trunks generally contains little tannin. Redwood, cedars, oak, walnut, hemlock, cherry, cypress and sassafras trees all contain high levels of tannin, with redwood and cedar having the most and therefore being most resistant to insect damage.

Naturally Rot-resistant Wood

The wood of many tree species can last 50 to 70 years when kept out of contact with the ground (see the next Construction Tip on how to accomplish this). The following trees produce the ideal kinds of wood for outdoor structures.

- Western Red Cedar (*Thuja plicata*), fast growing, strong, stable and decay-resistant, is one of the best choices for outdoor wood construction. Like redwood, it's grown in plantations, but cedar is preferable to redwood because of its greater flexibility and lower oil content, which make it easier to glue and stain. Cedar is an especially energy-efficient choice in the Pacific Northwest where transportation distances are shortest.

- Redwood (*Sequoia sempervirens*) is another of the great choices for outdoor construction, valued for its tight grain, dimensional stability and high level of tannic acid (along with its beautiful color). No longer produced by felling old-growth giants, most commercial redwood is now a renewable resource, with more seedlings planted every year than are harvested. Like Western Red Cedar, Redwood makes best energy sense on the west coast.

- Northern White Cedar (*Thuja occidentalis*), also known as arborvitae, is another of the extremely rot-resistant species. It's light and flexible, quite stable with changes in moisture, and it even lasts a long time *in contact with the ground*, so it can be used in fence posts. In the US, this wood is widely available in northern Midwest and the Northeast, as well as throughout eastern Canada.

- All Cedars (Atlantic White Cedar, Southern Red Cedar, Port Orford Cedar, etc.) are decay-resistant and suitable for outdoor construction. The best choice is always a local product, so be sure to ask about its species and origin. Eastern Red Cedar (*Juniperus virginiana*) is actually a juniper species, not a true cedar. It does contain decay-resistant heartwood, but this wood is not as strong as cedar.

- Black Locust (*Robinia pseudoacacia*) lasts longer in contact with the ground than any other North American wood; it's ideal for fence posts, landscape timbers, etc. It is not generally produced in dimensioned lumber due to

Fig. 15.10: *A perfect example of "re-use and recycle," this fence was designed for and built of redwood paneling that was removed from a house's interior, when the home's 1950's dark-wood decor didn't suit the new owner's modern taste.*

Tannins

Tannins, or tannic acid, are so called because they're the substance used in *tanning* leather. This process converts the proteins in raw animal hides into a form that resists decomposition, which turns the hides into leather.

its extreme hardness (difficult to saw, nail, machine and glue), wavy grain and crooked growth form. Once limited to the Appalachians and the southern Midwest, Black Locust has spread widely as an aggressive colonizer of dry, disturbed soils across the Northeast, so its availability is increasing.

- White oak (*Quercus alba*) is the only oak with closed pores, which make it very resistant to moisture absorption. Long used in boat building, white oak is probably too heavy for decks, but it makes excellent decay-resistant fence rails and outdoor furniture.

Tropical Wood

Many tropical woods have very tight grain and natural oils that repel insects. Recently, more of these woods have begun to be grown in plantations rather than harvested from the wild, which increases their appeal and acceptability to environmentally minded consumers. (Take care to find out whether the wood you're about to buy has actually been cut from a plantation rather than the wild.) The most widely available are ironwoods such as Ipe and Pau Lope, which can last up to 20 years with only one preservative treatment. All of these woods,

however, do have to be transported great distances to North American markets, so be sure to take this embedded energy cost into account when weighing all the factors about which wood to use.

Chemically Treated Wood

Wood that has to remain in contact with the ground for a long time is most vulnerable to both insects and moisture. Pine, which is the most widely available lumber in the US, has virtually no resistance to insect damage. To solve this problem, the lumber industry has worked for decades to develop ways to give pine some degree of resistance. The main effort has involved pressure-treating the wood in a process that forces chemicals into the wood's fibers, to make the fibers inedible or toxic to pests. A concoction of copper, chromium and arsenic was the first treatment used, but this CCA pressure-treated lumber was eventually revealed to be toxic not just to insects but also to its human users. In 2002, the US Environmental Protection Agency banned any further production of CCA lumber. Since then, several new products have been developed (ACQ, CA, MicroPro, Purewood), each with varying degrees of effectiveness and environmental safety.

With all these wood products, however, the treatment is primarily intended to repel insects. It does little to repel moisture, and it also makes the wood somewhat resistant to moisture-barrier preservatives. As a result, conventional treated wood still does absorb some moisture, still shrinks and swells, still does crack, twist, bend and cup, and all this movement can tear a structure apart. Real-life experiences show that

Fig. 15.11:
Ipe is so dense that building with it requires pre-drilling of holes, yet the wood holds up well for decades without any finishes or preservatives, making it a popular and energy-efficient choice for small outdoor projects like these steps.

many pressure-treated structures have ended up in landfills after as little as 10 years, despite manufacturers' claims of a 30-year lifetime. This fact, added to the high energy cost of manufacturing the product, make chemically treated wood less desirable in many situations than naturally resistant wood. If you must use treated wood for outdoor structures, try to find a product that has water-repellant chemicals injected into the wood fibers along with the insect-repellent substances.

Construction Tip:
Control Moisture Content

As noted earlier, many problems with wood are the result of moisture. But how much moisture is too much? There's no absolute answer to this, because different kinds of wood have different saturation points, and the moisture content of wood constantly shifts in response to surrounding conditions. Much of the lumber sold at lumberyards has been kiln-dried to a certain moisture percentage, but as soon as the wood leaves the kiln, it immediately begins to gain (or rarely, lose) moisture, until the water content of the wood exactly matches the amount of moisture in the air.

The main control you have over wood's moisture content is to make sure it's been stored, and continues to be stored, in a dry location. This means absolutely never storing lumber for any length of time directly on the ground; instead stack it on planks or blocks. It also means keeping wood covered to protect it from rain (though leaving the sides uncovered will help maintain air movement); not storing

How a Tree Becomes Lumber

After being cut to length and having its bark skimmed off, a whole log is roughly sliced into planks between one to four or six inches thick, depending on the size of the log and the wood's intended purpose. At this point, the boards have a rough surface and an irregular, "waney" edge.

The sides of each plank are then trimmed to make them even and to give the plank its maximum width; these dimensions generally range from 4 to 12 inches, in increments of 2 inches. Rarely anymore are trees wide enough to yield the old 16- and 20-inch wide planks common in historic homes. The finished board at this point is at its true, fullest size, represented by whole-number dimensions such as 2-by-4, 2-by-8 and 4-by-4.

Finally, boards are planed smooth on all four sides, in a process that removes yet another thin layer of wood. The resulting board, still called by its original or *nominal* dimension, is actually a half inch smaller in both thickness and width. Most building lumber then has its corners slightly rounded off, to prevent splinters and strengthen the edges.

Every stage in the process of lumber production consumes energy and turns some amount of the log into sawdust. So, when building outdoor structures, keep in mind that you can ask to buy wood in earlier stages of its processing, before it's been smoothed and eased, or even before its edges have been trimmed square, if this type of board will meet your needs.

wood near a large body of water, nor at the bottom of a slope (where cool, moist air descends in the evening); and making sure your supplier has taken good care of the wood.

Construction Tip: Minimize Damage from Ground Contact

Moisture from the ground has the greatest potential to damage wood structures. Beyond

Fig. 15.12: *For greatest durability, wood members should not be in contact with the concrete piers that support them. This is especially true for posts, whose open end grain acts like a giant straw, sucking moisture up into the wood.*

Setting Posts Directly in the Ground

When building any large, permanent structures, never set posts directly in the ground. No matter how rot-resistant the wood, its eventual decay is guaranteed, its replacement inevitable. This advice does not apply to fence posts and other small structures that can be easily repaired or partially replaced without great effort or expense.

the repeated shrinking and swelling that twists boards, loosens joints and gradually weakens overall integrity; beyond the fact that damp wood physically breaks down faster than dry wood, whether from insect action, fungus or simple cellular collapse, the big problem is that wood in contact with the ground is usually supporting the above-ground structure; therefore, its decay undermines everything. These supporting members are generally very difficult to repair or replace without a lot of trouble and expense. Worse, this trouble is compounded by the fact that most supporting members are either invisible, or virtually invisible, i.e., completely ignored, until they cause some sort of problem up above.

All permanent landscape structures need to be supported somehow. Most conventional decks, porches, gazebos, etc. rest on beams, which rest on posts that rest on (or in) the ground. The exceptions are when structures are built on a concrete or stone foundation, or when a cantilever — a beam that extends out beyond a building's wall to carry a load — eliminates the need for vertical supports. Fence rails and boards attach to fence posts that are set in or on the ground. In every situation except perhaps the most arid environments, these wood members that touch the ground are vulnerable to moisture damage. And this is damage that must be prevented, or at least kept to a minimum.

How can you do this? The following are three possible approaches: each one alone might be enough, and in some situations only one may work, but when possible, implementing all of them together is best.

• Minimize the number of wood posts that are needed in contact with the ground. This could involve designing the structure so the places that need support correspond to the maximum span a beam can carry, using stronger beams that can span longer distances or using a different material than wood posts for support, e.g., steel, concrete, etc.

• Rest posts on *piers*. These are structures that protrude at least a few inches above the ground's surface and extend down far enough to provide stability. In regions that freeze in winter, piers should extend below the normal depth of frost. Depending on the situation, piers may be concrete block, concrete poured into a form, a large or thick stone, etc. Ideally, whatever type of wood member will rest on a foundation, whether it's a post, beam, stair stringer, etc., a barrier or space should be between the wood and the foundation to prevent moisture absorption. Many companies provide an assortment of metal mounting brackets for this purpose. If a pier will directly support a post, without a barrier, shape the top of the pier so water drains off its surface.

• Use decay-resistant wood (see above), ideally naturally decay-resistant species such as black locust or cedar, which last longer than chemically treated wood.

The best way to minimize damage to wood from contact with the ground varies with every situation. Your own solution will depend on the nature of the ground in your region, the size and purpose of your structure, the local availability of materials, your budget and personal preferences.

Construction/Maintenance Tip: Treat Wood with Moisture-barrier Preservatives

Weathering is the deterioration of wood from ultraviolet rays that alter the chemicals in wood and destroys lignin, the natural glue that binds wood cells together. Raw wood sucks moisture from rain, dew and humidity. Then the sun dries out the surface and fibers shrink, starting a vicious cycle of deterioration.

Wood also breaks down due to the activity of fungi. Fungus spores are all around us, so it's impossible to eliminate them entirely, but they only become active in wood once the wood reaches a certain moisture content (around 28 percent). The best way to completely prevent fungus decay, and thus also eliminate the need to treat wood with chemicals, is to keep the moisture in wood below that threshold.

Many products are available to help wood's surfaces repel moisture. Whatever one you choose, keep in mind these essential steps:

• Before and during construction, apply preservatives to the top, bottom and sides of planks, along with all cut ends. Remember that the underside of a deck is exposed to moisture rising from the ground as well as rainfall, and the end grain of wood absorbs moisture more than the face of a board.

• Use corrosion resistant building materials, including screws, nails, brackets, etc.

• Provide regular, and thorough, preservative maintenance.

ACTION:
Use Alternative, Renewable Materials

Using alternative materials in landscape construction can save great amounts of energy. This

Fig. 15.13: *Small boulders, tightly stacked, form a low retaining wall that allows the adjoining driveway to be widened and re-graded for positive drainage. (Ferns and mosses now fill the cracks, and chipmunks use the wall as a highway.)*

Using Logs for Woodland Trails and Bridges

While it may seem convenient to simply cut trees and use the logs near where they're needed for trail support, this action has serious drawbacks. When the canopy gets opened, new sunlight will enter the woods, potentially encouraging the growth of weeds. Disturbing the ground layer will have the same effect, by reducing the native cover and providing conditions (compaction, etc.) more inviting to aggressive plants. Plus the logs themselves will rot in a few years, in contact with the ground. All of this results in added work — replacing the logs, managing invasive plants, repairing the ground — that would be avoided by building the project with naturally rot-resistant wood and leaving the surrounding ecosystem intact.

process may involve countless regional and local variations, but no matter how marvelously unique the results may be, the one common denominator in this approach is the need for an alternative attitude. This means being open-minded and creative about how to solve problems or accomplish goals, and being flexible about aesthetics.

Construction Tip: Use Local Materials

Materials that originate near the location of any project are always preferable to products that have been transported long distances. When purchasing stone or wood, always ask about its origin and, if possible, choose the local source.

If the only type of paving stone that works for your project has to be imported, consider redesigning the project to include an area surfaced with pea-stone or other local loose stone product. Many towns contain small stone-crushing operations that provide materials for local construction and road-paving projects, and much of what they produce can also work in your landscape.

Another local material that's so widely available it's often treated as a waste product in landscape construction is rock that is turned up during excavation and earthmoving. Whenever possible, plan to use these resources onsite, both to eliminate the need for new products and to cut out the energy cost of disposing them. Boulders can be set artfully into a bank to create an appealing retaining wall, perhaps with soil pockets for growing plants. Smaller rocks can be used as infill in stone walls or as backfill behind retaining walls.

Construction Tip: Use Recycled and Salvaged Products

Many options exist for reusing old products in new ways in our landscapes. Salvage yards can be a treasure trove of possibilities. When shopping for materials, be sure to check with local stone suppliers about any material that's been returned or left over from other jobs. And remember, even if you yourself can't use materials salvaged from other projects, your own project might be a source of products to donate or sell to salvage yards.

Instead of buying new stone for a patio, path or steps, a great alternative is to reuse granite curbstones from highway or road reconstruction projects. Most new roadwork contracts require new curbstones, and contractors must dispose of the old ones. If you ask, you might be able to have these waste stones delivered to your site for little or no cost. Curbstones are usually 4 inches thick and about 16 to 18 inches wide, so when laid on their sides, they can cover a surprisingly large area.

If your landscape contains an old concrete pad or surface, whether it's intact or crumbling, consider keeping it in place and simply building any new landscape features right on top of it. As long as the concrete isn't causing any problems, it's more energy efficient to leave it than to remove it. Old concrete can serve quite well as the base for a new patio. In some situations, you might also spread soil and plant lawn grass, herbs or a wildflower meadow on top of it, but keep in mind that this soil will dry out more quickly than normal, especially in full sun, so choose plants accordingly.

Other Recycled Materials

Crushed concrete and asphalt are commonly recycled and remixed as base materials for pavement projects. Most often, large chunks are laid in place as the drainage layer, and more finely crushed pieces are used to form the upper compacted layer. This is generally the work of excavators and large-scale landscape contractors, but be sure to check with your contractor about this option, especially if your project involves a substantial amount of paving.

Scrap tires may be one of the hardest materials to dispose of: they're completely non-biodegradable and toxic to incinerate. While not generally considered attractive, old tires can be used to build very durable, terraced retaining walls. By alternating their placement in each layer, just as you would with stone or brick, and filling the resulting holes with soil, the entire structure will be very stable. Beautiful plants can grow in these walls, and the tires themselves are about the perfect height to serve perfectly well as steps.

Old Brick

Aged brick may have a beautiful rustic appearance, but be aware that not all brick is suitable for outdoor use. It is naturally porous, and exterior brick is specifically produced to be moisture resistant. If you use old bricks from the interior of a house — a dismantled chimney, etc. — outdoors in your landscape, the water they absorb will quickly split their surface. The resulting loose brick chips and ragged surface may outweigh any satisfaction you might have from using salvaged material, and eventually they will have to be replaced.

Fig. 15.14:
*Structures built
of stacked
rubber tires
packed with
earth, the exte-
rior coated with
cans and bottles
set in mortar…
genius!*

Salvaged timber from dismantled buildings is widely available at salvage yards and even on the Internet. While much of this vintage timber might be best used for interior construction, it's likely to be denser and harder than present-day lumber, perhaps giving it some resistance to weather and so might also be suitable for some landscape construction projects.

Cautionary Note: **Railroad ties** used to be common in building landscapes. We now realize this is not a good idea, because the creosote soaked into these timbers, to make them resistant to insects and moisture, is toxic to all creatures in the natural world. In addition, railroad ties are difficult to build with due to their inconsistent shape, weight and extremely large dimension (8-by-8 inches, too big for comfortable steps). Plus, they should never be burned, due to the toxicity of creosote in smoke. Without exception, *never use railroad timbers near a vegetable garden*.

Construction Tip:
Use Remanufactured Products

The term "remanufacturing" often refers to assembling new machinery or equipment from the parts of earlier models, using recycled products in their current form but in new ways. In this discussion, though, it's about transforming discarded or waste materials to serve a different purpose. Remanufacturing does consume energy, but it also saves both the energy and resources used to manufacture new products, and it keeps many old products out of landfills.

For landscape construction projects, one of the most valuable remanufactured materials is **plastic lumber**. This product comes in standard dimensions and can replace wood in decks, boardwalks, tables and benches. Because it's rot resistant, plastic lumber can safely be used in contact with the ground. And because it's non-toxic, it's safe to use in wetlands. Unlike wood, it doesn't splinter or crack in the sun (especially if it's purchased as "UV stabilized"), it never needs painting or a preservative, and it resists insect damage. It can be sawed, drilled and nailed just like wood, but using plastic lumber saves the life of countless living trees.

Note: Some plastic lumber is made entirely from recycled plastic, most commonly from recycled milk jugs, while other products contain sawdust, fiberglass or other wood fibers. Composites are usually stronger and more stable than straight plastic lumber, but when sawed or drilled, the exposed wood fiber may be subject to fungus and insect attack just like untreated wood.

Plastic lumber costs more than wood but lasts longer, so may actually cost less in the long run. Its main disadvantages are that it's heavier and less stiff than wood, which means it needs more support, and it tends to shrink and swell more than wood, requiring more care during installation to accommodate that movement.

Construction Tip:
Use Alternative Landscape Materials

Grass paving systems offer an appealing alternative to stone, brick and other hard surfaces. Produced in a variety of forms, from thick pre-cast concrete grids to lightweight plastic mesh, grass pavers let turf grass grow in soil-filled cells while the overall system forms a surface that's stable and firm enough for walking, entertaining, occasional driving and temporary parking. Since grass is cooler than pavement, this kind of surface can also help reduce the heat-island effect in cities (see page 5) and keep your house cool. Note: many grass pavers are made from recycled plastic.

Soil cement or stabilized soil can also work as a replacement for stone surfacing or other hard pavement. These materials are made by mixing ordinary soil with a small amount of Portland cement or other type of binder. The resulting surface is firm and durable; trails and bridle paths constructed in the public works projects of the 1930s and '40s remain intact and a pleasure to use. Check with product manufacturers about the right amount of binder to use with different kinds of soil.

Adobe is a most effective, affordable and beautiful alternative to using stone to build walls. Made of just earth and water, it is a building material that makes particular sense in regions where little stone is otherwise available,

and where rainfall is scarce enough and the air is dry enough that the material will hold up well over time. In the American southwest, many traditional homes were, and increasingly are, built from earth that's been removed from within the building's footprint.

A major limitation is that not all soil is suitable for adobe. For best results, soil should be about half fine sand and the other half clay, silt and coarse sand in roughly equal parts.[1] It is possible, of course, to create this ideal mixture, but the most energy-efficient approach is to build with adobe only if onsite soil already

Fig. 15.15: *These pre-cast concrete grass pavers are commonly used for residential parking spaces as well as in large expanses of lawn that receive occasional vehicular traffic.*

Crumb Rubber

Also known as pulverized rubber, crumb rubber is made from shredding old tires. While it's a great example of recycling and remanufacturing a product that would otherwise be difficult to dispose, scientific conclusions about the toxicity of this material remain unclear. Crumb rubber may be a perfectly safe addition to asphalt pavement, and perhaps even for athletic tracks and fields, but it should be used with caution in home landscapes, play areas and natural environments.

contains desirable proportions of the right-sized particles.

Fig. 15.16: *Residents of the southwest US often find creative ways to use adobe and other locally-made earthen building products such as these rough "bricks."*

CHAPTER SUMMARY

This chapter presents the basic steps to take and facts to keep in mind while building landscape structures, with the goal being to create structures that save energy largely by being durable and low maintenance.

When building with stone, no matter the design or materials used, basic principles hold true in every project: good base preparation, positive drainage, solid construction techniques, attention to detail. Similarly, when building with wood, certain guidelines hold true regardless of the structure's size, shape or purpose: every step in the project should work toward protecting wood from moisture and decay. These guidelines apply equally to wood selection, building methods and wood treatments. Finally, the chapter offers suggestions for creatively incorporating alternative, energy-saving materials in all sorts of landscape construction projects. These include local, recycled, salvaged and remanufactured products.

By following the actions and construction tips presented here, the major built elements of any landscape will hold up well over time and rarely need to be fixed or replaced. This will make the most of any time and energy spent in their construction and prevent further costs.

CHAPTER 16

Constructing New Homesites

Now, having covered the topics of planting and building structures in the landscape, our discussion actually backs up a bit, to the subject of creating new homesites from the beginning. Like the two preceding chapters, this one presents ways to save energy both during the construction process and in the long run. Similarly, this chapter also doesn't offer detailed instructions about how to build things, but rather provides guidance about what and why.

Building a new home is an exciting but complex and often stressful process, full of choices that carry big consequences. If you intend to build on land that's sloped, hilly, rocky, wet or wooded, it's a good idea to get advice from a landscape design professional, *even before designing the house*, to create a good fit between what's there now and the new house and landscape you

imagine creating. This is also the time to incorporate ideas about orienting buildings and trees to save energy (presented in Sections II and III). Whatever your plans, consider taking the following Actions to make your whole project as successful and energy efficient as possible:

+ Protect the site before and during construction.
+ Use energy-efficient construction techniques.
+ Consider building an earth-sheltered home.
+ Heal the site after construction.

ACTION: Protect the Site Before and During Construction

Revegetating and restoring some semblance of health to newly developed landscapes requires a lot of work — shaping the ground, providing suitable soil, bringing in new plants and planting and nurturing them. A portion of this work, or in some cases most of it, can be eliminated by simply taking steps at the start to protect what is already there. In their book, *Building Inside Nature's Envelope*, Andy and Sally Wasowski explain this approach to construction and illustrate several projects where it worked beautifully.[1]

Construction Tip:
Save and Protect Trees

Trees are often one of the most valued features in a landscape. Whether solitary and majestic or in a grove with many companions, trees provide shade, cool the air, deflect winds, soften the soil and support wildlife. They can complement a building, frame a view, enclose a space or announce an entrance. They are also the source of countless intangible experiences: a sense of safety and protection; nostalgia and historic significance; the sound of wind singing through the leaves; a feeling of richness and abundance. Plus, trees make our world beautiful.

Fig. 16.1: *This mature sugar maple casts precious morning shade and shelters a garden rich in ferns and woodland flowers.*

Many of us may not even consciously notice the many services that trees provide, but when a tree is gone, we feel the loss acutely.

The problem with taking care of trees is that not only do they grow slowly, they generally die slowly too. And few of us know what an ailing tree looks like until the signs are so blatant we can practically feel the tree's pain ourselves. We don't notice the little signs: brown, yellow or mottled leaves; bare twigs at the ends of branches; cracks or splits in the bark; little drifts of sawdust around the base of the trunk. By the time these small indicators turn into major damage that we can't miss — peeling bark and falling limbs — the tree is in serious trouble.

Replacing a tree is no simple matter. Big trees are expensive to buy and difficult to handle, and they may not thrive in the places they're planted. Smaller trees may be affordable and a safer investment, but they grow slowly and we may have to wait a long time for the results we desire. To avoid all these difficulties, a better choice is simply to preserve as many trees as possible.

But here's the kicker: even though replacing trees is hard, protecting them is hard too. We have to avoid cutting or damaging their bark, so trees can continue to receive nutrients from their roots. Equally essential is pruning branches properly so scar tissue can develop quickly, letting the tree heal itself (see Chapter 14, page 161 for more on this subject). These are the common precautions most people think about when protecting trees, and they're the minimum steps to require of a contractor. But they're not the whole story.

Trees build themselves on the nutrients and water they receive from their countless little feeder roots, which are tender, easily harmed by compaction and usually quite near the surface. They hold themselves upright on the strength of large supporting roots, which may grow deep but often remain within a foot or so of the surface. And most root systems spread far beyond the extent of the canopy overhead.

In fact, preventing damage to just the visible portions of tree — the trunk and branches — while paying no attention to their invisible parts below ground is about as useless as pouring water into a bucket with a hole in the bottom. Your efforts won't succeed, and you'll have wasted energy in the process. Taking good care of a tree actually requires protecting a large amount of ground around the tree.

How can you save as many trees as possible?

Begin by assessing the condition of all your trees. Consult with an arborist if you have any questions about how to evaluate trees' health. If possible, include in this assessment the value of the trees' contribution to the surrounding ecosystem. Then assign each tree to one of three categories: those that absolutely must be saved, those that clearly should be taken out and those that are negotiable. Adjust your construction plans accordingly, shifting the location of a building or driveway, or even going so far as to relocate some elements altogether.

Clearly mark the trees that require protection. Whatever method you use, be sure your meaning is totally clear to everyone involved: the builder, subcontractors, excavators and the people who will actually remove the trees. Be aware that unspoken conventions

(e.g., certain colors of flagging tape) may have meaning to a forester that you don't realize. Always err on the side of too much explanation rather than too little. (Imagine... the huge oak tree that was going to shade the garage and driveway? the one with that nice horizontal branch where you were hoping to hang a tire swing? Well, "oops sorry, but orange tape means remove the tree" is a terrible way to end that dream.)

Protect the ground at least 15 to 20 feet all around the trunk of trees to be protected, using the following methods.

- Set up a physical barrier that everyone can see and recognize to prevent all vehicles, storage and construction activity in that zone.

Fig. 16.2: *Protecting tree roots on a small site may be difficult due to lack of storage space, but in these situations it's even more important, especially when the landscape contains only a few significant trees. In this case, compaction from stockpiled soil and heavy equipment will likely kill the tree.*

Save This Tree or That One?

In situations where construction might harm two valuable trees, the best choice will probably be to focus your protection efforts on one and sacrifice the other. Providing only partial protection for each tree is more likely to result in losing both.

Fig. 16.3:
Chain link fencing conveys permanence and a serious commitment to tree protection. This sign clearly explains the fence's unspoken message.

This might include a snow fence, yellow police tape, wood stakes driven into the ground or large immovable boulders.

• If a tree that's to be saved is very near a building, and vehicles absolutely have to drive over its roots, spread a deep layer (6 to 8 inches) of bark mulch over the root zone, then lay thick plywood on top as a driving surface, to cushion the ground and distribute weight over a wider area. If construction is taking place during the growing season, this mulch should be removed as soon as possible (maximum a few weeks) to make sure air and moisture can get to the roots. A safer time for this activity is during a tree's dormancy.

• Avoid all earth grading near a tree, and keep the ground surface intact in as much of the root zone as possible. Removing soil physically destroys roots, and piling new soil on top of existing roots is nearly as destruc-

tive because it smothers them. Be sure this precaution is also considered during your planning process.

• If you have to cut the roots of a tree, be very careful to cut them cleanly with a sharp saw or tool. Never tear or twist roots off, as this diminishes their natural ability to heal. And be sure to water the soil that covers any cut roots, thoroughly and regularly, to hasten the tree's recovery.

Assign a monetary value to the most important trees. Clearly state in your contract that you'll charge the assigned amount for any visible damage, or for violation of the barriers. Because harm to roots often doesn't reveal itself until several years later (after the contractor is long gone), this is an essential step, to back up your commitment and make sure it's taken seriously.

Construction Tip: Overall Site Protection

This book repeatedly notes that plants can thrive only in soil that contains nutrients, water and air. Chapter 14 discusses in detail the harmful (and frustrating) effects of compacted soil. In addition to protecting valuable trees, it's very important to minimize compaction everywhere on the site where plants — trees, shrubs, lawn and gardens — will be expected to grow.

Wherever heavy equipment will repeatedly work, or be left standing for a long time, prevent compaction by laying mats or thick plywood to cushion and distribute their weight. Even better, if site conditions allow, spread a thick layer of mulch below the mats. Then, after construction is done and all the equipment is gone, mechanically loosen all compacted soil (except in areas below a future driveway, patio or other hard surface). Skipping this step at the start will make your gardening efforts much less successful than you'd hoped or cost a tremendous amount to fix later, or both. And simply spreading topsoil over this hardpan will not solve the problem. Hence the need for the next tip.

Construction Tip: Designate a Work Zone

Vehicles driving on the land, vans and trucks delivering supplies, workers' trucks arriving and parking, lumber and supplies stacked in piles here and there — the normal activities of most construction projects often take up much more space than the structure itself. To minimize harm to the land, and hold down the cost of final landscaping, it makes sense to keep every construction area as small as possible.

This tip is especially important if your site contains trees, shrubs, grasses or other plants. Why? Because these plants are already thriving there, you've already paid for them when you bought the property. They require no energy to get established, and if you keep them you won't have to buy more plants to fill the landscape after construction is finished. Remember, also, that the movement of heavy vehicles results in compacted soil that will need repair or amendment or eventually cause plants to struggle or fail. So this tip can be equally important on sites that contain little or no vegetation.

To take best care of your property during the construction process, designate a work

Fig. 16.4: *Many new energy-efficient housing developments, like this one in Greenfield, Massachusetts, are especially committed to the idea of minimizing the "footprint" of our living spaces, both inside and out. (Here, where all the homes have a south-facing roof, workers are mounting solar thermal panels.)*

zone around the future building. Many contractors may automatically specify a 10- to 20-foot access strip around the entire structure, with claims that having any less space will raise the cost of the job. This may sometimes be true, but in many cases it's an oversimplification. It pays to carefully examine actual needs — for access, storage and parking — and find creative ways to meet those needs rather than accepting the first blanket solution.

Could one or two sides of the building (or all of them?) have a narrower access strip? Is there a way for vehicles to park in the street rather than on the land? Could the construction sequence be arranged so supplies are stored in one section of the building rather than outdoors, or so they're delivered in phases rather than all at once? Many contractors routinely follow these practices simply for the sake of efficiency in the project, but they may not be as concerned about minimizing harm to the land as you'd like. It makes sense to work through these issues ahead of time.

To maximize protection of the features you wish to preserve, erect a fence or other obvious boundary, to clearly define the edges of the agreed-upon work area. You might even wish to negotiate with your contractor some form of penalty or compensation if work encroaches beyond the designated construction zone.

ACTION: Use Energy-efficient Construction Techniques

This section provides suggestions to help with overall strategizing in the construction process. Like the rest of the book, these are not specific instructions but rather general guidelines for making the project as successful as possible while consuming the least energy.

Construction Tip: Plan Ahead

Lay out a sequence of work that minimizes the number of trips needed to pick up supplies and transport equipment to and from the site. This is almost like choreography: you just need to carefully think through the whole project as if it were a performance. The goal is smooth, steady forward movement, with as little repetition and backing up as possible.

Construction Tip: Use the Lightest Equipment Necessary

Instead of automatically using large equipment, on the assumption that big machines will be capable of more work, think creatively about using small equipment. In fact, big equipment often is more powerful and more harmful than necessary. If your site were constrained by slopes, wetness, lack of access or space limitations, wouldn't you be inventive about finding alternate ways to build your project? So let your desire to save energy be a similar motivation.

Hand labor and hand tools are often the most energy-efficient choice. Of course, they're not suitable in every job, but they might just be the best option on small jobs, in awkward spaces or when conditions won't allow larger machinery. For moving large objects such as boulders or trees and shrubs, consider these simple and very affordable tools:

- a ball cart, a sturdy two-wheeled dolly with an oversized, cupped base
- a pole sling, a strong strap that wraps around the object and loops over one or two poles that are suspended from the shoulders of two (human) carriers
- a come-along, a hand-powered winch that connects to an immovable anchor (tree, rock outcrop, etc.)

Resource-efficient machines save fuel in two ways:

- By having engines that power the function of the machine but not the wheels. Various models can be towed by a small tractor or even a person. Eliminating the self-propelled wheels makes the whole thing more fuel efficient.
- By consisting of a base machine that can take interchangeable attachments. Several

companies offer such versatile products that lower embedded energy costs. Manufacturing one machine with many optional extensions consumes less energy and resources than producing many whole machines for all the different jobs.

Mini-equipment is now being produced by many traditional heavy-equipment makers, in an assortment of models that perform a wide variety of jobs. Small tractors and loaders, mini-excavators and trenchers — the choices are vast and growing. Because much of this smaller modern equipment has a short turning radius, it can easily maneuver in constrained spaces, protecting more of the site. Compared to larger machines, mini-equipment is lighter in weight, which means it causes less compaction of the soil, *and* it needs less fuel both to run and to be transported to the job. Smaller machines are produced with a lower embedded cost (and consumption of resources) than large machines. Plus, many new models have been designed specifically for fuel efficiency and low emissions.

Other Equipment Notes to Keep in Mind

Concrete trucks don't need to drive up close to a building to deliver their load down a chute directly into the pour area. Instead, consider having your concrete delivered through a flexible hose that can be several hundred feet long, allowing the truck to remain parked quite far from the building or even off-site, in the street.

All machines run best when they're kept clean and tuned. On any power equipment that gets regular use, make sure to get a mainte-

nance check-up at least once a year, to maximize fuel efficiency.

When renting equipment, ask for information about fuel efficiency. Choose the most efficient models and favor companies that provide this information. This will send a message to suppliers that fuel efficiency matters, and it will encourage them to design and maintain equipment accordingly.

For more information on this subject, William Thompson and Kim Sorvig's book, *Sustainable Landscape Construction*, contains an excellent discussion of using appropriate machinery.[2]

Construction Tip: Balance Cut and Fill

Remember that the top layer of soil on any site is usually the most fertile soil, and therefore a valuable resource. Chapter 14 discusses the importance of preserving topsoil's structure and texture when moving and storing it for later use. No significant earth grading should take place in this layer of soil.

Ideally, your new landscape will have been designed to sit lightly on the land and require

Fig. 16.5: *Many residential landscape contractors routinely use small-scale equipment. What they do by necessity, either because of space or cost limitations, has the added benefit of energy-efficiency.*

little earth grading. Techniques for achieving this goal are presented in Chapter 11. It's likely, though, that at least some small amount of terrain will need to be reshaped — to improve drainage, access or usability — and this work should always be done at the level of the subsoil.

The terms "cut" and "fill" refer to how material is moved around on the land. Subsoil that has been excavated or removed from its long-time position has been *cut*; when this or any new material is then placed in another position, it is considered *fill*. A good way to save energy is to eliminate the need for trucking in new soil or hauling any away. Hence the notion of balancing cut and fill, or using just what exists on site to create the desired ground shapes.

This goal should also have been considered at the design stage, especially if your project involves complex terrain. Whether or not this has happened, you can balance cut and fill during construction, assuming your landscape doesn't require extreme alterations.

When planning earthmoving, it is important to know that cut soil, which has compacted in place over many years, will actually expand slightly once released from its position. It will fluff up a bit with the addition of air spaces between its particles. The amount of expansion differs with the type of soil, the duration of its compaction and the amount of handling it then receives, but you can expect about 20 percent more volume.

Similarly, newly placed fill soil will gradually compact itself back down to a smaller volume. As noted earlier, in discussing the preparation of the base for stonework, fresh fill can be compacted by hand or machine if it has to immediately support a landscape structure. For lawn and garden areas, though, newly placed fill should simply be left a little higher than its final intended level, and compaction will happen naturally, with the help of time and gravity. Keep this inevitable shrinkage in mind when creating garden beds or lawns adjacent to a patio, path or driveway.

Construction Tip:
Treat Waste as a Resource

The construction process always generates a certain amount of waste. Our society's conventional solution has been to haul this material away and dispose of it off-site. But this is really an inadequate solution: transportation consumes energy and simply transfers the problem to some other place, where the waste's presence or decay will eventually have to be managed. Instead of hauling this away, we can save fuel and prevent future problems by simply using site resources directly on the land where it came from. If you think creatively, keep an open mind and let go of outdated conventions about what "belongs" in a landscape, there's a place for nearly everything.

Brush, leaves and branches left over from clearing land can be piled and left to decompose naturally, meanwhile providing a living place or cover for various birds and small mammals.

A Note About Cut and Fill Slopes

The maximum angle an earthen slope will hold (its *angle of repose*) depends on the size and shape of the soil's particles. Because of compaction, though, cut slopes will usually stay in place at steeper gradients than looser fill slopes. When placing fill, expect it to slump into a gentler slope than the bank it came from.

These piles should be located out of the way of any future construction, ideally as close as possible to any natural areas that might provide larger habitat spaces or wildlife corridors.

Alternatively, brush and small branches can be chipped into mulch, which should age at least a few months before being spread on the ground. Many small brush-chippers are available for homeowners to buy or rent. Thick branches may require the larger machines operated by landscaping companies, foresters and highway crews. While running a chipper does consume energy, keeping resources onsite eliminates the cost of both hauling waste away and bringing new materials in, so the result can be a net gain.

Logs can be cut into cordwood if they're from suitable hardwood trees, or into kindling if from softwood trees (most evergreens). If you have no need for cordwood, consider taking this step anyway and then trading your cordwood for some other local product or service. Or instead, and especially if you have a tree that's crooked or hard to split, consider leaving a whole log on the ground, in a woodland garden or semi-wild part of the landscape. This rich resource will be a gold mine for the many decomposers that live in healthy soil, and it will further enrich the ground, reducing the need for imported fertilizers and nutrients. Logs can also be laid in the bottom of brush piles, where small mammals will dine on a smorgasbord of inevitable insects.

Undesirable soil, including sand or clay or other soil that's unsuitable for growing plants, may be mixed with other soil to improve its texture. Very rocky or gravelly soil makes an excellent sub-base for stone walls or backfill for retaining walls. Heavy clay might be used to waterproof a small natural pond. Soil that's filled with roots, weeds and fallen seeds should be composted (see page 153).

Boulders and stone turned up in the course of construction should be incorporated into the earth grading. As noted in Chapter 15's discussion of building with alternative materials, many of these materials will work in building stone walls, embankments, etc.

ACTION: Consider Building an Earth-sheltered Home

From the cone-shaped hills of Cappadocia in Turkey, to limestone caverns in Tunisia, subterranean settlements in northern China, and

Fig. 16.6: Sandy soil excavated for the driveway behind this house will now be used to create a level plateau in the front yard, to hold a small lawn and patio, making the yard more useful than if it were sloped.

Wetland Soils
Any soil that's extremely wet or mucky may be part of a wetland and therefore protected in most states. (Regulations, and their enforcement, shift with political tides.) Be sure to find out if this is true for your land, and avoid working in all wetlands.

DAVID SCHOCHET

Fig. 16.7:
In New Mexico, many creative homeowners are now building their houses as "earthships" nestled into the ground, with just their south walls exposed for solar gain in winter. Integrated ventilation stacks and internally-shaded windows prevent heat buildup in summer.

cliff dwellings in the American Southwest, millions of people have lived below ground for centuries. Many still do.

Subterranean spaces serve many purposes: defense and civilian protection; religious ceremony; and agriculture, both for food storage and as a way to save the land above-ground for growing food. Dwelling in the shelter of the earth itself has often been, and may continue to be, the best choice for some people in poor countries where few other options exist. By far the most widespread purpose for earth-sheltered dwelling, however, is to create shelter that's comfortable, in regions where outdoor temperatures are frequently harsh — either very hot, cold or humid. In these places, reliably moderate subsurface temperatures provide a haven from the discomforts above-ground. (See Chapter 20 for an explanation of this phenomenon.)

This discussion isn't about carving our homes directly out of the earth or living in caves. Rather, it's about designing and building structures that are either mostly or partly below ground. Here, the earth's constant temperature helps warm the house in winter and cool it in summer, while the surrounding soil insulates it from temperature fluctuations above.

Construction Tip: What's Involved

Building into the earth usually involves some combination of digging down and mounding up, depending on the terrain and soil conditions. If your site is pure bedrock or extremely wet, if it's in a floodplain or at the bottom of a steep slope, an earth-sheltered house probably won't be practical. Most other conditions can be accommodated with good design and careful engineering.

Earth-sheltered construction also usually involves some combination of masonry (concrete, adobe, etc.) and wood. Where the structure is in contact with the earth, masonry provides both strength and rot resistance. All buildings also need a moisture barrier between the structure and the surrounding soil. Any portion of the building that's above-ground may be made of wood, though many earth-sheltered homes are made entirely of adobe.

Subterranean living spaces often employ many passive solar heating and cooling strategies. Carefully placed openings bring light in from above as well as from windows in any exposed walls. Vents and windows are intentionally laid out to generate air flow and natural ventilation. Masonry floors and walls provide thermal mass for storing daytime heat and releasing it at night. Many of these homes also incorporate photo-voltaic modules, wind power and geothermal heat pumps (all described in Section VI).

Construction Tip: Where to Build

Earth-sheltered houses may be built in flat land, on slopes or at the top of a hill. For homes that are to be fully earth sheltered, the ideal location is on a hillside that's steep enough to contain the entire back wall of a building, but not so steep that the surface of the ground will tend to erode. Wherever the house is built, it should be designed so most of the windows are on one wall. On sloped topography, this front wall offers good views and a feeling of openness that compensates for the shortage (or absence) of windows in the rest of the house. Building on a slope allows for entrances at different levels. If the building has two stories that are set back as the slope ascends, sunlight can penetrate into rooms on each floor.

In cold climates, a slope that faces south allows the front wall to collect desirable warmth in winter, while overhangs and vegetation on this wall will prevent undesirable heat gain in summer. The slope rising behind the house to the north protects the living space from winter's cold northerly winds. Land that tilts down

and away in front of the house maximizes the cooling effect of summer's southerly breezes rising toward the house. In hot, dry climates, a north-facing slope may be preferable because it lets the house open toward light without also opening toward the hottest sun. Malcom Wells's delightful hand-illustrated book, *Underground Designs*, depicts dozens of intriguing earth-sheltered living spaces.[3]

The best soil for earth-sheltered construction is soil that offers good support and, if possible, can hold a moderate amount of moisture to help keep the ground cool. Coarse-grained soils like sand and gravel are easy to excavate, but they drain very quickly, need structural support, slump against the building and are difficult to vegetate after the house is built. Fine-grained soils like silt and clay provide good support when dry but tend to hold excess moisture that may increase pressure against the walls, as well as potentially being prone to landslide in heavy rains. Bedrock is self-supporting and puts no pressure on the walls, but it's expensive to excavate and difficult to move around. Whatever type of soils exists on-site, the first step toward your earth-sheltered home is a soil test and a sample excavation to discover just what's down there.

Hilltops and flat land will also work for earth-sheltered construction; both offer their own combination of advantages and drawbacks. Hilltop sites can offer feelings of loftiness along with marvelous views in all directions, but fairly often these sites are made of solid rock (the reason they haven't eroded away), which requires careful engineering and construction along with potentially expensive blasting. In contrast, lowlands and flat sites may contain

David Schochet

Fig 16.8: *Even a flat site can provide some degree of earth-shelter, if the soil can be moved and mounded against a structure that's been designed for that purpose.*

soils that are loose and easy to work, but they offer little opportunity for views and openness, and in general they're difficult to drain adequately. Level land may be the best place for partial earth-sheltering, in which earth is mounded up against just one wall or the lower portion of the building, to provide extra insulation and wind protection.

Other Building Issues

Regardless of *how* you intend to build your earth-sheltered home, whether it's mostly underground or only partially buried, you'll need to start with a thorough exploration of soil conditions. It's also a good idea to seek the advice of a professional experienced in this sort of construction, whether an architect, engineer or just a savvy person who's been through the process a few times, who knows the pitfalls and can be creative about solutions.

Regardless of *where* you intend to build, you may encounter some resistance in the permitting process. Building codes, fire codes and other local regulations probably won't address some of the issues of subsurface construction. When regulatory documents don't provide enough guidance, local authorities can tend to be overly negative, to protect themselves from the unknown. You should become familiar with all local regulations well ahead of time, so you'll be able to educate the people in charge and possibly work toward changing the codes so they address the alternative construction practices you plan to use.

The Pros and Cons of Earth-sheltered Building

Until recently, the whole concept of living below ground has had a slightly negative connotation. Some cultures associate it with low status and being disadvantaged, while other societies consider the underground to be the realm of demons and death. Perhaps the most widespread perception is that subterranean spaces are dark, damp and isolated from the world of light and space above-ground.

Despite these beliefs, many beautiful homes stand now as inspiration, and reassurance, to the rest of us. And in the last few decades, we've begun to see that the benefits of artfully designed, thoughtfully sited and well-built earth shelters far outweigh their perceived drawbacks. These buildings can have operating costs as much as 50 to 60 percent lower than conventional buildings.[4] Their maintenance costs are lower too, since only a portion of the exterior needs to painted and cared for, while the remaining structure is protected by earth.

And their benefits are more than just a matter of cost. Well-designed earth-sheltered structures are full of light and airiness. Outside noise is muffled by a thick blanket of soil, so they are quiet inside. When built right, they're safe from storm and wind damage, fire and even earthquakes. New technology and materials have made them easier to construct and maintain. Built in an endless variety of forms, earth-sheltered homes are quiet, beautiful and comfortable in every season.

ACTION:
Heal the Site after Construction

Before you can feel really at home in your new landscape, the final step is to repair, stabilize and revegetate any bare soil. Ideally, if your property originally held some vegetation, a significant portion of that natural wealth has been preserved. Some of the new landscape will, of course, be covered with a driveway, parking spaces and perhaps some paths, patios or other kinds of hard-surfaced outdoor living places. But the remaining land will probably need to be healed with some assortment of growing plants.

Section IV presents many ideas for designing the planted portions of our landscapes in ways that save energy. All of these ideas — conservation patches, reduced lawn areas, wildflower meadows — can work equally well in established grounds and new homesites.

One aspect of this discussion that is especially significant in new landscapes, however, is the goal to import as little topsoil as possible from off-site. A vast amount of bare and disturbed soil is often left exposed after a house is built, and because we're often behind schedule and rushing to get the job done and over budget, this is when we might be most tempted to sacrifice energy efficiency in favor of expedience. Although a load or two of fresh topsoil may seem like a perfect solution, try to avoid this temptation, by implementing some of the ideas in Section III. Or, better yet, plan ahead and protect as much established vegetation as possible and design the landscape specifically to import little or no topsoil.

Fig. 16.9:
This raw, sandy terrace has been transformed into a vibrant, lawn-free landscape, with plants selected to thrive in dry soil with a northern exposure, and with curving pathways inviting a daily stroll.

Finally, at the very end of the process, finish the job of healing your new homesite by planting a variety of regionally native vegetation. Chapter 14 presents a full discussion of how to accomplish this goal, to both save energy and make your new landscape a comfortable and beautiful haven for you, your family and the natural world.

CHAPTER SUMMARY

The process of building a new home can be very complicated and stressful. Quite often, builders and landowners focus narrowly on the design of the house. This may be a natural response to the complexity of the job and the difficulty of figuring out so many puzzles. But it's a disservice to the project if no attention is given to the land itself, and how to make the most of its precious resources. While Chapter 13 addresses the issue of *designing* new homesites, this chapter presents ideas for *taking care of the land, before, during and after construction* along with a summary of where and why it makes sense to design an earth-sheltered home.

Whatever sort of home you plan to build, the most important step in the process is protecting the site before construction begins, through taking an inventory of the site's assets, clearly identifying things to protect, designating a definite work zone beyond which workers must not tread and even adjusting the layout of major elements if necessary. During the building process, all of these Actions — taking steps to plan ahead, using the lightest equipment possible, using all the site's soil on-site and making the most of waste as a resource — will result in great savings.

This chapter concludes the discussion about landscape construction and care. The next section contains four chapters that explain various ways to generate energy at the relatively small scale of a home landscape.

Generating Energy in Your Landscape

WHILE THE PREVIOUS SECTIONS SHOW HOW we can shape our landscapes to help us *consume* less energy, this chapter focuses on how we can use our landscapes to actually *generate* some of the energy we use. Because the subject of generating energy is vast and complex, it presents an overview of possibilities rather than the specific advice found in other chapters.

Sunlight, wind, water and the heat of the Earth itself — these infinitely available resources (along with fire) were for millennia our only sources of energy. They warmed and cooled us; they powered early mills and fueled the Industrial Revolution. They were free, but unpredictable, and over the last two centuries, we gradually abandoned them in favor of fuels — kerosene, coal, oil, gas — that were easier to transport and manage.

Now we've come full circle. As carbon-based fuels have become scarce and expensive, utility companies and governments across the planet are again finding ways to generate power with solar, wind, hydro and geothermal energy, though now at a much larger scale than ever before. New technologies also make it possible

for us to capture energy from these old familiar resources in our own home landscapes.

To be useful to us, each of these energy sources requires its own unique set of conditions: a minimum amount of sunlight, winds that regularly blow at certain speeds, a stream or brook that's steep or deep or both, adequate space and workable ground. Each system also has an essential nature that may appeal to certain people more than to others. Do you love the freedom of the wind, the sound and power of it? Are you fascinated by water and its beautiful motion? Do you like to dig in the earth, to move it around or just know what's down there? Are you excited by solar panels, by their elegance and deep crystal blue surface, where sunlight seems magically to turn into electricity?

Is one of these energy systems right for you? Our purpose is to describe what's possible, to help you see the kind of opportunities your property might contain. If the ideas presented here appeal to you, and if your site has the necessary potential, see Appendix C's list of excellent books that offer step-by-step instructions for generating energy in your own landscape.

The following chapters present basic information about four energy resources that can work at a small scale, three of which — solar, wind and hydro — generate electricity. So, before we delve into the specifics of the different energy systems, let's review just what electricity is and how it works. This will provide a foundation for understanding what you're creating, and it will avoid repetition in the discussions below. If you're already familiar with this information, feel free to skip ahead.

WHAT IS ELECTRICITY?

To really understand electricity, you have to know a little bit about atoms. Everything in the world is made of atoms, and all atoms contain a nucleus of tiny particles called neutrons and protons, plus some much, much tinier particles called electrons. Not so long ago, electrons were imagined as invisible specks of energy rotating wildly around the nucleus, but that notion has been replaced in recent years by a new and improved definition: electrons are distributed in "energy levels" far removed from the nucleus. Whichever model makes sense to you, the essential fact is that protons and electrons carry an electrical charge: electrons are negative, while protons are positive (and neutrons

are neutral). Within an atom, the number of electrons usually equals the number of protons, creating a state of balance between positive and negative, resulting in a stable neutral charged atom.

Sometimes electrons jump from one atom to another, especially in materials whose atoms have a loose attachment to their electrons, as is the case in metals and other conductors. When this happens, the atom that has lost an electron is out of balance because it now contains more protons than electrons. This atom is positively charged; the atom that has gained an electron is negatively charged.

Nature always works to eliminate this sort of unbalance. So a positively charged atom attracts a negative electron to balance itself out, and in the process a negatively charged atom gets rid of its extra electron. This movement of electrons between atoms creates a flow of electric charge, an electric current that we call electricity.

Static (stationary charge) electricity is the buildup of electric charge on objects. When the amount of opposite charge buildup on adjacent objects is sufficient, electrons may cross the space and discharge the static charge imbalance. Lightning is a dramatically large discharge of this type when electrons jump between clouds, or between clouds and ground. A similar event on a smaller scale happens after you walk in socks across a carpet, picking up electrons that are then held in your body. When you come near a metal doorknob, or anything with a positive charge, these electrons jump across the gap and create a spark.

Current (moving or flowing) electricity is electrons moving through a conductor, such as copper wire, in two types of motion. Direct current (DC) is electrons flowing in one direction. Alternating current (AC) reverses the direction of electron flow, from 50 or 60 times per second to many billion times per second. Both forms play an important role in our lives.

Direct current is the type of electricity in the parts of your car's electrical system that are associated with the battery, your laptop computer battery, a flashlight and solar electric cells in watches and calculators. Power that is generated by solar panels, wind and hydro turbines is the only form of electricity that can be stored in batteries. One big problem with DC is that the voltage (electron force) is not readily changed, making long-distance transmission inefficient.

Alternating current is the type of electricity in most of the electric wires that stretch across the countryside, line our streets, and enter our homes. AC voltage can be increased or decreased as needed with a *transformer*. Since AC moves with the least energy loss at very high voltages, at the generating station AC voltage is stepped up before entering the long-distance transmission lines. Transformers at substations step the voltage down as it enters transmission lines around town, and then again on utility poles outside homes, ending with 240 volts in the wires that connect to electric meters and enter buildings. Because of this advantage, AC has become the usual type of electricity that safely runs our homes and most electrical appliances.

Fortunately, the DC electric energy that we get from solar photovoltaic modules, small wind and small hydro turbines, can be changed into AC electricity. This vital conversion takes place in an *inverter*, an essential ingredient in any renewable energy system. Let's take a closer look at a small-scale energy system, to see where the inverter fits in.

HOW IS ELECTRICITY GENERATED?

Large-scale electric generating stations produce electricity through the conversion of other forms of energy. The most common method is to create steam that turns the wheels of turbines, which are connected to electric generators, where the turbines' shafts spin inside coils of wire, creating electromagnetic fields and a flow of electrons. To produce the heat that turns water into steam, conventional power plants either burn fuel (coal, oil, gas) or split atoms (nuclear power). Modern solar thermal plants use the sun's energy to heat water to produce steam. Hydroelectric generating stations use the kinetic energy (energy of motion) of flowing or falling water, and wind generating stations use the kinetic energy of the blowing wind to turn their turbine-driven electric generators.

In all these systems, the end result is the same: different forms of mechanical energy are converted into electrical energy. The small-scale wind and hydro systems you install in your landscape will also work on the same principle. Mechanical energy will spin a turbine's wheel, and the energy of the turbine's spinning shaft will be converted to electricity inside a generator.

The photovoltaic (PV) cells of solar panels operate on a completely different principle, one that involves no turbines or mechanical energy. Instead, PV systems directly convert the energy of sunlight into electricity, described in more detail in Chapter 17.

HOW IS ELECTRICITY MEASURED?

Wherever it comes from, the electricity you use at home (or in your camp, RV, boat or anywhere) is calculated in *watts*. A watt is simply a measure of power, the amount of work that's being done. All electric energy systems are designed to generate a particular wattage of power, and if you decide to produce electricity on your property, you may need to understand a few basic terms and concepts.

Like water in a stream or hose, electricity in a wire flows at a certain rate of speed and with a certain amount of pressure. The rate of speed of the electric charge (electrons) that passes a certain point in a given amount of time, or the electric current, is measured in amperes or amps. The pressure, or electric force, of the flowing charge is measured in volts.

The arithmetic product of the current times the voltage yields the electric power in watts: **amps x volts = watts**

Power and Energy

Power multiplied by time equals energy. Since power is measured in watts or kilowatts, and time is measured in hours, electric energy is measured in watt-hours or kilowatt-hours.

The power rating of a device is a characteristic of its design. The energy consumed or produced depends on how long the device operates and the circumstances of that operation.[1]

Voltage Comparison

Low-voltage landscape lighting is delivered at a relatively harmless 12 volts, while the wiring in your house delivers current at 110 to 120 volts, enough to kill you if you accidentally touch a bare wire or outlet. Overhead power transmission lines generally carry electricity at tens to hundreds of thousands of volts.

Light bulbs indicate the amount of watts needed to power them. All electric devices also have labels that indicate how much electricity they use. If a label only states the number of amps, multiply this figure by 120 (the typical voltage of most US homes) to find total wattage. For example, a hot plate may use 6 amps x 120 volts, or 720 watts.

One watt of electric power being used for one hour equals one *watt-hour* of electric energy, and one thousand of these equals one *kilowatt-hour (kWh)*. Your power company measures your electricity consumption by the kWh of power you use in a month.

WHERE DOES THE ELECTRICITY GO?

If you do decide to generate electricity in your landscape, you'll need to begin by making one central decision: will your system be *off-grid* and dependent on batteries to store the electricity, or will it be *grid-tied* and connected to the public utility system? Your answer will depend on many physical realities such as location and budget, as well as the less tangible but equally important reality of your own natural inclinations and philosophy. Keep in mind that an off-grid system with batteries is more costly and less efficient than a grid-tied system.

Off-grid systems make sense in remote locations, and for people who desire self-reliance and complete independence from conventional power. Grid-tied systems let you use power from the utility company when your own system can't produce quite enough. If you occasionally produce more power than you need, some utilities will also buy this extra electricity from you (though not always at the same price at which they'll sell it back to you later). Some grid-tied systems also include batteries that provide power during a blackout. In his highly readable book, *Power with Nature*, Rex Ewing neatly describes the details of these various arrangements.[2]

Whatever system you use — off-grid, grid-tied or grid-tied with batteries — each involves a similar set of components:

- energy source: the sun, wind or stream
- collector: the PV cells, wind turbine or water pipe
- battery bank for storage, if desired
- inverter, to convert DC power to AC
- transmission lines
- energy sink: the appliance, light, etc. that uses the electricity

All of these components come in various sizes, styles, capacities and arrangements. This is not the place for a detailed discussion of your specific needs, the best size for your system or any technical calculations. Again, if you decide to pursue any of the energy possibilities described below, you'll find the guidance you need in resources listed in Appendix C.

Legal Issues

Generating electricity, whether from the sun, wind or water, will almost certainly involve local laws or covenants that restrict what you're allowed to do. Every town and state will have its own set of regulations that you'll need to discover before proceeding with your plans. Local energy associations may help guide your process, and you might even end up working to change existing regulations that seem unreasonable or hopelessly out of date. For your safety and to keep your insurance company satisfied, be sure you follow the National Electric Code regulations for installation of a renewable energy system. Your installer should obtain an electrical permit and have the electrical inspector sign off on it before you start and when finished.

SUMMARY

Your property may be the largest investment you'll ever make. Doesn't it make sense to use your land to its maximum potential, to get the greatest return on your investment? One way is by generating electricity directly from a natural process freely taking place within your landscape. If you do this, you'll not only save money and cut down on CO_2 emissions, you'll also feel good about being part of the solution to the world's energy problems.

CHAPTER 17

Making Electricity from Sunlight

SOLAR ENERGY IS HARDLY A NEW IDEA. Prehistoric people chose to live in caves that opened toward the sun, to capture as much warmth as possible during the winter. Ancient Egyptians, Greeks and Romans built their houses to face the sun for the same reason. In every part of the planet where winters are cold, people have found ways to take advantage of the sun's free heat, to help make their living spaces more comfortable.

These passive solar strategies are still the most economical way to use the sun's energy; many guidelines are covered in Chapters 2 and 3. This chapter explains the basic principles of active solar power, transforming solar energy into electricity (and to hot water) that we can store and use even when the sun's not shining. (See Information Box on page 222

for a more complete discussion of solar hot water.)

Scientists have been fascinated by the idea of harnessing the sun's energy since long before the oil crisis of the 1970s. Even in the mid-1800s, at the height of the Industrial Revolution, engineers devised ways to actively use solar power,

Fig. 17.1:
These passively solar-heated caves in eastern Turkey were historically used for shelter.

217

including a steam engine that ran purely on sunlight and parabolic trough collectors that operated on many of the same principles that solar thermal power plants use today. Since those early inventions, progress toward practical solar energy has been slow but persistent.

The first *solar cell* that could produce a steady, measurable electric current was developed in 1953 by scientists at Bell Laboratories (now AT&T). Early solar cells were used by NASA to power spacecraft during the 1950s and 60s, because no other energy supply could perform that unique job. However, like the solar steam engine of the 1860s, which worked fine and contained great potential, the first solar cells couldn't compete with the cheaper and more accepted energy sources of their time.

Fortunately, at last, things have changed. In response to widespread new understanding about the reality of finite resources and the costs — financial, environmental and political — of importing fuel, solar energy has finally entered the mainstream. Higher demand for solar products has made it possible to produce them in larger quantities, which has lowered their cost. Solar or photovoltaic cells have been dramatically improved from their original form. They've become both more efficient and more adaptable to a wide range of uses.

Now solar modules, assemblies of solar cells linked together, appear all around us. They power road construction signs, entry gates and the lights in gardens and parks. They're integrated into roof shingles and the glass walls of skyscrapers. Tiny solar modules are even sewn into handbags, to charge tiny gadgets inside. Perhaps where we mostly see solar modules is on building roofs, where they're equally as common on traditional ranch houses and Victorians as they are on modern structures built by innovative pioneers.

You may be asking yourself, why are we talking about solar electricity and solar modules on roofs in this book about landscape design? Well, beyond the fact that solar cells are affected by shade trees in the landscape, many rooftops may not actually be the best place for your solar array. A roof might face in a direction that doesn't receive enough sunlight to make the PV cells work efficiently. It might be tilted at the wrong angle or may even be too weak to support the system. For these and other reasons, it sometimes makes sense to place solar modules out in the landscape, either near the house or even some distance away. This *landscape-based solar electricity* is the subject of our discussion.

WHAT'S INVOLVED?

Sunlight generates electricity when it hits the surface of a photovoltaic (PV) cell and excites electrons inside the cell. When these energized electrons jump back and forth between the cell's layers, the electricity they create is captured in

Fig. 17.2:
Photovoltaic arrays set up in the yard can even be a beautiful element in the landscape.

wires running through the cells. The direct current (DC) electricity produced by PV cells can be stored in batteries and sent through an inverter before going to your appliances as alternating current (AC). Or it can be immediately converted to AC and sent to the public utility grid.

Solar modules consist of photovoltaic cells laid out on a metal frame (usually aluminum for lightest weight) and sealed with a layer of glass or other transparent material to protect them from moisture and damage. Modules are connected together to form a *solar array* that's designed to generate a specific wattage. For example, a single module might contain 50 cells that each produce 2 watts; this 100-watt module might be linked with nine others to create a 1,000-watt (1 kW) solar array.

For a brilliant explanation of how solar cells work, get Rex Ewing and Doug Pratt's book, *Got Sun? Go Solar* and read Chapter 3, "Riding Herd on Electrons: Electricity and Solar Cell Basics."[1]

WHAT'S REQUIRED?

All solar modules require sunlight to work. How much sun is enough? Solar modules need to be able to receive, *on average throughout the year*, at least four hours of direct sunlight during midday, when the sun is most powerful. To discover whether your site has enough potential solar energy to justify the cost of installing PV, you can start by visiting the website chooserenewables.com. When you enter your address, a program will calculate the average amount of sunlight available, based on the latitude and prevailing weather of that location.

This, of course, is not quite enough information for a final decision, but it's a good place to start.[2]

What may be even more important to know is how much sunlight is available during the least sunny time of the year. This information is provided in several websites, in *insolation maps* that show the solar radiation falling on a south-facing surface that's tilted at an angle equal to the latitude of its location, as your solar modules would probably be.

If both of these estimates show that your region offers a reasonable solar resource, or if you already know this because all your neighbors have PV modules on their roofs, your next steps will be to get more specific. Solar modules have to be oriented toward the south,

Fig. 17.3:
This 5 kW array is mounted on a custom-built rack because the barn roof, despite being oriented properly, is in poor condition and needs future repair.

Modules vs Panels

The term "solar module" refers to an assembly of photovoltaic cells linked together, while the term "solar panel" technically refers to the structure that holds pipes for producing hot water. In everyday talk, many people use the two terms interchangeably. This book uses "modules" when discussing electricity and "panels" when discussing hot water.

or at least within 25° to the east or west of south (also see Appendix A for guidance about finding south on your property). Once you've decided on a likely location, you'll need an accurate measure of the hours of sunlight falling there.

For many of us, some of the sunlight that could reach our solar modules is blocked by shade trees or other structures nearby. (Chapters 2 and 5 present detailed guidance about where to position shade trees for solar gain.) You can find out the hours of sunlight that will actually reach your solar array simply by paying careful attention throughout the year, watching the movement of shadows and perhaps keeping a chart or diagram of the result. Or you could go through the laborious process, used for decades by old-school landscape planners, of calculating the length of shadows cast by objects of various heights and then projecting these shadows on an accurate scale drawing of your landscape. (This exercise is not for the faint of heart!)

A far easier way to determine your solar potential (although it's also more expensive) is to hire a professional to perform a solar assessment. This job will probably involve using a *solar pathfinder*, a clever gizmo with a glass dome that arches over a chart that illustrates the hours of the day in every month. When the pathfinder is held level and oriented properly, in the location of your planned solar array, objects that will block the sun show up as shadows on the glass dome. By carefully comparing this shadow outline with the chart below, the evaluator can determine an exact tally of solar gain throughout the year.

WHERE SHOULD YOU PUT YOUR SOLAR ARRAY?

You may decide to install just a single 3-by-5-foot module or dozens of modules linked together in one or more arrays in different places. The potential arrangements are nearly endless. Many solar arrays are mounted on rooftops because sometimes that's the place that receives the most sunlight. But there's no requirement that the modules be mounted on a roof, and there are actually some reasons not to do so.

Latitude and Longitude

Latitude is your position north or south of the equator. It's represented by degrees, with the equator being zero, the poles being 90°, and locations in between indicated by both degrees and direction, as in 30° north latitude, 30° south latitude. Alternatively, latitude is sometimes indicated by positive and negative signs, with the northern hemisphere being positive and the southern hemisphere being negative.

Longitude is your east-west location, measured relative to an arbitrary starting point, the prime meridian that passes through Greenwich, England. Longitude is also measured in degrees, with zero at Greenwich, positive degrees to the east across Europe and Asia, and negative degrees to the west across the Atlantic Ocean, North and South America. How can you find your latitude and longitude? It's simple.... just Google those words on the Web (see Appendix A).

Dust that naturally accumulates on the surface of the array can reduce the cells' efficiency. Roof-mounted systems will probably rarely be cleaned, except by rainfall, whereas solar arrays in the landscape are easy to monitor and clean. Snow removal, which can be difficult or impossible with modules on a roof, is a snap when the solar array is near the ground. And, as the sun's angle changes with the seasons, a pole-mounted system can be manually tilted to keep the modules oriented as perpendicular as possible to the sun's rays. This benefit, too, is completely unavailable with most roof-mounted systems.

The type of material that covers your roof may also be a factor. While ordinary asphalt shingles and metal roofing pose no problem, wood shingles and tiles can be difficult and expensive to work with. In addition, if for any reason you ever need to replace your shingles or work on the structure of the roof itself, roof-mounted photovoltaics can be quite inconvenient.

If you decide to put your PV array out in your landscape, it may be mounted on poles or racks, positioned just a few feet off the ground or quite high up, depending on what else needs to happen there. It can be attached to the side of a south-facing deck or other sturdy fence. You might even build a shed or small structure that's specifically designed to hold a solar array on its roof (and a rain collection tank inside?).

Of course, you may not have enough space on your property, or perhaps not enough sunlight at ground level, to support a solar array in the landscape. Maybe you'd rather not look at, or work around or worry about preventing damage to solar modules near ground level.

Every situation will require its own unique evaluation and solution.

CHAPTER SUMMARY

The sun shines everywhere on the planet, showering us with enough energy in a single day to meet the entire world's needs for years. Solar power is the renewable energy that's most available to the largest number of people worldwide. It isn't affected by being harvested, and nothing we silly humans do can change its awesome power. All we can do is find ways to make the most of it.

At the moment, our best choice is to use photovoltaics. PV modules can be used anywhere the sun shines. Reliable, sturdy and lightweight, they contain no moving parts to wear out and require very little maintenance. Small arrays can easily be expanded later or used in conjunction with other systems, especially with wind generators.

Fig. 17.4: Pole-mounted PV arrays are becoming increasingly common in residential landscapes, in both new construction and long-established homes.

Fig. 17.5: The owners of this pole-mounted solar module further reduce their demand for electricity by drying their clothes outdoors and heating with propane.

While the initial cost of a solar array may be high, the payback may be shorter than you think, especially as the cost of carbon-based energy rises. Many states offer tax incentives, and numerous organizations provide grants to help pay for PV or other renewable energy systems. In some situations, especially in remote regions, the cost of installing PV will be lower than bringing in conventional electricity. The great advantage of solar power, true as well for the wind and hydro systems described later, is that it produces no pollution, causes no harm to the environment and frees us from the costs of conventional energy.

Solar Hot Water

Have you ever burned your fingers on the hot water that pours out of a hose after it's been lying in the garden or across your yard during a sunny day? If so, you've felt the same thing that inventors of solar hot water systems felt right before they had their eureka moment and thought, hey, we could use this hot water!

Solar hot water systems may be simple or complex. The simplest systems (also called batch, open-loop or direct systems) expose a tank of water to the sun, let it get hot and then pipe this water directly to a building's faucets, where it's used for bathing, washing, laundering, etc. Cold water is piped into the tank to replenish the hot water that's been used. This basic system, in which heat is both collected and stored in the same place, works best in regions that don't freeze in winter.

More complex solar hot water systems collect heat in one place and store it in another. These indirect or closed-loop systems consist of flat panel collectors containing pipes or tubes that are filled with water or other fluid. After being heated by the sun, this fluid is piped through (not into) a conventional household water tank. Here it transfers its heat to the surrounding water and then returns to the collector, cooler but otherwise unchanged, where it will start the cycle again. The sun-heated liquid never mixes with the household water supply. Because the heat-storage area is inside the house, these systems work fine when outdoor temperatures are cool, and some function even more efficiently when the air is cold than when it's hot.

In Chapter 3 of *A Homeowner's Guide to Renewable Energy*, Dan Chiras presents an excellent discussion of both direct and indirect solar hot water systems, along with their various advantages and drawbacks.[3] Keep in mind that hot water collector panels need to be exposed to a generous amount of sun, and to accomplish this, they may be placed on the side of a house or even on the ground near it, thereby becoming an element in landscape design.

Figure 17.6:
Although mounted on the side of a house, this solar thermal panel should also be considered as part of the landscape, since the position of landscape trees and shrubs will affect its power.

CHAPTER 18

Generating Electricity from the Wind

WINDMILLS HAVE BEEN SPINNING for hundreds of years; the earliest pumped water in Persia (Iran), from about 500 to 900 AD. In the Western world, they commonly powered sawmills, gristmills and wells for irrigation and drinking water. Windmills that generated electricity, first invented in the late 1800s, became a widespread source of lighting for homes across rural America, until the 1930s and 40s, when public utility lines were extended countrywide, and most windmills became unnecessary.

Since then, wind power in the US has developed in fits and starts, with a surge of attention after the oil crisis of the 1970s, followed by waning interest as the political and financial climate changed. Now, with the rising cost of carbon-based energy, and on the heels of European advances during the 1980s and 90s, the US has

focused again on the great potential of wind energy. Large-scale wind power today contributes a significant and growing portion of the world's renewable energy supply.

Gone, though, are the familiar old-fashioned windmills, with their giant paddles and sail-covered frames that used to spin majestically in a breeze. Modern windmills are no longer made of wood, and in fact, we call them wind turbines or wind generators, not windmills. Today their blades, shaped like propellers or wings, employ the same aerodynamic principles as airplanes, with wind providing lift that makes them spin faster. New technology and a contagious enthusiasm about the potential of wind power have produced a vast array of wind energy products.

Huge turbines that stand 200 to 400 feet tall generate megawatts of electricity. Medium-sized wind turbines hold their 60 to 80 foot rotors up to 200 feet high and generate hundreds of kilowatts. In recent years, small-scale wind power has also become a successful industry: to meet the needs of homes, farms and small businesses, countless new "micro wind turbines" have been developed (with more certainly on the way) that generate from as little as 20 watts to as much as 20 kilowatts. These small turbines are the subject of this chapter.

Fig. 18.1: *Like so much of technology, modern wind generators would be unrecognizable to the users of early windmills.*

HEALTH-EOLTEC-3: PVSQUARED

WHAT'S INVOLVED?

In appearance, micro wind turbines seem to vary almost as much as snowflakes, but they all do essentially the same thing: convert the kinetic energy of wind into electrical energy. They accomplish this by placing propeller blades (rotors) in the path of the wind. When the wind blows, the rotors turn, which spins a shaft that's connected to a generator. (For more information about electricity generation, see the introduction to this section.)

Wind turbines are specifically designed to harness certain wind speeds and generate certain amounts of electricity. Long rotor blades, which cover a large *sweep area*, generally work best in low winds, while shorter blades can handle faster winds. Some turbines work equally well in a wide range of wind speeds. While there's no direct relationship between a rotor's diameter and the power produced, in his book *Wind Energy Basics*, Paul Gipe categorizes small wind turbines as:

+ Micro: 2- to 4-foot diameter, which generate 20 to 300 watts
+ Mini: 4- to 9-foot diameter, which generate 500 to 800 watts
+ Household: 9- to 23-foot diameter, which generate 1 to 10 kilowatts
+ Small: 23- to 29-foot diameter, which generate 10 to 20 kilowatts[1]

The basic components of all wind turbines are: the rotors; a housing (called the nacelle) behind the rotors, which contains a generator that's connected to the rotor shaft; and a tower that holds the whole assembly above the ground and contains transmission lines for sending the electricity to its destination. Some wind turbines generate AC power, eliminating the need for the DC inverter that's required in both solar and hydroelectric systems (see pages 212-213).

This discussion doesn't cover the exact measurements and calculations involved in designing your own small wind system; several excellent resources, listed in Appendix C, provide that information. However, you will have enough information to help you decide whether your site has the potential to generate electricity from wind.

WHAT'S REQUIRED?
Wind

To make your small wind turbine a viable source of energy, you need, well, enough wind. What's enough? Wind speed is measured on the Beaufort scale from 0 to 12, in which 0 represents calm air and 12 is a hurricane. Most small wind turbines will produce electricity in "force 2 winds," what the Beaufort scale describes as light breeze (or about 7 to 11 mph), and some will even work with 7 to 8 mph winds. More than half of the continental US experiences winds that are at least this strong.

To find the potential wind power in your area, check the Wind Energy Resource Atlas of the United States (nrel.gov/rredc) or the US Department of Energy's wind map (windpoweringamerica.gov). Both resources show average annual wind speed for every state, along with the Pacific Islands, Puerto Rico and the Virgin Islands. Another online program (chooserenewables.com) will give an even more detailed assessment of the potential wind (and solar) resource for any address. Bearing in mind that any wind speed estimate is necessarily approximate, this information is a great place to start.

In addition to the prevailing wind speeds in your regions, the power of wind is affected by the density of the air itself: denser air carries more power than lighter air. So, for example, at equal wind speeds, the same turbine will generate as much as 20 percent more electricity during winter than in summer (typically the effect is less than this). Density increases in colder temperatures and at lower elevations, so winter winds at sea level generally have the greatest potential force. The wind's ability to generate most power during the winter, when days are short and the sun is low in the sky, makes wind systems a handy complement to solar electric systems, which are usually most

Fig. 18.2:
Wind generators contain hundreds of hidden parts, but their main visible components are the rotor, the nacelle or housing for the turbine, and the tower.

Fans
Although they may look quite similar, wind turbines are the opposite of fans. Fans produce a breeze by using electricity; wind turbines produce electricity by using breezes.

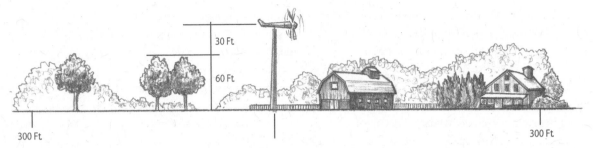

30 Ft

60 Ft

300 Ft

300 Ft

Fig. 18.3: Placing the wind turbine at least 30 feet above any obstruction within 300 feet of the tower will reduce power loss due to turbulence, maximizing generator output.

efficient during the summer, when days are long and the sun shines from high in the sky.

If you do decide to proceed with plans to install a wind turbine, you'll need to get more data about wind speeds at the specific location and height of your proposed tower. Ideally, this will involve setting up an anemometer and taking measurements over the course of a whole year (which may be required for any tax credit or rebate programs), but you may find other ways to obtain the information, e.g., checking with a nearby weather station, or talking to neighbors about their systems.

A Tower

Wind power is affected by the shape of the ground. Smooth terrain like ice, snow and grasslands contain no obstacles that will unsettle the wind flow. Buildings and forest interrupt the wind and produce turbulence

Wind in the City

The crowded buildings and odd-shaped open spaces of cities create a tremendous amount of turbulence. Some parks or athletic fields may support small wind turbines, and will certainly work fine for education or demonstration purposes. But for generating substantial amounts of electricity, wind energy in urban areas doesn't work very well.

that reduces wind speed. In these rough wind regions, turbines need to be mounted on towers that lift them high above the ground into smoother, faster wind.

How tall should a tower be? While turbulence is greatest immediately downwind of an obstacle, the region of disruption may extend upwind by a distance up to 2 times the obstacle's height, and downwind up to 20 times its height. A rule of thumb for tower height (as true today as it was for the old-timers who proposed it), is that a turbine should be placed at least 30 feet higher than the top of any obstruction within 300 feet of the tower.

Shorter towers may be appropriate in some situations: when a turbine is quite small and not expected to be the only source of energy, when the cost of a tall tower isn't justified by a low power output or when a tower may need to be moved occasionally (for example, to charge a movable electric fence that's powered by the turbine).

Towers come in three basic forms: wide at the base and hence self-supporting, slender at the base and relying on guy wires for support and free-standing poles set in deep foundations and needing no guy wires (generally used for utility-scale wind turbines). Most wind turbine manufacturers sell towers that provide the proper clearance and other design specifications to make them work best with their own turbines. Some towers may also be built from do-it-yourself kits.

Suitable Space

Small wind turbines should generally be set up only in sites that are at least a half-acre. This is especially important if you're using a tower with guy wires, which need to be spaced far enough apart to give the tower maximum stability. If your property contains a hill, remember that it is an obstacle that can reduce the wind's energy. The best way to manage a hill is simply to put the tower on top of it, even if your turbine will then be farther from the house, because this will take advantage of the smoother air high up.

Wind towers, like trees, have the potential to blow over in strong gusts and storms. Although this happens *extremely* rarely, it's best (and some regulations require this) if the distance between the tower and any structures, property boundaries or electric lines is at least 1.5 to 2 times the height of the tower. Before proceeding with any plans, make sure to check whether this distance is specified in any local ordinances.

OTHER ISSUES

Noise

Wind turbines make no noise when they're standing still and potentially a lot of noise when the wind is strong and their rotors are spinning fast. The American Wind Energy Association claims that "small wind turbines do make some noise, but not enough to be found objectionable by most people. A typical residential wind system makes less noise than the average washing machine."[3]

Roof-mounted Towers

You may wish to mount a turbine on the roof of your house, barn or other outbuilding. However, vibrations from the spinning propeller will actually transmit through the entire frame, magnifying its sound and perhaps eventually taking a toll on the structure itself. Wind expert Paul Gipe says about roof-mounted towers: "Don't bother; they're not worth the trouble."[2]

Turbine Safety

Many wind turbines are designed with "over-speed" protection mechanisms that immediately brake a turbine if it's spinning too fast or if the generator overheats. Some also have sensors that detect high levels of vibration and automatically switch off the turbine. Large-scale wind turbines contain rotors that are able to rotate along their longitudinal axis, to provide aerodynamic braking.

For comparison, a small wind turbine operating at full speed generally produces sound between 50 and 60 decibels, while the noise level inside a car is about 80 decibels, people's whispering is 20 decibels, and a jet engine produces about 150 decibels. For both safety and sound, it's best to place your turbine as far as reasonably possible from living areas.

Legal Issues

If you decide to generate electricity from the wind, you'll need to educate yourself about the various rules and regulations that govern this new source of energy. Can you feed your extra electricity into the public utility grid? Is generating alternative energy even allowed by the utility? How tall can your tower be, and how far must it be from your boundary? Are there any noise level restrictions? Does your town require a stamped engineer's drawing of the construction plans?

State and local authorities everywhere are working to keep up with advances in home-based energy, but at this moment no widely accepted standards yet exist. To find out more about regulations (and financial incentives) in your region, and to learn where else to look for answers, visit the Database of State Incentives for Renewables and Efficiency (DSIRE) at www.dsireuse.org.

Fig. 18.4:
Located high in the hills of Hawley, Massachusetts, this 1.8 kW Skystream turbine serves the power needs of an apple grower's processing plant. It's mounted on a 50' tilt-up monopole, installed in 2007 by PV2 (pvsquared.coop), of Greenfield, Masschusetts.

CHAPTER SUMMARY

Wind power does involve a few drawbacks that could make it unattractive to some homeowners or unsuitable in some situations: the whooshing sound of spinning rotors, absence of power when the wind is still, rotors stilled by ice during certain winter conditions and the need for regular maintenance. And, while the energy of full sunlight is steady and unchanging, wind energy depends on many variables, some of them entirely unpredictable.

With steady wind flow, however, wind energy is one of the most economical forms of energy available. And it's an excellent addition to other sources of energy, especially solar, which can share the same storage and transmission equipment. This is especially true because winds are stronger in the morning and late afternoon, when sunlight is weak, and they carry more kinetic energy in winter, when solar energy systems are least productive.

Wind is a locally available source of energy that consumes no water or carbon-based fuels and emits no greenhouse gases or toxic particles. Like the sun (in fact as a product of the sun's heat), it is inexhaustible and infinitely renewable. Using wind power frees us from the unpredictable costs of conventional power and requires no regular expenses beyond occasional maintenance. What was true for early civilizations is true for people today all across the globe: we can live, farm, work and thrive on the power of a good strong breeze.

CHAPTER 19

Harnessing the Energy of Flowing Water

HYDROELECTRIC GENERATION is based on a beautifully simple idea: capture the energy in flowing water, convert this energy into a usable form, and return the water to its source. Early industry was powered by water, through the use of dams, millponds and millraces. Spinning waterwheels turned the shafts of sawmills, grain and textile mills and eventually the vast network of factories that created the Industrial Revolution. Since then, from its humble, often picturesque beginnings, hydroelectric power has become the primary form of renewable energy used around the globe. As of 2007, the seven countries with the greatest production of hydropower are, in order: China, Canada, Brazil, US, Russia, Norway and India.[1]

Micro-hydro simply adds new technology, equipment and knowledge to this old, original idea. Now, homeowners and communities can generate energy at a scale that seems miniature compared to modern hydroelectric plants. Instead of damming large rivers to form reservoirs that push water with great force through a giant pipe to generate gigawatts of electricity, micro-hydro, often called *run of river* systems, simply taps into the flow of streams and brooks and uses natural current (rather than concentrated, falling water) to generate modest amounts of electricity.

Large-scale hydroelectric stations can be built only in places with large rivers and the right sort of terrain; in many of these locations, concern about the environment often further limits their suitability. Micro-hydro systems, in contrast, can be set up in countless locations on every continent. All that's required is water that flows throughout the year with enough volume and force to justify the cost of capturing its energy.

WHAT'S INVOLVED?

In a typical micro-hydro system, a pipe collects water directly from a watercourse, without any sort of dam. Water in the pipe flows downhill, gaining energy as it's pushed by the water behind it. At the lower end of the pipe, the water passes through a turbine. Inside the turbine, it turns a wheel that's connected to a shaft, which in turn spins magnets inside the coils of a generator. This transforms the turbine's rotational energy into electricity. After the water has done its work, it simply flows back into the stream that it came from (at a lower point, of course).

The basic components in a micro-hydro system — intake, pipeline (called the penstock), turbine, outlet, generator, batteries, transmission lines — come in a wide variety of forms that depend on the nature of the flow and the amount of energy being generated. This discussion doesn't cover all the myriad details you'll need to know if you decide to install a micro-hydro system. It does, however, give you enough information to help you decide whether or not your site has the potential to be used for micro-hydro power.

WHAT'S REQUIRED?

The power your stream can generate depends on two vital characteristics:

- *Flow*, the amount of water that courses down the stream, and how fast it's going. This figure is usually measured in cubic feet per second (cfs) or gallons per minute (gpm).
- *Head*, the amount of vertical drop (or fall) between top and bottom. This figure is usually measured in feet (although it's sometimes shown as the amount of pressure created by the difference between top and bottom, measured in pounds per square inch (psi)).

Micro-hydro energy is the combined result of head and flow working together. Your stream may be steep or gentle; it may gush and gurgle or just flow steady and full. A short steep stream might work as well as a long gentle one.

Fig. 19.1: Throughout the 1900's, much electricity in North America was generated by large hydro power plants like this one, TransCanada's six-megaWatt Station Number Four on the Deerfield River in western Massachusetts.

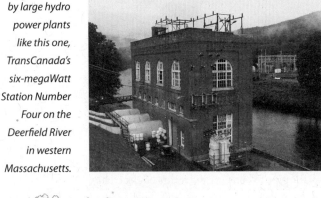

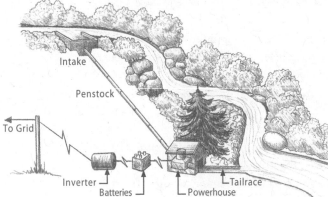

Fig 19.2: *Whatever their design and arrangement, the basic components of all hydro systems are: an intake point; a pipeline; the turbine itself; an outflow; and a means for either transmitting or storing the generated electricity.*

The only kind of water supply that definitely won't work is a stream that's both short *and* gentle, because this water source just won't provide enough energy to make the system cost-effective. Micro-hydro power requires a certain minimum amount of water flowing at a certain minimum rate, or at least enough to generate an amount of electricity that will meet your needs.

A micro-hydro stream must also flow continuously all year long. Low water during the summer is okay as long as the stream doesn't dry up; ice and snow in winter are okay as long as water continues to flow beneath them. Of course, if you want to use your micro-hydro systems only during certain months — as in a summer camp — this year-long flow may not matter.

Most micro-hydro systems need some sort of structure or shed (often called the powerhouse) where the turbine and generator receive the incoming water pipe, and where the outgoing water (called tailwater) can be released back to the stream. This building must be located in a place relatively near the stream but out of the way of any potential flooding.

Few of us are lucky enough to have a stream right next to our house, though that would be the ideal location for micro-hydro. In reality, we can still take advantage of a stream's power even if it's up to a mile away from our home, keeping in mind that a greater distance between where the electricity is produced and where it ends up getting used will always equal a loss of energy (unless you use very large wire for the transmission, which could cost too much to make sense).

WILL YOUR STREAM WORK?

Assuming your stream runs year-round and is reasonably near your house, your next step is to find out whether it's got the flow and head needed to generate enough electricity to justify your investment. Although you can get a rough measurement of both yourself, if and when you decide to move ahead with developing a hydro system, you'll need to get exact measurements, which will determine the size of the system's components.

Measuring Flow

You'll need a large portable container of a known size, such as a 5-gallon bucket, and you'll definitely need a helper because this is a two-person job. Find a place in the stream where you can collect all the flow into the bucket: this could be a natural drop-off area where the bucket will fit under the flow, or a temporary dam that's set up with a pipe to direct flow into the bucket. Have one person insert the bucket all the way into the flow while the helper immediately starts keeping track of time on a stopwatch. As soon as the bucket gets completely full, note how much time has elapsed, in seconds.

Fig. 19.3: *This small stream that feeds the Connecticut River in western Massachusetts provides just enough electricity to meet the limited power needs of a small summer cottage (not pictured here).*

To calculate flow in gallons per minute, divide the size of the container by the time (in seconds) needed to fill it up, then multiply by 60. For example, a 5-gallon bucket that filled up in 4 seconds would indicate a flow rate of 75 gallons per minute (5 gal/4 seconds x 60 seconds = 75 gpm).

This method works best in a small or medium-sized stream. To determine the flow rate of a large stream or small river, you may find it easier, and your results may be more accurate, if you use one of several other methods described in Scott Davis's book *Microhydro: Clean Power from Water*[2] or in Daniel New's "Guide to Hydro Power" on his website (canyonhydro.com).[3]

A flow rate between 2 and 100 gpm is generally considered sufficient for a micro-hydro system. Rates at the lower end of this range will work best in streams with higher head (see below), and may require specially designed turbines. A rate below 2 gpm just won't have enough oomph to make your investment worthwhile.

Three Ways of Measuring Head

The following three methods involve supplies that most people already own. There are other, potentially more accurate ways to measure head, including using a surveyor's transit or builder's level (and if you own one of these, you probably already know how it works), or an accurate altimeter. If a pipe is already in place in the stream, you can use a pressure gauge and convert pressure into feet of head (by multiplying psi times 2.31). For more detailed advice, see Scott Davis's book *Microhydro: Clean Power from Water*.[4]

Higher head means more power. As a general rule, you'll need at least 20 to 30 feet of head to generate cost-effective electricity for use at home. New technologies, however, are steadily being developed that may soon make it feasible to generate electricity from low-head micro-hydro.

Method One: Stepping Down the Slope

You'll need some stakes, a hammer, a long string or plank, a level and a yardstick or tape measure. You may be able to do this job alone, but a helper will make it easier. Start at the highest point that you believe you'll be able to capture water, and measure in increments down the slope, by following these steps:

1. At the top, drive a stake in the ground.
2. Attach a string to the stake at ground level, or rest a plank on the ground.
3. Extend the string or plank out over the land that's sloping down, using a level to be sure you're holding it perfectly flat, not tilted uphill or downhill.
4. At the end of the string or plank, drive another stake in the ground. Mark where they cross. Then measure the distance from this mark down to the ground.
5. Repeat steps 1 through 4, working your way down the slope until you reach the point where you'll capture the flow (where the turbine will be set up). You may follow the stream course closely, or take a shorter route; in either case the total *vertical drop* from top to bottom will be the same.
6. Keep track of each individual measurement as you go along, then add them together at

the end. This sum is the total change in elevation from the top to the bottom of your system.

Method Two: A Water Level

This method simply requires a hose and a measuring tape, and, like the previous method, you can probably do it solo but it'll be easier if you have a helper. Follow these steps:

1. Lay a length of hose in the stream bed, with one end at the top of your intended hydro system.

2. Hold the upper end in place while the hose fills with water.

3. When water flows from the lower end, pick up that end and raise it to a height where water stops flowing out. Because of the laws of fluid dynamics, this height is level with the upper end of the hose. (If your stream is very steep, you'll have to use a short length of hose, to be able to hold the end high enough.)

4. Measure the distance from the hose end to the ground.

5. Repeat steps 1 through 4 to the bottom of the stream, adding each incremental measurement to get the total vertical drop from top to bottom.

Method Three: Sighting up the Slope

This method requires a level, a measuring tape and two people. Starting at the *bottom* of your future micro-hydro system, follow these steps:

1. Stand facing up the stream and hold a level up to your eye, with its length extended out toward the slope rising up in front of you. Stand with a good straight posture that you'll be able to do again.

2. Have the second person measure the distance from your eye to the ground. Then have him or her stand to the side and confirm the level is....well, level.

3. Sight along the level and note where your line of sight meets the ground upstream.

4. Have the second person go to that point and mark it.

5. Move uphill to that new point and repeat steps 1 through 4, standing up as tall each time, multiplying the heights of yourself by the number of times you move.

HOW MUCH ELECTRICITY?

Your preliminary head and flow measurements will give you a *rough approximation* of the amount of electricity your stream might produce. The *actual amount* of electricity generated will be determined by several factors, including friction and turbulence in the pipe; the efficiency of turbines, generators, etc.; and by other issues too complex for this discussion.

In his book, *Power with Nature*, Rex Ewing provides a formula for estimating the total electricity your stream has the potential to generate:

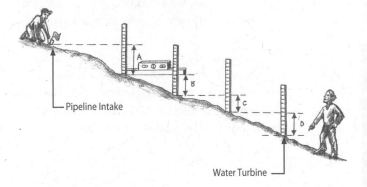

Pipeline Intake

Water Turbine

Fig. 19.4: *If done with a moderate amount of attention to detail, this non-technical method for measuring head can produce quite accurate results.*

Kilowatts = Head (in feet) x Flow (in cfs) x Efficiency (0.55) x C (0.085)

Note: If you measured your stream's flow in gallons per minute (gpm), convert this into cubic feet per second (cfs), by dividing your gpm figure by 448.8 (the number of gpms equal to one cfs).

For example, assuming a head of 50 feet and a flow rate of 75 gpm (0.167cfs):

50 x 0.167 x 0.55 x 0.085 = 0.390 kW (390 watts)[5]

OTHER ISSUES

To get a realistic sense of your stream's potential, you should measure flow during each season and then average the results. Summertime flows

Fig 19.5: *Many rivers have the potential to generate electricity. The goal is to capture this potential in a way that causes no harm to the waterway and violates no conservation regulations, and to produce enough electricity to justify the investment.*

are almost always lower than during the rest of the year.

The amount of water in your stream should be enough that redirecting a small portion of the water into your hydroelectric system will have no effect on the health of creatures living in the stream and the natural processes taking place there. Also, before you proceed with your plans, remember that in most states, working in a river, stream or any body of water may require a permit from local authorities (Conservation Commission, Wetlands Committee, etc.).

CHAPTER SUMMARY

Like all types of renewable energy, and in fact like all sorts of conventional energy, micro-hydro has its own unique set of disadvantages and benefits. On the down side, micro-hydro will only work if a site provides adequate head and flow, and if it's located generally within a mile from its destination. Taking care of a micro-hydro system requires knowledge and some mechanical ability, and a willingness to pay attention; again, this isn't for everyone.

However, if you have a suitable stream, micro-hydro can provide the cheapest electricity available. It doesn't need a dam or reservoir in a river, and it provides a continuous energy supply all day long and all year. Even when the sun is weak — early and late in the day throughout winter — water is still flowing. Even when the wind is quiet — in mid-day, during summer doldrums — water is still flowing. Micro-hydro systems can also be built in conjunction with solar and wind systems, offering the possibility of supplying your house entirely with renewable energy.

Is Your Stream Too Small?

If you don't have enough head or flow to power your house, there are a number of companies that produce small DC generators that run off small turbines. You probably won't be able to power your house with these, but for off-grid dwellers, you can charge some batteries pretty easily, or use an inverter to power a couple of electronics.

CHAPTER 20

Capturing the Warmth of the Ground

T HE EARTH IS HEATED BY THE SUN, day
after day, all year long. Because the
ground itself is an insulator that holds this heat
well, its temperature just a few feet below the
surface remains at about 50° to 60°F (about 10°
to 15°C) throughout the year, regardless of
daily fluctuations in air temperature. Ground
temperatures, which vary slightly depending
on a region's prevailing climate conditions, generally equal the average annual air temperature
of that region.

In most parts of the world, this means that
during the winter the ground is warmer than
the air, and in summer it's cooler than the air.
We can take advantage of this handy situation
by installing *geothermal heat exchange systems*.
This sort of system, sometimes termed a
ground-source heat pump, takes warmth from the
ground and uses it to heat living spaces in winter, and puts heat back into the ground to cool
living spaces in summer. This process uses that
ground as a heat source in winter and a heat
sink in summer.

WHAT'S INVOLVED?

The most common kind of geothermal heat is
called a *closed-loop system*. In this system, a fluid

Air-source Heat Pumps
Some heat pumps use the air instead of the ground as both the
heat's source and sink. The operating principle is the same in both
systems, though the components differ slightly. Air-source heat
pumps are less efficient than ground-source heat pumps and work
best in warm climates.

Fig. 20.1: *In a horizontal geothermal system, a slinky tubing lay out maximizes the amount of fluid exposed to, and moderated by the ground's temperature.*

What's in the Closed-loop Pipe?

The fluid inside a geothermal loop can be ordinary water in warm climates where the ground doesn't freeze. Otherwise, it should be either an antifreeze solution or a mixture of water and antifreeze, with a freeze point at least 10° below the lowest projected temperature in that area.

circulates through a loop of pipe that's laid below ground, absorbing the heat of the ground. From here the fluid flows through a pump that works like a reverse refrigerator, raising the 50 to 60°F temperature of the fluid up to the 70 to 80°F needed in a building. The building's own heating system distributes the heat to where it's needed, and the fluid returns to circulate again through the buried loop. In closed-loop systems, the fluid is self-contained and constantly recycled.

Less commonly used is the *open-loop system* that draws water from a well or water body rather than using antifreeze, and returns this water to its source after the heat has been extracted. Open-loop systems are more efficient than closed-loop systems, but minerals, iron and minute particles of organic matter can clog pipes and damage this system, and the entire process has the potential to affect the water table or harm an aquifer.

All geothermal systems are capable of cooling a house in summer as well as heating it in winter. Usually the expense of installing this type of heat only makes sense if air conditioning is also desired in a home. Within the house, geothermal systems may operate in any of several different ways, all of which are beyond the scope of this book. The important thing for our discussion is the loop of pipe itself, which is buried out in the landscape.

WHAT'S REQUIRED?

The loop's size and shape depend on several factors, including the soil's thermal conductivity, the depth of bedrock, regional climate conditions, the heating and cooling demands of the building and the amount of space available in the landscape.

Ideally, if your property is large enough and the soil conditions are suitable, the easiest and least expensive method is to install the pipe horizontally underground, in a trench or trenches dug below the winter frost level. The pipe may be laid in any of several different configurations, including multiple parallel trenches, a single deep trench in which the loop is aligned vertically or in a *slinky* arrangement, with the pipe curling around itself continuously, like a squashed slinky.

If your property is too small or if the ground is too rocky for trenches, the pipes may be installed vertically, in drilled holes that may extend from 100 to 400 feet below ground, as needed. For more information about the characteristics of soil in your location, contact the Natural Resources Conservation Service Soil Survey (soils.usda.gov). In any case, before you proceed too far in your hopes and dreams, you'll definitely need to consult with a heating contractor who specializes in installing this type of energy system.

Geothermal heat pumps can be installed in both new and existing houses. Their equipment takes up less space than conventional HVAC (heating, ventilation and air conditioning) systems. This saves space in existing homes and allows new homes to be designed differently, with smaller equipment rooms. Geothermal systems contain no outside condensing units, so they're very quiet, both inside and outside the house. And they have few moving parts, most of which are located inside the shelter of a building, making them safe from harm and

Fig. 20.2: *In a vertical geothermal system, pipes extend deeply below ground, in holes drilled by conventional well-drilling rigs.*

easy to maintain and service. These systems are extremely durable; underground piping usually carries a warranty of 25 to 50 years, and the pumps themselves routinely last more than 20 years.

CHAPTER SUMMARY

If your property is suitable, and if you need or intend to use this system for both heating and cooling, geothermal heat pumps can be a great investment. The US Department of Energy says that, as of December 2008, there are approximately 50,000 geothermal heat pumps installed in the country each year. These systems use 25 to 50 percent less electricity than conventional heating and cooling systems and can reduce energy consumption by 50 to 70 percent over standard heating and cooling equipment.[1]

Fig. 20.3: *Vertical geothermal tubes connect to a system of short horizontal tubing that carries the fluid into the building's heat exchanger system. Note the small birch tree near the top of the image on the left, and the same tree in the image on the right, four months later. Landscapes show no sign of geothermal systems functioning silently below.*

Lights in the Landscape

A BIT OF LIGHTING HISTORY

WE'VE COME A LONG WAY since the start of outdoor lighting. In the beginning, lighting was simply fire. In time, fire evolved into candles and whale oil lamps, which soon gave way to kerosene and gas-fueled lamps. These were used primarily to light the interior of our dwellings, usually just one or a few lamps per room, at first just in the wealthiest homes and then more widely through the middle classes and onward across all of society.

The earliest lamps burned upward with a wick and open flame. Later, the invention of light fixtures with a mantle allowed the flame to burn downward and generate an even hotter, brighter light. All early lighting involved some danger of fire. The greatest danger came, however, when gas pipes were installed in the walls to fuel lamps in each room. In the late 1800s, gas explosions and fires burned many homes to the ground.

As a result, when electric light became available in the early 1900s, the public eagerly embraced this new, safer technology. Homeowners at first chose to convert their existing gas fixtures into combined gas/electric lights. This helped the gradual transition to purely electric lighting, the standard since 1920.

Outdoor electric lighting was originally a luxury reserved for cities and the wealthiest homes, mainly for security and property protection. During the mid-1900s (the age of cheap oil), lighting our landscapes became the norm. People everywhere relied on it for safety and comfort and, increasingly, for social status, as the purpose of landscape lighting grew to include beauty, drama and visual effect.

Today the outdoor lighting industry is huge. One Internet search engine shows more than 14 million related entries, with countless companies offering an infinite variety of fixtures, bulbs and installation techniques. As a society, we illuminate oceans of pavement, whether or not they're being used. We floodlight the façades of churches, town buildings and even some homes. We embed fixtures in stone walls, tuck them under deck railings, hide them in fern beds beside our entry paths. We float glowing globes across our swimming pools. We uplight, downlight, frontlight, sidelight, backlight and crosslight. And now, as outdoor lighting has expanded in every city and across the countryside, we've come to realize, belatedly but not too late, that more light and brighter lamps actually harm ourselves, our neighbors and the natural world.

SOME PROBLEMS: BEYOND THE ENERGY SPENT ON LIGHTING

In densely populated areas of the industrialized world, buildings, vehicles, shopping malls and vast expanses of lit pavement throw glowing auras far into the night sky. For the millions of us who live in cities, this excessive light, often called *light pollution*, eliminates our human experience of darkness and the stars. Debate continues on whether or not it harms our circadian rhythms — our internal sense of time that influences our physiological processes — but without a doubt the absence of darkness diminishes the richness of our lives. Our ancestors could see the Milky Way on any clear night…when was the last time you saw it?

In commercial and manufacturing regions, unshielded floodlights shine all night long across parking lots and entryways, as property owners attempt to prevent theft, break-ins and vandalism. Now, however, light in the darkness has become so commonplace that much security lighting does a better job of lighting a criminal's work area than of alerting a witness. And just outside any zone of bright light lies a perfect hiding place, made invisible to us by our eyes' inability to see well after adapting to glare.

Across the countryside, residential high-wattage security lights shine far beyond one property boundary into neighbors' yards and windows. This *light trespass* pierces sleep and strains relations. It also wastes a tremendous amount of energy, as outdated fixtures and oversized bulbs continue to be sold when they should be replaced with energy-efficient, thoughtfully designed and appropriately sized products.

Worldwide, artificial nighttime light harms and kills insects, amphibians, birds and mammals. Moths instinctively circling a light may become too exhausted to mate or migrate, or their navigation and flight may be disrupted. Bats that prey on these defenseless moths may unnaturally displace other faster-flying bat species. Frogs and salamanders temporarily blinded by light cannot see prey, while they themselves become vulnerable to predators aided by the light. Thousands of migrating birds (including several species of songbirds) that often fly at night and at low altitudes become disoriented and collide with communications towers and tall buildings. In these several ways, and in many more that we don't fully understand, artificial light disrupts the functioning of natural ecosystems and damages environment.

THE SOLUTION

We need to pay attention to lighting in more appropriate ways. Landscape lighting should put light where it's needed, when it's needed and with the least amount of waste. Ideally, this means not blazing constantly across empty pavement, not glaring disruptively into natural areas, not shining into a neighbor's yard or window, not beaming up into the sky. What really matters is not how bright a space is, but rather how well people in that space can see.

CHAPTER 21

Lighting with Energy in Mind

THIS CHAPTER PRESENTS ACTIONS for lighting our landscapes as efficiently as possible. Of course, not every landscape *needs* outdoor lights, and skipping them altogether will save the most energy. But if you choose to install lights outdoors, either for security or pleasure, the ideas in this chapter can be applied in any landscape. These include the following Actions:

+ Use the right energy source for the job.
+ Arrange electrical circuits to allow maximum control.
+ Install various kinds of controls.
+ Use the most appropriate light bulb.
+ Point lights downward, not at the sky.
+ Clean and maintain light fixtures.

ACTION:
Use the Right Energy Source for the Job

There are three basic options for powering your outdoor lighting: line voltage, low-voltage and solar power. Your choice depends on where your lights are (or will be) located and what you want them to do. To save energy, choose the power source most suited to the job.

Design Tip: Line Voltage

For lights that need to be very bright, especially for safety or security, the best power is likely to be the 120-volt AC current, called line voltage that's supplied by your electric company. Wires in the building carry this current to various outlets and switches, and these wires can also be arranged to power outdoor light fixtures.

241

Using line voltage for outdoor lighting has the advantage of its inherent strength, along with great familiarity for professional installers, an abundance and wide variety of available fixtures and well-established standards governing the performance of those fixtures. Circuits for lighting have an upper limit of 20 amps, but this is enough power for about 2,000 watts, which should be plenty for most landscape lighting.

Line voltage does, however, involve some constraints with regard to outdoor lighting. All wires must be buried at least 24 inches deep or placed in a protective conduit; both solutions require careful planning, and the wires are difficult to relocate once in place. All fixtures must be completely waterproof, to prevent shock and short-circuits. And finally, the amount of light produced by line-voltage fixtures may be brighter than absolutely necessary. Since the power supply itself imposes no limits, homeowners may tend to be less careful in their bulb choices than would be ideal for efficiency.

Fig. 21.1: A simple design found in many home landscapes, this low-voltage fixture puts light just where it's needed: on the path.

Design Tip: Low-voltage Power

Low-voltage power is very easy to use and is appropriate in residential settings, where lighting requirements are generally less intense than in large-scale commercial, institutional or urban situations. Low-voltage systems reduce your house's 120-volt power to 12-volt power. This is made possible by plugging a *transformer* into an existing outdoor receptacle (outlet). For homeowners living off the grid, or for homes in remote locations, low-voltage systems may also be powered by solar panels or wind generators, with electricity stored in DC battery banks.

Low-voltage (L-V) lighting has several benefits over line-voltage lighting. Perhaps the greatest advantage is its extreme ease of installation. Most systems can be installed by homeowners using the instructions provided, along with basic common sense and reasonable attention to detail. In addition, L-V fixtures can accommodate either incandescent or halogen bulbs.

L-V wires can be buried in a shallow trench (National Electrical Code specifies six inches minimum depth) and are safe to operate even

What Size Transformer Should You Use?

Transformers come in a range of sizes, with varying wattage ratings available to handle different lighting loads. To figure out the right size for your system, lay out your planned lighting arrangement and add up the wattages of all the lamps you intend to use. Choose a transformer with a capacity as close as possible to that total, but in no case should it be less. If your wattage is too high, divide the load between two transformers, or select a more powerful transformer. Also, the total wattage should not be less than one-third of the transformer's wattage rating.

when exposed to moisture; this allows for great flexibility in planning and layout. The 12-volt wires are completely safe and hold no risk of shock if accidentally touched or cut. In general, low-voltage lamps are a lower wattage than would be used with line voltage, allowing several separate fixtures and more precise lighting effects, or just a more economical use of light in the landscape.

The primary disadvantage of low-voltage lighting is the potential voltage drop (causing dimmed lights) if too much demand is placed on any given system. This can be prevented by making sure individual cable runs aren't too long and by using heavier gauge wire.

Design Tip: Solar-powered Lights

The concept of solar lighting is simple: put a solar collector on or near a light in a position to receive sunlight, put a rechargeable battery inside the fixture and the light will be powered at night by stored solar energy. It costs nothing to operate!

Solar-powered lighting technology is growing fast, and hundreds of companies are keeping pace by offering countless new products and services. Most modern solar light systems have become extremely efficient due to the development of the Light Emitting Diode (LED, see page 250). This type of light bulb converts power into lumens so efficiently that even small amounts of stored solar energy can keep an LED light shining for many hours. Most new LED bulbs last over ten hours on a full charge and have a lifetime of about ten years.

Solar lighting systems are easy to set up and easy to move. The disadvantages of using solar

lighting are that the solar panels need to be placed in a sunny location (at least six to eight hours of exposure), the lights gradually dim as the charge runs out, and they don't work very well after a cloudy day. For these reasons, solar lighting is most appropriate in situations that don't require full bright lights all night.

ACTION: Arrange Electrical Circuits to Allow Maximum Control

The easiest way to save lighting energy and minimize light pollution is simply to make sure we turn lights on only when they're needed and turn them off when they're not. (See Sidebar on page 251, When Should You Turn off Your Lights?) To save the most energy, you should be able to turn on only the specific lights you need. Lighting your front porch shouldn't also mean illuminating the whole driveway. Using

Fig. 21.2: *While this solar-powered light does keep light from shining upward, its design may make it more effective as a landscape ornament than as a fixture that illuminates the walkway beside it.*

your patio, deck or pool at night shouldn't also require lighting your entry path. You get the idea. Whatever your situation, the layout of circuits in your house can significantly influence how easy or hard it is for you to light only certain areas and not others.

A Review of Electrical Circuits

Electrical power, or current, flows into a building through a meter that measures usage, then to a panel that distributes it throughout the building. The current is carried, in the form of flowing electrons, through wires arranged in circuits, which connect to outlets and switches and return to the panel.

Electrical switches may take several different forms (toggle, push-button, selector, lever, etc.), but whatever its form, when a switch is turned on, electrical conductors — wires — are brought into contact with each other, allowing current to flow past the switch, to power lights and appliances, then return to the wire and complete its circuit. When a switch is turned off, that contact is broken and current stops.

Most circuits provide current to several different outlets and switches in a building, up to a certain limit determined by voltage, wire size and other technical considerations. These circuits are laid out during new construction, but

they can be changed or augmented during house renovations or to meet new needs. Determining the best layout for your circuits is the responsibility of your electrical contractor. Your job, as an energy-conscious homeowner, is to specify that outdoor lighting switches be intentionally designed to let you control a single light, or small groups of lights, rather than lighting several areas from one switch.

ACTION:
Install Various Kinds of Controls

We lead busy lives. Few of us are always available to turn lights on or off when we should, and even if we are in the right place at the right time, we may forget or not notice we've left lights on. To help save energy in these situations, it makes sense to install a device that can automatically turn lights on and off as needed.

Design Tip: Motion Detectors

A motion detector measures optical or acoustical changes caused by movement in the field of view and transforms this detection into an electronic signal that may be used to switch on a light or sound an alarm. Motion detectors allow a portion of the landscape — the driveway, entry path, sidewalk, porch, etc. — to be lit only when someone is approaching, leaving that space dark the rest of the time.

For the purpose of home security, motion sensor lighting is far more effective than leaving a light on all night. Security professionals have learned that motion sensors actually reduce crime, because the sudden illumination of a previously dark area attracts much more attention to that place than happens with simple movement within an area that's constantly lit. Some motion detectors can be set to activate not just a conventional light but also a rapidly flashing strobe light. Would-be intruders are both surprised and disoriented, and attention is drawn to the area from blocks or even miles around.

Three kinds of sensors are used in different motion detectors:

- Passive infrared (PIR) sensors that emit no energy and respond to body heat
- Ultrasonic sensors that emit extremely high-frequency sound pulses and measure their reflection off a moving object
- Microwave sensors that emit microwave pulses and measure their reflection from a moving object (as in police radar guns)

Some motion detectors combine two types of sensors, using the passive infrared that draws no energy as a first source of detection. Only when the PIR sensor is tripped does the second sensor activate a more accurate signal. Most residential motion detectors are of the passive infrared type, with programmable settings to provide immunity for pets (or children) up to 80 pounds.

The motion detector industry is constantly improving its products to make them more versatile and effective. New detectors contain optics that respond to motion both near and far from the unit and microprocessors that self-test the system, cover multiple zones and distinguish subtle differences in signals to reduce the number of false alarms. Also, many companies provide whole-house controls that can be programmed to meet an infinite variety of

schedules, and many of these require no line-voltage wiring but instead are controlled wirelessly or with lightweight computer wiring.

Design Tip: Install Photo-sensors

Photo-sensors save energy by turning outdoor lights on and off in response to changes in ambient light conditions. This prevents lights from staying on all day when they're not needed and is especially useful in places where no one is present to operate them manually.

Photo-sensors contain a light-sensitive photocell, optics, an electrical circuit to convert the photocell signal to an output signal and a housing. They are usually quite small and varied in shape, ranging from about the diameter of a golf ball to the size of a standard light switch. Since photo-sensors are frequently used for interior lighting, the product selection for this purpose is vast. Many of these simple devices come with do-it-yourself installation instructions; some may be solar-powered.

Fig. 21.3:
Modern security lights, many of them triggered by motion- or photo-sensors, are designed to be tiltable rather than fixed in place, to minimize glare and sky-lighting.

Design Tip: Timers

Like motion detectors and photo-sensors, timers help us reduce unnecessary lighting. These simple mechanisms can be set to turn lights on at dusk and off at dawn, and they're particularly useful in situations where nighttime lighting may be overlooked or forgotten and then remain on all day.

As with motion detectors and photo-sensors, timers are available in a wide array of styles for a wide variety of purposes. Many simple plug-in devices are used with aquariums, grow lights and, most commonly, to create the illusion that a house is occupied when people are on vacation or away from home for an extended period.

Timers that control low-voltage outdoor lighting may be simple units that are plugged into the system's transformer (see low-voltage discussion above). These outdoor devices may also contain photo-sensors that turn lights on for different lengths of time throughout the year as days lengthen and shorten.

For lights that are powered by standard house current, a professional electrician must install a timer in the circuit that serves them. In these situations, the timer will be placed in a convenient location, often near the circuit panel if possible. Some devices are designed to fit invisibly inside the switch box in the wall, replacing the switch itself.

ACTION:
Use the Most Appropriate Light Bulb

When most of us think about light bulbs, the term that frequently comes to mind is "watt," such as in a 60-watt bulb and 200-watt floodlight. But to find the most appropriate type and size of bulb for a certain job, watts don't tell the whole story. A bulb's brightness is the result of several factors: its design, its condition and age and its inherent ability to transform energy into visible light. Yes, a 100-watt bulb is brighter than a 60-watt bulb, but watts just tell us how much power is being used. The bulb's brightness, the light we can actually see, is measured in *lumens*.

To really understand lumens, we need to look all the way back to fire and the first unit of light measurement, the *foot-candle*. One foot-candle is the amount of light generated by a candle flame when observed by a viewer one foot away from it. (For total accuracy, the candle in question must contain exactly 0.167 troy pounds of whale blubber and be of a consistency thick enough to burn at a specific rate for exactly eight hours …. but who's counting?) A lumen is a measurement of light equal to *the light of one foot-candle falling on one square foot of area*. You can probably imagine a single lumen: picture young Abe Lincoln in his log cabin, eagerly reading *Aesop's Fables* by the light of one dim candle.

Bulb or Lamp?

To lighting engineers and electricians, the actual light-producing part of a light fixture is called a *lamp* while the term *bulb* refers only to the glass or plastic housing for the lamp. To most of the rest of us, the word "bulb" means the entire unit, whatever its shape or size, and whatever sort of light it produces. (And "lamps" are those things that stand on a table that we switch on when entering a room.) In line with common parlance, this book generally uses the term "bulb" to mean the whole light-producing object.

Design Tip: Choose Efficient Bulbs

One of the best ways to save energy and money is to use bulbs that put out the most light for the least input of power. This efficiency is measured in *lumens per watt*. A standard 60-watt incandescent bulb gives about 800 lumens of visible light. You could get those same 800 lumens of light from one 13-watt compact fluorescent light bulb. Compact fluorescent bulbs are clearly more efficient than incandescent bulbs; 60 watts vs. 13 watts used to produce the same amount of light. This is why Vice President Al Gore ended his Nobel Prize winning movie, *An Inconvenient Truth*, by flatly stating that the one thing we should all do is convert our incandescent bulbs to fluorescents.

Fluorescent bulbs, however, aren't necessarily the best solution in every situation. Other bulbs are even more efficient than fluorescents, and you should consider additional factors when making the choice for greatest efficiency and appropriateness.

Design Tip:
Choose Bulbs with a Long Lifetime

Thomas Edison didn't exactly invent the light bulb. What he did instead was improve upon an existing idea for creating light, and then he devised several essential new components that made incandescent bulbs practical, affordable and safe. Together these inventions led to making the humble light bulb an essential part of our everyday lives (while also making Edison rich and famous).

While they are undoubtedly a monumental invention, sadly, incandescent light bulbs have never been efficient. They create light by heating a filament until it's so hot (about 4,500° F) that it glows. Since the purpose of the bulb is to create light, the heat is essentially wasted. And because they're so hot, the bulb filaments rather quickly burn out. (Actually the tungsten in the filaments gradually evaporates, making thin spots in the filaments that eventually break.)

Since the early 1900s, lighting engineers have strived to develop bulbs (or rather, "lamps") with higher levels of efficiency and longer lifetimes. The table below compares various lamp efficiencies and lifetimes. The most efficient lamps are variations on the concept used in fluorescent bulbs, in which light is produced by passing an electrical current through a gas in some sort of tube. One exception to this rule is the most recently developed idea, the light-emitting diode (LED), which uses an entirely different technology. All the lamps on this list are described later in greater detail.

How Much Light Do You Need?

The amount of lighting appropriate for various purposes is subjective, and also quite complex. It depends on many factors, including how much daylight is available, the color of surrounding objects or structures, the viewer's distance from the source and even the age of the viewer's eyes. However, as a rule of thumb, when selecting bulbs, choose the size that will give:

- for low light: 10 to 20 lumens per square foot of area being lit
- for ordinary tasks: 30 to 50 lumens per square foot of area being lit
- for reading or fine work: 50 to 100 lumens per square foot of area being lit

Light bulb packaging states the amount of lumens delivered by an individual bulb. Keep in mind that all light fixtures have a maximum size of bulb (watts) they can safely accommodate.

Lumens and Lamp Life of Various Lamps		
Type of Lamp	Lumens per Watt	Avg. Lamp Life (hrs.)
Incandescent	8–25	700–1,000
Halogen	12–36	2,000–4,000
Fluorescent (compact)	44–80	6,000–10,000
Fluorescent (tubular)	33–100	10,000–20,000
Mercury Vapor	20–60	1,600–6,000
Metal Halide	60–125	6,000–10,000
High Pressure Sodium	45–110	12,000–24,000
Low Pressure Sodium	80–180	10,000–18,000
Light-emitting Diode (LED)	60–130	30,000–50,000

These comparative figures are approximate. Exact specifications depend on complex factors involving voltage, temperature and various details of manufacture.[1]

Design Tip:
Use the Bulbs Most Suited to the Job

Some kinds of bulbs are best-suited for industry and urban lighting. Many very efficient bulbs are also suitable for use inside and outside the

Fig. 21.4:

This contemporary light employs reflective glass above a halogen bulb, to maximize both down-lighting and energy-efficiency.

house. In addition to efficiency and lifetime, factors to consider in choosing the most appropriate type of bulb for various purposes include heat generation, cost of bulb, color of light and method of disposal. There is no single type of bulb that's perfect for every situation.

Incandescent Bulbs

The most common bulb in use in most homes, the incandescent bulb is the least efficient light source available. Only about ten percent of the energy it uses goes into producing light. This bulb's great advantages are that it is currently the cheapest bulb available, it produces a pleasing warm-tone light that is very familiar and appealing to most people, and it is easy to dispose of in any landfill. Its disadvantages include its extreme inefficiency (though a dimmer switch can save some energy), a short lifespan and its heat, which means it must be used with care near any flammable material.

Halogen Bulbs

Like incandescent bulbs, halogens use a tungsten filament enclosed in an outer casing. However, inside this casing is a gas, which at high temperatures will combine with tungsten atoms as they evaporate from the hot filament. These atoms are then redeposited on the filament instead of accumulating on the surrounding glass, so the halogen bulb filaments last much longer and can be run at much higher temperatures, making the bulbs more efficient. Halogen bulbs are smaller than incandescent bulbs and are encased in quartz envelopes instead of glass.

Their advantages include bright white light and high efficiency. Their greatest disadvantage is extremely high heat, so they should never be operated in small spaces, and the bulbs shouldn't be turned on when near any objects.

Fluorescent Bulbs

Whether tubular or compact, fluorescent bulbs produce light by passing energy through gas in a tube. They require a *ballast* to start and run the lamp at the correct voltage and current levels. Fluorescent bulbs are substantially more efficient than incandescent bulbs, they're available in a variety of colors, and they operate at a cool temperature, making them safe in a wide variety of situations. Their disadvantages include the fact that they're generally not dimmable (unless specifically designed for that purpose), their fixtures may be costly (due to the ballast), they have a tendency to flicker (especially as they age), and their efficiency declines with frequent switching on and off.

Older fluorescent bulbs contain small amounts of mercury gas in the tubes and other toxic materials (including PCBs) in the ballast. These units must be disposed of in a hazardous waste management facility. The ballasts of newer fluorescents are electronic and so contain no toxic chemicals.

High-intensity Discharge (HID) Lamps

The following four types of bulbs produce light by causing energy to flow through pressurized gas in a glass casing. They all need to be disposed of with great care, though for differing reasons. Please check packaging materials for guidance about their disposal.

Mercury Vapor: Often used for security lighting, these bulbs have the lowest efficiency of the HID-type lamps. They are, however, more efficient than incandescent and halogen bulbs, they have a long life, and they're frequently sold in home-security lighting products. Their main disadvantage is their distinctly blue-green light, and that they're often sold in poorly designed fixtures that produce a lot of glare.

Metal Halide: These bulbs are twice as efficient as mercury vapor. The whitest of the white light sources, they are the best choice for accurate color rendering. Their drawbacks are the high cost of both the bulb and its fixture and their very hot operating temperature.

High Pressure Sodium: Widely used for street lighting and parking lots, these bulbs have a long lifetime and are more efficient than metal halide, but their output is a distinctly

Fig. 21.5: *Replacing an incandescent bulb with a fluorescent one in this traditional globe light may save a small amount of energy, but the fixture itself wastes light by shining it upward. (Plus, the fluorescent bulb in this situation insults the original design intent, and simply looks rather sad.)*

pinkish-orange-gold color. Some lighting engineers claim that the way they distort color actually makes people feel uncomfortable and less secure.

Low Pressure Sodium: These are among the most efficient HID lamps available, and they have a long lifespan. They have a low-intensity discharge source and a linear lamp shape, so they emit a soft luminous glow that reduces glare. LPS bulbs cast a yellow light that renders most colors at night in black, white and shades of gray, making them a poor choice for creating attractive visual effects in the landscape.

Light Emitting Diodes (LEDs)

The newest lighting product on the market, LEDs are little light bulbs illuminated by the movement of electrons in a semiconductor. Originally, when they weren't bright enough for actual lighting, they were used primarily as

Fig. 21.6: Because LED bulbs are so small, their light fixtures can also be quite compact; because LED's are so efficient, they operate easily on solar power alone. This simple 3-inch round unit is mounted on a 12-inch pipe that can be inserted into the ground anywhere it's needed.

on-off indicators in TVs, telephones, calculators, etc. Recently, however, their technology has advanced so far that LEDs are now bright, efficient and reliable enough to be used for many purposes, including outdoor lighting.

The advantages of LEDs are many. In addition to being one of the most efficient bulbs available, they have an exceptionally long life, are extremely resistant to damage and are ideal in situations that involve frequent on-off cycling. They fit standard fixtures and can replace incandescent or halogen bulbs. LED light is close to the color of daylight, which is both relaxing and helps people stay alert, but they are also available in many colors. LEDs give off directional light, so light goes only where it's aimed, reducing light pollution. They light up quickly, don't get hot and fail very gradually instead of burning out abruptly. They contain no gas or hazardous materials.

The primary disadvantage of LED bulbs is their initial purchase cost. However, when the lifetime cost is considered, they actually surpass incandescent and halogen sources and are even beginning to be competitively priced with compact fluorescents. Other disadvantages include the bulb's quirkiness when operating in extreme temperatures, their specific voltage requirements and the possibility that some intensities of light may exceed safe limits.

ACTION:
Point Light Downward, Not at the Sky

Lights that shine up into the night sky cause a form of light pollution called *sky glow*. This phenomenon reduces our view of the night sky and diminishes our pleasure in (and perhaps biological need for) darkness. It also seriously compromises astronomical observations. More serious than this, though, is that sky glow wastes both light and the energy spent to create light.

Design Tip: Use Full Cut-off Fixtures

Fortunately, there's an easy solution to light pollution. The key is to use only fixtures that are designed to direct light downward. Not sideways, and never upward. These fixtures are called *full cut-off* or *full shut-off*. When in use, no light is allowed to leak out above the nadir, or horizontal plane of the fixture. Generally this means that the bulb, whatever its shape or size, is tucked up inside a hood, shield or cover. Some full cut-off fixtures direct light only downward, in a cone of varying size, and in some the light is further enhanced and directed with reflectors inside the shield.

Particularly wasteful types of fixtures are unshaded floodlights or bulbs of any kind, globe lights, barn lights, the common security wall packs sold by many home supply stores, and the ubiquitous drop-lens cobra-head street light. All of these fixtures direct light where it's not needed, and some of them produce so much glare (extreme contrast between light and dark) that they actually fail to improve overall visibility and security.

Many styles of full cut-off fixtures are now available, and the variety is growing steadily in response to demand. Cobra-head fixtures are being redesigned with recessed bulbs; security lights are made with Hubbell Skycap hoods; streetlights are tucked into flat-lens shoebox-shaped fixtures; wall packs can now be purchased

Fig. 21.7:
This full cut-off light fixture does its job exceedingly well: it illuminates the entry post at night, without sending wasted light upward, and the lamp itself looks beautiful by day.

BARBARA KEENE/RICHARD BURCK ASSOCIATES

When Should You Turn Off Your Lights?

All types of bulbs have an expected operating life that is affected by the number of times they are turned on and off. Incandescent bulbs, because they are inefficient to begin with, hot to operate and inexpensive to replace, should be turned off whenever they're not needed. By contrast, the efficiency of turning off fluorescent bulbs is a bit more complex. Although their operating life is strongly affected by being turned on and off, they require a slightly higher amount of energy to start up, and they're relatively expensive to replace, so frequently turning them on and off may shorten their lifetime enough that it saves neither energy nor money. As a rule of thumb, turn fluorescent lights off only when they won't be needed for at least 15 minutes. When an off period is expected to be shorter than 15 minutes, leave them on. In any case, even when frequently turned on and off, fluorescent bulbs are still more efficient than incandescents.

as shaded sconces; canister lights illuminate the underside of eaves and porches. We simply need to ask our lighting suppliers for fixtures that cause no light pollution; the ability exists to create them, and soon the motivation will exist as well.

ACTION:
Clean and Maintain Light Fixtures

Maintenance is vital to lighting efficiency. Aging lamps and dirt on fixtures and bulbs can reduce total illumination by 50 percent or more, while these lights continue to draw full power. To get the most out of your lights, follow these maintenance suggestions, provided by the US Department of Energy's Office of Energy Efficiency and Renewable Energy:[3]

Lighting Codes, Ordinances and Standards

Many communities are actively involved in implementing new programs to keep light from shining pointlessly into the night sky. This is especially important in any area near an astronomy observatory. The biggest problem in controlling light pollution is generally the public's lack of awareness, so it's important to educate our elected officials as well as our neighbors about the problem of light pollution. Most people respond positively once they understand the problem.

For more information about light pollution, or to help change lighting policies in your region, contact (or join) the International Dark Sky Association in Tucson, Arizona.[2]

- Clean fixtures, lamps and lenses every 6 to 24 months by wiping off the dust. However, never clean an incandescent bulb while it is turned on because the water's cooling effect will shatter the bulb.

- Replace lenses if they appear yellow.

- Consider replacing lamps in groups. Common lamps, especially incandescent and fluorescent lamps, lose 20 to 30 percent of their light output over their service life. Many lighting experts recommend replacing all the lamps in a lighting system at the same time. This saves labor, keeps illumination high and avoids stressing ballasts with dying lamps.

CHAPTER SUMMARY

We can save a significant amount of electricity simply by making sure our outdoor lighting systems are designed to be as efficient as possible. This involves making informed choices about every element of the lighting system: we should use the appropriate type of power supply, we should arrange circuits and controls to make sure lights are turned on only when they're needed, and we should choose the most suitable bulbs for every type of lighting job. Finally, this chapter explains the importance of selecting fixtures that direct light only toward the space that needs to be lit, downward toward the ground rather than upward into the night sky.

Conclusion

THIS BOOK IS BASED ON three fundamental ideas. First, no matter where we live, our home landscapes are full of opportunities for conserving energy. This might involve: using less fuel directly, in everyday activities; or building things so they last a long time and rarely need maintenance or replacement; or choosing materials with the least embedded energy costs. In many cases, it could even involve all of these actions.

Second, every homeowner can take at least a few steps toward consuming less energy by intentionally designing and building landscapes with that goal in mind. From shading a house and cooling summer air, to welcoming winter sun and blocking cold wind...from mowing less lawn to using more of nature's free services...from terracing a hillside to harvesting rain...from planting trees properly to building stone walls that endure...from generating energy to lighting a driveway...every decision can be guided by this over-arching purpose: to use less fuel.

And finally, if some of us implement a few of the suggestions presented here, as individuals we'll save money, time and effort, and we'll also make a small contribution to a healthier world. Even better, if many of us everywhere implement several of this book's ideas, our actions will produce enormous savings and create a dramatically different world.

The main differences, of course, will be conservation of the planet's natural resources, an easing of our need to import or find other sources of oil and perhaps a change in the world's political balance. Another difference, one that's more subtle, less urgent and potentially much more controversial and emotionally charged, involves a shift in how our landscapes look.

Here it's time to say a few words about beauty. As a society, and maybe just because we're human, many of us try to make our surroundings aesthetically pleasing, to delight the eye and lift the spirit. But what, really, is this beautiful effect we're trying to achieve? It's certainly not one absolute unchanging thing. In 13th century Moorish gardens, beauty involved colonnades, mosaics, canals and pools of still water. Five hundred years ago, Italian Renaissance beauty required elaborate fountains, sculpture and ornate balustrades. Around the same time in France, highly manicured hedges and vast geometric gardens were considered beautiful. Then in the 19th century, landscape aesthetics shifted to value the bucolic greenswards and majestic trees of English estates. Does this last image sound familiar? If so, it's because this 200-year-old ideal of landscape beauty, this "prestige aesthetic," persists even now in the minds of 21st century Americans.

All of us act, both consciously and unconsciously, in accord with the political, economic and social currents that surround us. We choose our cars, houses and clothes based on the conventions of our time and place. The same is true for our landscapes: they reflect the values of we who create them. This discussion is not meant to be a treatise on beauty, value judgments or the complexity of human perception. That would require a much different book. Rather, it's a reminder that just as people change, and social norms change, so too can our landscapes change.

In the face of current economic and cultural realities, isn't it time for us to update our ideas about what makes a landscape attractive? Everyone knows that beauty is not just in the eye of the beholder, that it's also in the *mind* of the beholder. Might we imagine a new notion, one in which beauty is more than a pretty picture? Can we aim to do more than imitate a magazine image, a neighborhood standard or a centuries-old convention? Is it possible for us to create something entirely new, that's an expression of our values now?

The book describes how to design for energy efficiency in any type of landscape, regardless of its size, shape, location or style. Almost all of the book's ideas can be applied even in the most traditional sort of landscapes, where the main ingredients are open lawn, single trees growing here and there and tidy beds of favorite plants. However, many of the suggestions presented here tilt toward a slightly different look, so that even while a landscape is well tended and cared for, its overall appearance becomes a bit more loose and relaxed, less about effect and more about effectiveness.

Instead of trees standing alone in lawn, imagine them in groves, growing close together as they do in a forest, in rich soil that's constantly replenished by the rain of falling leaves.

Picture garden beds where plants intertwine instead of standing in isolated clumps, where the ground is shaded by overhanging foliage and mulch is a sponge that keeps the ground cool and moist.

Think about filling our landscapes with plants that simultaneously serve the natural world *and* our own gratification, so a million invisible interactions are keeping whole ecosystems healthy while we also get to watch and delight in the show, without needing any ultra double blooms, two-tone leaves or extreme peeling bark.

Consider the unexpected beauty of graceful meadow grasses and flowers rippling in the breeze. Or front yards full of fruit trees and vegetable gardens. And what about a solar array as garden sculpture? How about orienting a house toward the sun instead of lining it up with the road?

It's time for us to dream a new idea of home, one in which beauty is not just a conventional norm or a familiar picture, but also an expression of our social values. Now in the 21st century, we can shape our landscapes so that, in addition to looking attractive, they will work for our own good and the good of the larger world.

Energy efficiency is a major part of that goal, an important new reality and responsibility that all of us share. This book provides hundreds of ways to purposely design our landscapes so they save energy. Its main message is simply this: before taking any step in our landscapes (where many things will cost a lot of money, last a very long time and be expensive to undo), get informed about the energy your action will consume, both now and in the future. Slow down, think about the options, understand the underlying purpose and implications of every choice, keep an open mind and weigh the pros and cons of each possibility. Then, based on your own best judgment, implement the ideas that make the most sense in your own situation, according to your own budget, tastes and lifestyle.

This book aims to teach and inspire, to encourage and reassure and to nudge us all toward a new understanding. Every property — no matter how casual or ornate, simple or complex, modest or grand — is a place where we can save energy and contribute to a better world *while also* satisfying our own dreams and ideals. I wish you all the best of success in this new approach to designing and caring for your home landscape.

APPENDIX A: Details and Calculations

THIS APPENDIX CONTAINS INSTRUCTIONS for finding (or figuring out) additional information that will help in more detailed planning of your landscape. Specifically, this knowledge is for readers who want to go beyond the basic guidelines and Actions explained in the text, and/or those who live in regions other than the 40° latitude covered in this book. The following subjects are covered here:

+ Finding true north
+ Knowing your latitude
+ Figuring out the height of a tree
+ Calculating shadow lengths
+ Finding the direction a shadow will fall
+ Reading a solar path diagram
+ Determining slope

FINDING TRUE NORTH

Most of us know that a compass works by letting a magnetized needle rotate in response to the magnetic pull of the Earth's poles. What many don't realize, though, is that these poles are skewed slightly off center and don't exactly line up with the north-south axis of the planet. So what does this mean?

First, because a compass needle responds to magnetism, it points toward a direction called *magnetic north*, which is different from *true north* by an amount called the *magnetic declination*. Declination varies depending on geographic location and actually shifts gradually over time. Within the continental US, it ranges from 0° near the center of the country to about 20° in the upper northeast and northwest.

Second, as a result of declination, if you're trying to find north for the purpose of designing with the sun, the information on a compass may not correspond to what the sun is actually doing. For example, at noon the sun always shines from due south (except in the southern hemisphere), but your compass needle might point in a slightly different direction at that time, depending on where you live.

If you're building a house or planting trees for energy efficiency, it probably pays to know the location of true north and south. Of course, much of what we do in our landscapes doesn't require absolute precision: even solar arrays can be off by five degrees or so without causing a noticeable loss in solar gain. But if you live in a place where declinations are greater than five to ten degrees, this can make a big difference in the success of your plans.

You can find your own declination at a number of websites, including the National Geophysical Data Center (ngdc.noaa.gov). Click on Geomagnetic Data and Models, then go to Declination. Then, if you want to use your compass to find north, you'll have to adjust for this declination, by either rotating a movable ring on the compass or by simply correcting each reading the appropriate amount.

This process may be necessary when hiking or using a map to find your way, but in your own landscape, there's an alternative non-technical way to identify the direction of true north. Just use the stars as your guide, as follows.

- Find the North Star. If you don't know where it is, find the Big Dipper in the sky and draw an imaginary line between the two stars of its outer edge. Then extend that line outward (in the direction that liquid would pour out of the dipper) until you see a star that seems to be standing alone. This is the North Star, the last star in the handle of the Little Dipper.
- Choose a point in the landscape that lets you sight toward the North Star. You can use a fence post or drive a stake into the ground.
- Have a friend take a second stake and walk toward the North Star. Ten or 20 or 30 feet out, have him or her, at your direction, drive that stake into the ground at a point *on the line you're sighting*, the line between you and the North Star. If you tie a string or draw a line between these two stakes, this will represent an accurate north-south direction.

KNOWING YOUR LATITUDE

Shadows are created by objects of various heights blocking the sun's rays. If your aim is to design your landscape so that trees will cast shadows where you want them, and no trees will cast shadows where you don't want them, you'll need to know two basic pieces of information: the length of shadow cast by trees (or structures) in your landscape; and the direction in which those shadows are cast.

Both of these facts are affected by the position of the sun, which itself is entirely dependent on your latitude. You can find your own latitude (and longitude) by using various online services, including GoogleEarth, GoogleMaps, TerraServer, or perhaps even by checking your car's GPS unit. NASA provides a useful website for this purpose (mynasadata.larc.nasa.gov).

CALCULATING TREE HEIGHT

Combined with the position of the sun, the height of an object determines the length of its shadow. One easy way to find the height of a tree is to create a ratio between the shadow cast by the tall thing that you *can't* measure directly and the shadow cast by a short thing that you *can* measure directly. You'll need a measuring tape (or some other way to measure), a stick at least three to five feet long, a sunny day and generally level ground beside whatever object needs to be measured.

It's also desirable, though not necessary, to have an assistant to help with the measuring while the sun is still in one position. A calculator may also be needed, to make the results as accurate as possible. Units of measurement don't matter, as long as the same units are used throughout. Follow these steps, taking care to be precise:

1. Choose a time of day when the shadow of the tree is falling on level ground. Close to midday may be easiest, as this is when shadows are shortest, but level ground is more important.

2. Drive the stick into the ground, in a place where its shadow also falls on level ground and you can see it (not in the shade of the tree), then measure its height from the ground up to its top.

3. Measure the length of the shadow cast by the stick.

4. Measure the length of the tree's shadow, from the base of the trunk to the tip of the treetop.

5. Multiply the length of the tree's shadow by the height of the stick, then divide this number by the length of the stick's shadow. The result is the height of the tree or tall object. If you're mathematically savvy, you'll see that this derives from the equation: tree shadow/tree height = stick shadow/stick height.

CALCULATING SHADOW LENGTH

In order to know specifically where shadows will fall, on your house and in your landscape, you'll need to know the length of shadows being cast by objects of various heights at various times of day throughout the year. This information derives from the height of the object, as described above, and the *altitude* (or height) of the sun above the horizon. The sun's altitude, at any particular time of day, can be found by reading a "solar path diagram" (described below) or by visiting any of various websites and following their detailed directions.

One accurate source is the US Naval Observatory website (usno.navy.mil/USNO). Go to Astronomical Applications, then Data Services, and then find Position of Selected Celestial Objects (listed under More). Choose Altitude and Azimuth of the Sun or Moon, enter the name of your city or town and the date you're interested in, click Compute Table, and you will be given a chart that shows the sun's altitude at every hour of that day. This chart also provides information that will come in handy in the next step, so keep the Web page handy.

Once you know the altitude of the sun at the times of day when you want to know more about shadows, you could, if you're adventurous, perform some trigonometric calculations to find exact shadow lengths, using the formula: shadow length = height of the object ÷ tangent of the altitude angle. Or, more simply, you can plug this information into various "shadow calculator" websites that will compute them. A particularly easy website is one designed for public schools, the Sandburg Center for Sky Awareness, in Fairfax County, VA (wsanford.com/~wsanford/shadow_ length.html).

FINDING A SHADOW'S DIRECTION

After determining the length of a tree's shadow at any particular time of day, you'll need to discover precisely where it falls in the landscape. Go back to the USNO website mentioned in the previous step, and find the sun's *azimuth* (or direction relative to north) during the hour of the day when you're trying to find out more about shadows.

Then, take a compass, hold or place it beside the tree or object in question and line it up with true north (see above for guidance about adjusting for declination). Read on the compass the angle that corresponds to the sun's azimuth and project a line out in that direction.

Using a tape measure, mark off the length of the shadow (determined in the previous step). And remember that although shadow *length* varies depending on the height of an object, the *direction* of a shadow is the same for every object (at any hour of the day).

READING A SOLAR PATH DIAGRAM

Because the sun's passage across the sky is consistent from year to year, scientists have devised ways to accurately depict (and predict) its position. Various software programs help designers and engineers determine this information, and some of them may be useful to non-professionals. A low-tech (and free) way to figure out the sun's location is to use a "solar path diagram," which projects the dome of the sky onto a flat surface, then illustrates the sun's path across that dome, in every month of the year.

Below is an explanation of how to read a solar path diagram. The diagram in this example represents the sun's pattern at a geographic latitude of 40° north. Find the appropriate diagram for your own latitude by searching the Internet for solar- or sun-path diagrams. One of the simplest websites to use is www.luxal.eu/resources/daylighting/sunpath.shtml.

The notes below deconstruct the diagram into its four components and explains each part separate from the others. Then a final image shows all the components merged together.

Figure A-1: Concentric rings represent **altitude,** or the sun's height above the horizon. Each circle stands for 10° of altitude. Remember that this is a projection of the sky's dome onto a flat surface.

Fig. A-1

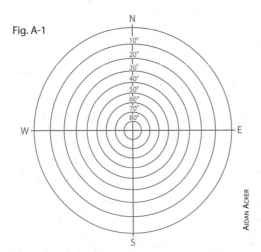

AIDAN ACKER

Figure A-2: Radiating lines represent **compass direction**, also know as *azimuth*, with each line indicating 10° on a compass (and north being 0°).

Figure A-3: Dashed, gently curved lines that fan across the diagram designate **hours of the day**, with the noon line being vertical (pointing north-south), morning hours on the right (east) and afternoon hours on the left (west). Remember that during Daylight Savings Time, from March to October, our clocks shift one hour ahead, so the sun is highest in the sky at 1 PM, not noon.

Figure A-4: The long curved lines that arc across the entire width of the diagram represent the **sun's path, on the 21st of each month**. The top line represents the summer solstice (June 21st in the northern hemisphere), and the bottom line is the winter solstice (December 21st). The five lines between these extremes each represent *two months*, in pairs that mirror their relationship to the solstices: May/July, April/August, March/September, February/October and January/November. Finally, in **Figure A-5,** all these lines are overlaid together, showing the sun's place in the sky at every moment of the year.

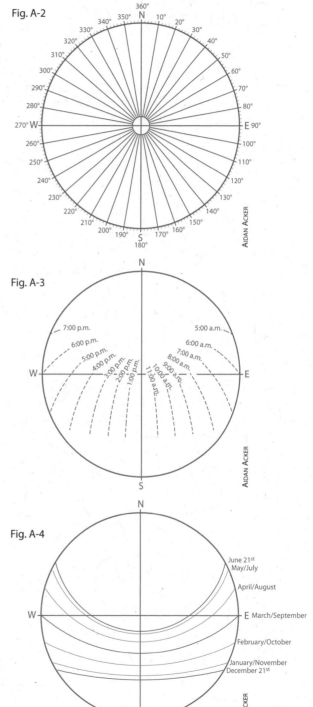

Fig. A-2

Fig. A-3

Fig. A-4

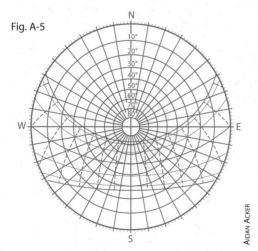

Fig. A-5

To read your own diagram, so you can obtain information about the sun's altitude and direction at any time of day throughout the year, follow these steps:

1. Decide on a particular **month** to be analyzed and find that month's line on the diagram.

2. Decide on a particular **hour** of day in that month when you want to know the sun's position and find that hour line.

3. Identify the **point where the month line and the hour line intersect.** Marking this point with a dot will be helpful as you move ahead.

4. Now, trying to ignore the month and hour lines, look through them to the concentric rings and radiating lines.

5. Find the **altitude** of the sun by locating your point's position within the altitude rings. Keep your eye clearly on the labels that identify these rings, distinct from any other component of the diagram. Your point will probably fall somewhere between two rings, for example not exactly on 30° or 40° but perhaps 32° or 35° or 38°.

6. Find the sun's **compass direction** in the same manner by finding your point's location within the radiating lines. Again, you may need to estimate the degree based on your point's position between two lines, i.e., not exactly 150° or 160° but perhaps 154° or 157°, etc.

As a demonstration, points marked on the diagram shown in Figure A-6 indicate the sun's position as follows:

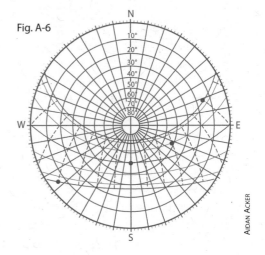

Fig. A-6

AIDAN ACKER

A: June, at 6 AM: altitude 15°, direction 72°

B: August and April, at 9 AM: altitude 42°, direction 113°

C: October and February, at noon: altitude 38°, direction 180° (due south)

D: December, at 4 PM: altitude 6°, direction 234°

Once you've determined the sun's altitude and direction, you can use this information to determine the length and location of shadows cast by various objects, as explained above.

DETERMINING SLOPE

As explained in the Information Box in Chapter 10 (page 115), *slope* is the amount that land rises vertically within a certain horizontal distance. In common terms, it's the relationship between *rise* and *run*. This ratio is often expressed in two different ways. Some people describe slope as a ratio, as 10:1, or ten to one. Others describe the very same slope as 1:10, or one in ten. To be absolutely clear about what is meant, it's a good idea to indicate which side of the ratio refers to the rise, and which to the run, as in 1v:10h (one vertical to ten horizontal).

A simpler way, the one used by landscape professionals, is to use percentages, which eliminate any confusion (the example above would be called a 10% slope). To find the percentage of a slope, divide the vertical rise by the horizontal distance and multiply by 100. This is the formula: $\% = V/H \times 100$.

How can you figure out the rise (vertical) and run (horizontal) of a slope? Chapter 19 describes three ways to measure the vertical, or height, of a slope (for calculating a stream's hydro potential). Each of these methods involves establishing some sort of level line (or line of sight) that extends out over the slope, then measuring the distance from the ground up to that level line. This method only works if the line is truly level, so be sure to use some sort of builder's level or string level; simply guessing by eye will not give a good result.

To calculate slope, you also need to measure the horizontal distance. Be sure to measure this along the level line, *not along the ground itself.*

Then follow the formula stated above. In Figure A-7, V= 4' and H=28.5', so percent = (4÷28.5) x 100, or 14%. Keep in mind that you must use the same units of measurement on both sides of the equation. If necessary, convert inches to feet by dividing your inch measurement by 12, Example: 27.5" = 2.3'.

Alternatively, if you have a topographic map of your site, you can calculate slope by using its contour lines, rather than by taking direct measurements on the ground. This method can be especially helpful on very large sites, or in places that you can't access. Bear in mind that most large-scale topographic maps are based on aerial photometry and therefore don't show small irregularities in terrain. A surveyed map of your property will be more accurate.

To calculate slope from a map, you'll need to know the *scale* of the map, i.e., the ratio between real-life measurements and the dimensions shown on the map. You'll also need to know its *contour interval*, the vertical change in elevation from one contour to the next. Both are usually indicated on the map, often in its legend. If the contour interval isn't defined, you may have to figure it out by reading the labels on the contour lines themselves.

Fig. A-7

To determine slope of any area, find the vertical difference (V) between the top and bottom of that slope by counting the contour lines between those points and then multiplying by the contour interval. Then, to find H, use a scale that matches the scale of the map and measure, on the map itself, the total distance between the top and bottom of the slope. Convert all figures to the same units (feet, meters, etc.), then plug them into the formula.

You can use this method to find the slope of one small section or very large areas. Keep in mind that the spacing of contour lines represents the degree of slope (contours close together represent steeper land than contours farther apart), so when contour spacing changes, this indicates a change in slope. If your measurements encompass many different kinds of contour spacing, your result will be an average of several individual slope percentages.

APPENDIX B: Plant Lists

THE TREES AND SHRUBS in the following lists may be planted in your landscape to provide shade or wind protection or both. They are native to various portions of the temperate US. However, because this book recommends that you garden with plants that are native to your own particular region (see Chapter 7 to be reminded about why), these lists should be just a starting point in your selection process. Information about the specific range of any species may be found at the USDA Plants Database website (www.plants.usda.gov).

These lists are not intended to be all-inclusive. Rather, they contain plants that are reasonably adaptable to domestic landscapes and relatively easy to grow. Many other local native plants may also meet your needs. Not shown here are any horticultural varieties or species that are native to other countries (although some of the plants listed here may also be native outside the US).

Plant hardiness zones worldwide appear to be shifting in response to climate change. Hardiness designations, therefore, are not included here. Be sure to check with a local nursery or other reliable source to discover whether a particular plant will tolerate the climate extremes in your region. Also, these lists provide only a basic description of each plant's physical characteristics and behavior. Before buying any tree or shrub, learn a bit more about its unique traits, by reading or visiting some of the resources listed in Appendix C. Keep in mind that mature heights and widths of plants will depend, of course, on actual growing conditions.

This information is derived in large part from Gary Hightshoe's delightfully clear and comprehensive book, *Native Trees, Shrubs and Vines for Urban and Rural America* (Van Nostrand Reinhold, 1988). Many of the observations about plants' physical characteristics have been further verified by the author.

TREES: Deciduous Trees Taller than 50 Feet

Common Name (Botanical name)	Growing Conditions	Appearance/Comments
Red Maple (*Acer rubrum*)	Sun to moderate shade; moist to average soil; prefers acid (pH 4.5-6.5).	50-75-foot-wide canopy; moderately dense branches; bright red fall color; medium to fast-growing.
Black Maple (*Acer nigrum*)	Very shade tolerant; moist to average soil; slightly acid to neutral (pH 6.0-7.5).	50-75-foot-wide canopy; very dense; orange fall color; medium to slow growth rate.
Sugar Maple (*Acer saccharum*)	Sun to deep shade; moist to average soil; needs slightly acid to neutral (pH 6.0-7.5).	50-75-foot-wide canopy; very dense; orange and red fall color; slow-growing.
Sweet Birch (*Betula lenta*)	Sun to moderate shade; tolerates dry but prefers moist; needs acid soil (pH 4.5-5.0).	35-50-foot-wide canopy; moderately dense; golden yellow fall color; slow-growing.
Yellow Birch (*Betula alleghaniensis*)	Very shade tolerant; moist to average soil; wide pH tolerance (4.5-8.0).	35-50-foot-wide canopy; moderately dense; golden yellow fall color; medium growth rate.
Paper Birch (*Betula papyrifera*)	Requires sun; tolerates dry soil; wide pH tolerance (5.0-8.0).	35-50-foot-wide canopy; moderately dense; lemon yellow fall color; medium growth rate.
Bitternut Hickory (*Carya cordiformis*)	Sun to moderate shade; moist to dry soil; wide pH tolerance (5.6-8.0).	50-75-foot-wide canopy; moderately dense; yellow-brown fall color; slow to medium growth.
Shagbark Hickory (*Carya ovata*)	Sun to moderate shade; wet to dry soils; very narrow pH tolerance (6.1-6.5).	35-50-foot-wide canopy; open branching; yellow-brown fall color; slow-growing.
Mockernut Hickory (*Carya tomentosa*)	Needs sun; average to dry soil; slightly acid (pH 6.1-6.5).	35-50-foot-wide canopy; open branching; yellow-brown fall color; slow-growing.
Common Hackberry (*Celtis occidentalis*)	Sun to moderate shade; wet or dry soil; neutral to alkaline (pH 6.6-8.0).	75-100-foot-wide canopy; moderately dense; lemon yellow fall color; medium to fast growth.
Common Persimmon (*Diospyros virginiana*)	Needs sun; average to dry soil; slightly acid (pH 6.1-6.5).	35-50-foot-wide; open branching; yellow-orange fall color; slow-growing.
American Beech (*Fagus grandiflora*)	Sun to deep shade; moist to average soil; needs moderately acid soil (pH 5.5-6.5).	50-75-foot-wide canopy; very dense; yellow fall foliage that persists; slow to medium growth.
White Ash (*Fraxinus americana*)	Sun to deep shade; moist to average soil; slightly acid to neutral soil (pH 6.1-7.5).	50-75-foot-wide canopy; moderately dense; yellow-purple fall color; medium growth rate.

Common Name (Botanical name)	Growing Conditions	Appearance/Comments
Honeylocust (*Gleditsia triacanthos*)	Needs sun; moist to dry soil; slightly acid to neutral soil (pH 6.1-7.5).	50-75-foot-wide canopy; open branching; pale yellow fall color; fast-growing.
Kentucky Coffeetree (*Gymnocladus dioicus*)	Needs sun; prefers wet to average soil; neutral pH (6.6-7.5)	50-75-foot-wide canopy; open branching; lemon yellow fall color; slow to medium growth.
Eastern Larch (*Larix laricina*)	Needs sun; prefers wet soil but will tolerate dry; strongly acid (pH 4.8-7.5)	35-50-foot-wide canopy; open; orange gold in fall; fast-growing; needles resemble an evergreen.
Sweetgum (*Liquidambar styraciflua*)	Needs sun; moist to average soils; slightly acid (pH 6.1-6.5)	50-75-foot-wide canopy; dense; scarlet fall foliage; slow to medium growth rate.
Tuliptree (*Liriodendron tulipifera*)	Sun to moderate shade; moist to average soils; slightly acid (pH 6.1-6.5).	35-50-foot-wide canopy; moderately dense; lemon yellow fall color; medium to fast growth.
Black Tupelo (*Nyssa sylvatica*)	Needs sun; demands moist soil; slightly acid (pH 6.1-6.5).	35-50-foot-wide canopy; dense; glossy scarlet fall foliage; slow-growing.
Sycamore (*Platanus occidentalis*)	Sun to moderate shade; needs moist soil; neutral to alkaline (pH 6.6-8.0).	75-100-foot-wide canopy; open branching; tan-brown fall foliage; very fast-growing.
Black Cherry (*Prunus serotina*)	Needs sun; prefers moist, tolerates dry; slightly acid to neutral (pH 6.1-7.5).	35-50-foot-wide canopy; open; yellow-orange fall color; fast-growing.
White Oak (*Quercus alba*)	Sun to moderate shade; tolerates dry soil; slightly acid to neutral (pH 6.1-7.5).	75-100-foot-wide canopy (or wider); moderately dense; burgundy fall color; slow-growing.
Scarlet Oak (*Quercus coccinea*)	Needs sun; average to dry soil; slightly acid (pH 6.1-6.5).	50-75-foot-wide canopy; moderately dense; scarlet fall foliage; medium to fast growth.
Bur Oak (*Quercus macrocarpa*)	Needs sun; moist or dry soils; acid to alkaline (4.6-8.0 pH).	75-100-foot-wide canopy; open branching; yellow-brown fall color; slow-growing.
Chestnut Oak (*Quercus montana*)	Sun to moderate shade; average to dry soil; slightly acid (pH 6.1-6.5).	75-100-foot-wide canopy; moderate to open branching; dark red fall foliage; slow-growing.
Pin Oak (*Quercus palustris*)	Needs sun; average to moist soil; slightly acid (pH 5.5-6.5).	50-75-foot-wide canopy; deep red fall color; medium to fast-growing.
Northern Red Oak (*Quercus rubra*)	Tolerates shade; moist to average soil; acid soil (pH 4.8-6.5).	75-100-foot-wide canopy; dense; yellow-brown fall color; medium growth rate.
American Linden (*Tilia americana*)	Very shade tolerant; moist to average soil; neutral soil (pH 6.5-7.5).	50-75-foot-wide canopy; dense; golden yellow fall foliage; medium growth rate.

Deciduous Trees 35-50 feet tall

Common Name (Botanical name)	Growing Conditions	Appearance/Comments
Striped Maple (*Acer pensylvanicum*)	Requires shade; demands moist to average soil; strongly acid (pH 4.0-5.0).	10-20-foot-wide canopy; open; lemon yellow fall color; medium to slow-growing.

Common Name (Botanical name)	Growing Conditions	Appearance/Comments
Ohio Buckeye (*Aesculus glabra*)	Sun to moderate shade; moist or dry soil; slightly acid (pH 6.1-6.5)	20-35-foot-wide canopy; moderately dense; orange-red fall color; slow-growing.
Shadblow Serviceberry (*Amelanchier canadensis*)	Sun to deep shade; moist to average soil; slightly acid (pH 6.1-6.5)	35-40-foot-wide canopy; dense, may be multi-stemmed; orange-red fall color.
American Hornbeam (*Carpinus caroliniana*)	Sun to deep shade; moist to average soils; slightly acid to neutral (pH 6.1-7.5).	35-50-foot-wide canopy; very dense branching; orange-red fall color; slow-growing.
Flowering Dogwood (*Cornus florida*)	Sun to moderate shade; moist to dry soil; moderately acidic (pH 5.5-6.5).	35-50-foot-wide canopy; dense branching; scarlet red fall foliage; medium growth rate.
Red Mulberry (*Morus rubra*)	Sun to moderate shade; moist to dry soil; acid to alkaline (6.3-8.0).	35-50-foot-wide canopy; very dense; yellow fall color; fast-growing.
American Hophornbeam (*Ostrya virginiana*)	Tolerates sun or deep shade; moist or dry soil; slightly acid (pH 6.1-8.0).	20-35-foot-wide branches; dense but thin; yellow fall color; slow-growing.
Sourwood (*Oxydendron arboreum*)	Sun to moderate shade; moist to average soil; acid (pH 4.5-6.0).	20-35-foot-wide; moderately dense; scarlet fall color; slow-growing.
Sassafras (*Sassafras albidum*)	Needs sun; moist to dry soil; acid (pH 6.0-6.5).	35-50-foot-wide canopy; very open branching; multi-hued fall foliage; medium growth rate.

Deciduous Trees 20-35 feet tall

Common Name (Botanical name)	Growing Conditions	Appearance/Comments
Mountain Maple (*Acer spicatum*)	Needs shade; moist to average soil; strongly acid (4.0-5.0).	20-35-foot-wide canopy; moderately dense; orange fall color; medium to slow-growing.
Red Buckeye (*Aesculus pavia*)	Sun to moderate shade; moist to average soil; acid to neutral (pH 5.5-7.5)	12-20-foot-wide canopy; moderately dense; yellow-green fall color; slow-growing.
Common Pawpaw (*Asimina triloba*)	Sun to moderate shade; moist to average soil; acid to neutral (pH 6.1-8.0).	20-35-foot-wide canopy; open branching; pale yellow fall color; slow-growing.
Eastern Redbud (*Cercis canadensis*)	Sun to moderate shade; prefers moist soil, tolerates dry; acid to alkaline (pH 6.1-8.0).	20-35 feet wide or wider; moderately dense; golden yellow fall color; slow-growing.
White Fringetree (*Chionanthus virginicus*)	Sun to deep shade; moist to average soils; acid (pH 4.6-6.5)	20-35 feet wide; moderately dense; may be shrub-like; bright yellow fall color; slow-growing.
Pagoda Dogwood (*Cornus alternifolia*)	Sun or shade; moist to average soil; neutral (pH 6.6-7.5).	20-35 feet wide; open branching; maroon fall color; slow-growing.
Carolina Silverbell (*Halesia carolina*)	Sun to moderate shade; moist to average soil; acidic (pH 4.6-6.0).	20-35 feet wide, dense branching; lemon yellow fall foliage; medium growth rate.
Common Witchhazel (*Hamamelis virginiana*)	Sun or shade; moist to average soil; slightly acidic (pH 6.1-6.5).	20-35 feet wide; moderately dense; yellow fall foliage that persists in winter; medium growth rate.

Common Name (Botanical name)	Growing Conditions	Appearance/Comments
American Plum (*Prunus americana*)	Needs sun; average to dry soil; prefers neutral soil (pH 6.6-7.5)	20-35-foot-wide canopy, often wider than tall; dense; yellow fall color; fast-growing.
Common Hoptree (*Ptelea trifoliata*)	Moderate shade; moist to dry soil; neutral (pH 6.6-7.5)	20-35-foot-wide canopy; open branching; pale yellow fall color; medium to slow-growing.
Showy Mountainash (*Sorbus decora*)	Needs sun; moist to average soil; acid to neutral (pH 5.1-7.0).	20-35-foot-wide canopy, often less; open branching; red-purple fall color; medium growth rate.
Nannyberry Viburnum (*Viburnum lentago*)	Sun to moderate shade; moist to dry soil; slightly acid to alkaline (pH 6.1-7.5).	20-35-foot-wide canopy; dense branching; orange red purple fall color; fast-growing.
Blackhaw Viburnum (*Viburnum prunifolium*)	Needs sun; average to dry soil; neutral to alkaline (pH 6.6-8.0).	20-35-foot-wide, often multi-stemmed; dense; scarlet fall color; slow-growing.

Evergreen Trees Taller Than 40 feet.

Common Name (Botanical name)	Growing Conditions	Appearance/Comments
Balsam Fir (*Abies balsamea*)	Very shade tolerant; demands wet to moist soil; acidic soil (pH 4.0-6.5).	20-35-foot-wide branches; conical, spire shaped; very dense; slow-growing.
White Fir (*Abies concolor*)	Shade tolerant; tolerates average to dry soil; prefers acidic (pH 4.0-6.5).	20-35-foot-wide branches; fat conical shape; very dense; slow-growing.
Eastern Redcedar (*Juniperus virginiana*)	Needs sun in youth, shade tolerant later; moist to dry soil; slightly acid to alkaline (6.1-8.0).	35-50 feet wide; broadly conical; very dense; slow-growing.
White Spruce (*Picea glauca*)	Sun to moderate shade; moist to average soil; acid to alkaline (pH 4.6-8.0).	20-35 feet wide; conical; dense; slow to medium growth rate.
Red Pine (*Pinus resinosa*)	Thrives in sun; moist to dry soil; acidic (pH 4.6-6.5).	50-75 feet wide, oval shaped crown; moderately dense; medium growth rate.
Pitch Pine (*Pinus rigida*)	Needs sun; average to dry soil; acid (pH 4.6-6.5).	50-75 feet wide, round canopy; open branching; fast-growing.
Eastern White Pine (*Pinus strobus*)	Best in full sun; moist to average soil; acid (pH 4.5-6.5).	50-75-foot-wide canopy; moderately dense, branching; medium growth rate.
Douglas Fir (*Pseudotsuga taxifolia*)	Sun to moderate shade; moist to dry soil; slightly acid (pH 6.0-6.5).	20-35-foot-wide branching, dense; medium growth rate.
Canada Hemlock (*Tsuga canadensis*)	Moderate to deep shade; needs moist to average soil; acid (pH 4.5-6.6).	35-50 feet wide, very dense branching; short, soft needles and pliable twigs; medium growth rate.
Eastern Arborvitae (*Thuja occidentalis*)	Sun to light shade; moist to dry soil; slightly acid to alkaline (pH 6.0-8.0).	35-50-foot-wide spread; very dense; needles in soft fans; fast to medium growth.

Note: There are no native evergreen tree species with a mature height less than 40 feet.

SHRUBS

The dimensions given below represent the height and width of a plant at maturity. Bear in mind that many shrubs continue to widen as they send up new shoots from their roots.

Deciduous Shrubs 6 to 20 feet tall

Common Name (Botanical name)	Growing Conditions	Appearance/Comments
Bottlebrush Buckeye (*Aesculus parviflora*)	Sun to moderate shade; moist to average soil; acid to neutral (pH 5.5-7.5).	6-12 feet tall; 6-12 feet wide; dense; yellow-green fall color; slow-growing but spreads by suckering.
Red Chokeberry (*Aronia arbutifolia*)	Sun to moderate shade; moist to dry soil; acid (pH 5.1-6.5).	6-12 feet tall; 3-6 feet wide; moderately dense; orange-red fall color; slow-growing.
Common Sweetshrub (*Calycanthus floridus*)	Shade tolerant; moist to average soil; acid to neutral (pH 6.1-7.5).	6-12 feet tall; 6-12 feet wide; dense; yellow fall foliage; slow to medium growth.
Summersweet Clethra (*Clethra alnifolia*)	Shade tolerant; wet to moist soil; acid (pH 4.5-6.5).	6-12 feet tall; 3-6 feet wide; open; yellow fall foliage; slow to medium growth.
Redosier Dogwood (*Cornus sericea*)	Needs sun; wet to average soil; acid to alkaline (pH 6.1-8.5).	6-12 feet tall; 6-12 feet wide; moderately dense; purple fall color; fast-growing.
American Filbert (*Corylus americana*)	Sun to moderate shade; moist to dry soil; acid to neutral (pH 6.1-7.5).	6-12 feet tall; 6-12 feet wide; moderately dense; yellow fall foliage; medium to fast-growing.
Vernal Witchhazel (*Hamamelis vernalis*)	Sun to moderate shade; wet to average soil; acid to neutral (pH 5.5-7.0).	6-12 feet tall; 6-12 feet wide; dense; yellow tan fall color; fast to medium growth.
Common Winterberry (*Ilex verticillata*)	Sun to moderate shade; wet to moist soil; acid to alkaline (pH 4.5-8.0).	6-12 feet tall; 6-12 feet wide; dense; yellow fall foliage; slow-growing.
Virginia Sweetspire (*Itea virginica*)	Shade to deep shade; wet to moist soil; acid to neutral (pH 5.0-7.0).	6-12 feet tall; 6-12 feet wide; open; scarlet fall color; slow to medium growth.
Common Ninebark (*Physocarpus opulifolius*)	Needs sun; moist to dry soil; acid to neutral (pH 6.1-8.0).	6-12 feet tall, 6-12 feet wide; dense; purple fall color; fast-growing.
Smooth Azalea (*Rhododendron arborescens*)	Part shade; wet to moist soil; demands acid (pH 4.5-6.0).	12-20 feet tall; 12-20 feet wide; moderately dense; deep red fall color; slow growth.
Flame Azalea (*Rhododendron calendulaceum*)	Part shade; moist to dry soil; acid (pH 5.1-6.0).	6-12 feet tall, 6-12 feet wide; moderately dense; yellow-green fall color; medium to slow growth rate.
Pink Azalea (*Rhododendron periclymenoides*)	Part shade to shade; moist to dry soil; demands strongly acid (pH 4.5-5.5).	6-12 feet tall, 6-12 feet wide; moderately dense; dull yellow fall foliage; slow.
Early Azalea (*Rhododendron prinophyllym*)	Part shade; moist to dry soil; acid to alkaline (pH 5.1-8.0).	6-9 feet tall; 6-12 feet wide; moderately dense; purplish fall color; slow.

Common Name (Botanical name)	Growing Conditions	Appearance/Comments
Pinkshell Azalea (*Rhododendron vaseyi*)	Part shade to deep shade; wet to moist soil; demands acid (pH 4.5-6.0).	6-12 feet tall; 6-12 feet wide; open; red-purple fall color; medium growth rate.
Highbush Blueberry (*Vaccinium corymbosum*)	Sun to part shade; wet to dry soil; demands acid (pH 3.5-6.5).	6-12 feet tall, 6-12 feet wide; dense; orange-red fall color; slow-growing.
Common Deerberry (*Vaccinium stamineum*)	Sun to part shade; moist to dry soil; demands acid (pH 4.5-6.0).	6-12 feet tall; 6-12 feet wide; moderately dense; red-purple fall color; slow-growing.
Hobblebush (*Viburnum alnifolium*)	Shade; moist to average soil; acid (pH 5.5-6.5).	6-10 feet tall; 8-12 feet wide; open; red-purple fall foliage; medium growth rate.
Arrowwood Viburnum (*Viburnum dentatum*)	Sun to shade; moist to average soil; acid (pH 5.1-6.5).	6-12 feet tall; 8-12 feet wide; moderately dense; purple fall color; medium growth rate.

Deciduous Shrubs 3 to 6 feet tall

Common Name (Botanical name)	Growing Conditions	Appearance/Comments
Roundleaf Serviceberry (*Amelanchier sanguinea*)	Sun to moderate shade; average to dry soil; acid to alkaline (pH 6.1-8.5).	3-6 feet wide; open; orange-red fall foliage; medium growth rate but spreads by suckering.
Dwarf Fothergilla (*Fothergilla gardenii*)	Sun to shade; wet to average soil; acid (pH 5.1-6.5).	3-4 feet wide; dense; yellow-orange-scarlet fall color; slow-growing.
Smooth Hydrangea (*Hydrangea arborescens*)	Moderate to deep shade; moist to average soil; acid to alkaline (pH 6.1-8.5).	3-6 feet wide, spreads easily; dense; yellow-tan in fall; fast-growing.
American Fly Honeysuckle (*Lonicera canadensis*)	Part sun to shade; moist to average soil; acid to alkaline (pH 6.0-8.5).	3-6 feet wide; wider than tall; open; yellow fall color; fast-growing.
Carolina Rose (*Rosa carolina*)	Needs sun; wet to dry soil; acid to alkaline (pH 6.1-8.0).	6-12 feet wide; forms colonies; orange fall color; fast-growing.
Maple-leaf Viburnum (*Viburnum acerifolium*)	Shade; moist to dry soil; acid (pH 5.1-6.0).	3-6 feet wide; open; red-purple fall color; slow to medium growth rate.

Broadleaf Evergreen Shrubs

Common Name (Botanical name)	Growing Conditions	Appearance/Comments
Inkberry (*Ilex glabra*)	Sun to part shade; wet to moist soil; acid (pH 4.5-6.0).	6-12 feet tall; 6-12 feet wide; dense when young, open when older; evergreen in south; slow-growing.
Mountain Laurel (*Kalmia latifolia*)	Part sun to part shade; wet to average soil; needs acid (pH 4.5-6.0).	12-20 feet tall; 12-20 feet wide; dense when young, open when older; slow-growing.
Mountain Andromeda (*Pieris floribunda*)	Part sun to shade; moist to average soil; demands acid (pH 4.5-6.0).	3-6 feet tall, 3-6 feet wide; dense; slow-growing.

Common Name (Botanical name)	Growing Conditions	Appearance/Comments
Carolina Rhododendron (*Rhododendron carolinianum*)	Moderate to deep shade; moist to average soil; demands acid (pH 4.5-6.0).	3-6 feet tall; 3-6 feet wide; moderately dense; medium to slow growth rate.
Rosebay Rhododendron (*Rhododendron maximum*)	Best in moderate shade; moist to average soil; needs acid (pH 4.5-6.0).	10-20 feet tall and 20-30-foot-wide, open branching; medium growth rate.

APPENDIX C: Resources

THESE LISTS CONTAIN BOOKS and websites that provide useful information about the following subjects:

* Native Plants and Gardening Inspired by Nature
* Invasive Plants
* Renewable Energy
* Green Roofs
* Passive Solar Design and Construction
* Porous/Permeable Paving

Native Plants and Gardening Inspired by Nature

Not included here are the countless books and plant identification guides written for specific states and regions, all of which may easily be found by searching the Internet.

Brooklyn Botanic Garden. *Gardening with Native Plants*. Brooklyn Botanic Garden, 1989.

Condon, Marlene. *The Nature-Friendly Garden: Creating a Backyard Haven for Plants, Wildlife, and People*. Stackpole Books, 2006.

Cox, Jeff. *Landscaping with Nature*. Rodale Press, 1991.

Cullina, William. *Growing and Propagating Wildflowers*. Houghton Mifflin, 2000.

Cullina, William. *Native Trees, Shrubs and Vines*. Houghton Mifflin, 2002.

Cullina, William. *Native Ferns, Moss and Grasses*. Houghton Mifflin, 2008.

Darke, Rick. *The American Woodland Garden*. Timber Press, 2002.

Diekelmann, John and Robert Schuster. *Natural Landscaping: Designing with Native*

Plant Communities. University of Wisconsin Press, 2002.

Johnson, Lorraine and Andrew Leyerle. *Grow Wild!: Low-Maintenance, Sure-Success, Distinctive Gardening with Native Plants.* Fulcrum, 1997.

Jones, Samuel B. and Leonard E. Foote. *Gardening with Native Wildflowers.* Timber Press, 1997.

Junker, Karan. *Gardening with Woodland Plants.* Timber Press, 2007.

Kingsbury, Noel and Nicola Browne. *Natural Garden Style: Gardening Inspired by Nature.* Merrell, 2009.

Lewis, Pam. *Sticky Wicket: Gardening in Tune with Nature.* Frances Lincoln, 2007.

Lovejoy, Ann and Allan Mandell. *Naturalistic Gardening: Reflecting the Planting Patterns of Nature.* Sasquatch Books, 2002.

Marinelli, Janet, ed. *Going Native.* Brooklyn Botanic Garden, 1994.

Pollan, Michael. *Second Nature.* Grove Press, 2003.

Roberts, Edith and Elsa Rehmann. *American Plants for American Gardens.* University of Georgia Press, 1996.

Roth, Sally. *Natural Landscaping: Gardening with Nature to Create a Backyard Paradise.* Rodale Press, 1997.

Sauer, Leslie Jones. *The Once and Future Forest.* Island Press, 1998.

Smyser, Carol. *Nature's Design: A Practical Guide to Natural Landscaping.* Rodale, 1984.

Sternberg, Guy and Jim Wilson. *Landscaping with Native Trees.* Chapters, 1995.

Tallamy, Douglas. *Bringing Nature Home: How Native Plants Sustain Wildlife in Our Gardens.* Timber Press, 2007.

Wasowski, Andy. *The Landscaping Revolution: Garden with Mother Nature, Not Against Her.* Contemporary Books, 2000.

Organizations

Lady Bird Johnson Wildflower Center: wildflower.org

Native Plant Societies: michbotclub.org

New England Wild Flower Society: newfs.org

Plant Conservation Alliance: nps.gov

Society for Ecological Restoration International: ser.org.

Invasive Plants

Burrell, C. Colston. *Native Alternatives to Invasive Plants.* Brooklyn Botanic Garden, 2006.

Kaufman, Sylvan Ramsey and Wallace Kaufman. *Invasive Plants: A Guide to Identification, Impacts, and Control of Common North American Species.* Stackpole Books, 2007.

Lawn Weeds. Turf IPM Fact Sheets, umassturf.org

Randall, John M. and Janet Marinelli. *Invasive Plants (Weeds of the Global Garden).* Brooklyn Botanic Garden, 1996.

Organizations

National Invasive Species Information Center. invasivespeciesinfo.gov/resources/lists.shtml

WeedsUS: Database of Plants Invading Natural Areas in the United States. nps.gov/plants/alien/factmain.htm

Renewable Energy

Bartmann, Dan and Dan Fink. *Homebrew Wind Power*. Buckville Publications, 2008.

Chiras, Dan. *Lessons from Nature: Learning to Live Sustainably on the Earth*. New York: Island Press, 1992.

Chiras, Dan. *The Homeowner's Guide to Renewable Energy*. New Society, 2006.

Craddock, David. *Renewable Energy Made Easy: Free Energy from Solar, Wind, Hydropower and Other Alternative Energy Sources*. Atlantic, 2008.

Davis, Scott and Corrie Laschuk. *Microhydro: Clean Power from Water*. New Society, 2003.

Ewing, Rex. *Got Sun? Go Solar: Get Free Renewable Energy to Power your Grid-Tied Home*. PixyJack Press, 2005.

Ewing, Rex. *Power with Nature: Alternative Energy Solutions for Homeowners*, 2nd ed. PixyJack Press, 2006.

Gipe, Paul. *Wind Energy Basics: A Guide to Small and Micro Wind Systems*. Chelsea Green, 1999.

Gipe, Paul. *Wind Power: Renewable Energy for Home, Farm and Business*, rev. ed. Chelsea Green, 2004.

Gleason, Carrie. *Geothermal Energy: Using Earth's Furnace*. Crabtree, 2008.

Harvey, Adam and Andy Brown. *Micro-Hydro Design Manual: A Guide to Small-Scale Water Power Schemes*. Practical Action, 1993.

Kemp, William H. *The Renewable Energy Handbook: A Guide to Rural Energy Independence, Off-Grid and Sustainable Living*. Axtext Press, 2006.

Morris, Neil. *Geothermal Power*. Franklin Watts, 2008.

Ramsey, Dan and David Hughes. *The Complete Idiot's Guide to Solar Power for Your Home*, 2nd ed. Alpha, 2007.

Rodriquez, Luis and Teodor Sanchez. *Designing and Building Mini and Micro Hydro Power Schemes: A Practical Guide*. Practical Action, 2009

Savage, Lorraine. *Geothermal Power (Fueling the Future)*. Greenhaven Press, 2006.

Schaeffer, John. *Real Goods Solar Living Source Book*, 30th anniversary ed. Gaiam Real Goods, 2007.

Stanley, Tomm. *Going Solar: Understanding and using the Warmth in Sunlight*. Stonefield, 2005.

Wengenmayr, Roland and Thomas Bührk. *Renewable Energy: Sustainable Energy Concepts for the Future*. Wiley, 2008.

Green Roofs

Cantor, Steven L. and Steven Peck. *Green Roofs in Sustainable Design*. W.W. Norton, 2008.

Dunnett, Nigel and Andy Clayden. *Rain Gardens: Managing Water Sustainably in the Garden and Designed Landscape*. Timber Press, 2007.

Dunnett, Nigel and Noël Kingsbury. *Planting Green Roofs and Living Walls*. Timber Press, 2008.

Luckett, Kelly. *Green Roof Construction and Maintenance*. McGraw-Hill Professional, 2009.

Margolis, Liat and Alexander Robinson. *Living Systems: Innovative Materials and Technologies for Landscape Architecture*. Birkhauser Basel, 2007.

Osmundson, Theodore H. *Roof Gardens: History, Design and Construction.* W.W. Norton, 1997.

Snodgrass, Edmund C. and Lucie L. Snodgrass. *Green Roof Plants: A Resource and Planting Guide.* Timber Press, 2006.

Passive Solar Design and Construction

Chiras, Dan. *The Solar House: Passive Heating and Cooling.* Chelsea Green, 2002.

Gevorkian, Peter. *Solar Power in Building Design: The Engineer's Complete Project Resource.* McGraw-Hill Professional, 2007.

Johnston, David and Scott Gibson. *Green from the Ground Up: Sustainable, Healthy and Energy-Efficient Home Construction.* Taunton, 2008.

Kachadorian, James. *Passive Solar House: The Complete Guide to Heating and Cooling Your Home.* Chelsea Green, 2006.

Roaf, Sue. *Ecohouse*, 3rd ed. Architectural Press, 2007.

Wilson, Alex. *Your Green Home.* New Society, 2006.

"Passive Solar Guidelines." *A Sourcebook for Green and Sustainable Building.* October 20, 2008. www.greenbuilder.com/sourcebook/passsolguide1-2.html

Porous/Permeable Paving

Calkins, Meg. *Materials for Sustainable Sites: A Complete Guide to the Evaluation, Selection and Use of Sustainable Construction Materials.* Wiley, 2006.

Larson, Mike. *New Porous Pavement Comes from Recycled Glass.* Associated Construction Publications, April 6, 2009. www.acppubs.com

McCormack, Tony. *Driveways, Paths and Patios: A Complete Guide to Design, Management and Construction.* Crowood Press, 2006.

"Porous Pavement: A Win-Win Stormwater Strategy." *Environmental Building News*, Vol. 13, no. 9. September, 2004.

"Porous Pavement," *Environmental Building News.* Vol. 14, no. 8. August, 2005.

"Porous Paving," *Environmental Building News.* Vol. 18, no. 4. April, 2009.

Thompson, William and Kim Sorvig. *Sustainable Landscape Construction: A Guide to Green Building Outdoors.* Island Press, 2007.

Endnotes

Section I: Introduction

1. *Heat Island Effect.* [online] US Environmental Protection Agency. May 11, 2009. epa.gov/heatisland/mitigation/trees.htm.
2. Alex Wilson. *Your Green Home.* Gabriola Island, BC: New Society, 2006, p. 80.

Chapter One

1. Arthur Guyton. *Basic Human Physiology.* W.B. Saunder, 1971, p. 586.
2. *Global Humidity Zones.* [online] University of Arizona, College of Agriculture and Life Sciences. November 11, 2008. cals.arizona.edu/oals/soils/surveys/legend.html.
3. *Arctic Climatology and Meteorology.* [online] National Snow and Ice Data Center. March 13, 2009. nsidc.org/arcticmet/factors/pressure.html.
4. *National Weather Service Windchill Chart.* [online] National Oceanic and Atmospheric Administration. weather.gov/os/windchill.
5. *Landscaping and Your Regional Climate.* [online] US Department of Energy. May 2, 2009. energysavers.gov/your_home/landscaping.

Chapter Two

1. *Heat Island Effect.* [online] US Environmental Protection Agency. May 11, 2009. epa.gov/heatisland/mitigation/trees.htm.
2. *End Use Consumption of Electricity 2001.* [online] Energy Information Administration. May 11, 2009. eia.doe.gov/emeu/recs/recs2001/enduse2001/enduse2001.html>.
3. *Energy Efficiency and Renewable Energy: Energy Savers.* [online] US Department of Energy. May 11, 2009. energysavers.gov/your_home/landscaping.

Chapter Three

1. *Energy Efficiency and Renewable Energy: Energy Savers*. US Department of Energy. May 11, 2009. energysavers.gov/your_home/landscaping.
2. US Department of Energy. National Renewable Energy Laboratory. *Tomorrow's Energy Today for Cities and Communities*, 1993.
3. Anne Simon Moffat and Mark Schiler. *Energy-Efficient and Environmental Landscaping Cut Your Utility Bills by Up to 30 Percent and Create a Natural Healthy Yard*. Hamilton: Appropriate Solutions Pr, 1994, p. 16.
4. *Earth Center Global Climate Change*. [online] Missouri Department of Natural Resources. May 11, 2009. dnr.mo.gov.

Chapter Four

1. *Earth-Sun Relationships and Insolation*. [online] The Encyclopedia of Earth. March 6, 2009. eoearth.org.
2. Brochure on the Use of Cool Pavements to Reduce the Urban Heat Island Effect. [online] Town of Gilbert, Arizona. May 11, 2009. ci.gilbert.az.us/planning/urbanheatisland.cfm?style=print
3. Henry Fountain. "Concrete Is Remixed with Environment in Mind." [online] *New York Times* (March 31, 2009). April 3, 2009. nytimes.com.

Chapter Five

1. *Energy Kid's Place*. [online] Energy Information Administration. May 12, 2009. eia.doe.gov/kids/energyfacts.

Chapter Six

1. *How Windbreaks Work*. Natural Resources Conservation Service. October 29, 2008. nrcs.usda.gov/technical/ecs/forest/wind/how.pdf.

Chapter Seven

1. Yvonne Baskin, Paul R. Ehrlich and Jane Lubchenco. *The Work of Nature: How the Diversity of Life Sustains Us*. New York. Shearwater Books, 1997, p. 134.
2. *Chronicle Online*. April 1, 2006. Cornell University. January 26, 2009. news.cornell.edu/stories/march06/insect_value.ssl.html.
3. Douglas W Tallamy. *Bringing Nature Home: How Native Plants Sustain Wildlife in Our Gardens*. New York. Timber Press, 2007, pp. 42-47.
4. William Cullina. *The New England Wild Flower Society Guide to Growing and Propagating Wildflowers of the United States and Canada*. Boston: Houghton Mifflin, 2000, p. 1.
5. Sara Stein. *Noah's Garden: Restoring the Ecology of America's Backyards*. Boston: Houghton Mifflin, 1993, pp. 250-252.
6. Nigel Dunnett. *Dynamic Landscape Design, Ecology and Management of Naturalistic Urban Planting*. Dallas: Taylor & Francis, 2004.
7. William Cullina. *The New England Wild Flower Society Guide to Growing and Propagating Wildflowers of the United States and Canada*. Boston: Houghton Mifflin, 2000, p. 19.

Chapter Eight

1. Virginia Scott Jenkins. *The Lawn: A History of an American Obsession*. Washington, D.C: Smithsonian Institution, 1994, ch. 2.

Chapter Nine

1. William McDonough. *Green Roofs: Ecological Design and Construction*. Schiffer, 2004.

Chapter Fourteen

1. Leslie Sauer. *The Once and Future Forest*. New York: Island Press, 1998, p. 156.

2. *Wastes, Resource Conservation, Composting.*
[online] US Environmental Protection
Agency. May 13, 2009. epa.gov/osw/
conserve/rrr/composting.

3. *American Standard for Nursery Stock.* American
Nursery and Landscape Association, 2004.
(ANSI Z60.1-2004) Section 1.6.1, Table 6,
Root Ball Diameters.

4. Céline Caron. "Regenerating Soils with
Ramial Chipped Wood." *The Ecological
Landscaper,* 7, 2000, pp. 5-8.

5. Paul Tukey and Nell Newman. *Organic Lawn
Care Manual.* Grand Rapids: Storey, LLC,
2007, p. 31.

6. Ibid., p. 120.

Chapter Fifteen

1. William J. Thompson and Kim Sorvig.
*Sustainable Landscape Construction: A Guide to
Green Building Outdoors, 2nd Edition.* New York:
Island Press, 2007, p. 231.

Chapter Sixteen

1. Andy Wasowski, Sally Wasowski and Darrel
G. Morrison. *Building Inside Nature's Envelope:
How New Construction and Landscape
Preservation Can Work.*

2. William J. Thompson and Kim Sorvig.
*Sustainable Landscape Construction: A Guide to
Green Building Outdoors, 2nd Edition.* New York:
Island Press, 2007, pp. 59-64.

3. Malcolm Wells. *Underground Designs.*
Malcolm Wells, 1977.

4. Gideon Golany. *Earth-Sheltered Habitat:
History, Architecture and Urban Design.* New
York: John Wiley & Sons, 1983, p. 44.

Section VI: Introduction

1. Walton Congdon, Renewable Energy
Instructor at Greenfield Community College,
Greenfield, MA; personal interview, January
2009.

2. Rex Ewing. *Power with Nature: Alternative
Energy Solutions for Homeowners.* New York:
PixyJack Press, 2006, pp. 85-94.

Chapter Seventeen

1. Rex Ewing and Doug Pratt. *Got Sun? Go
Solar: Get Free Renewable Energy to Power Your
Grid-Tied Home.* New York: PixyJack, 2005.

2. *My Watts Renewables Estimator.* [online]
Choose Renewables. December 3, 2008.
chooserenewables.com/estimator_start.php.

3. Dan Chiras. *The Homeowner's Guide to
Renewable Energy: Achieving Energy
Independence Through Solar, Wind, Biomass and
Hydropower.* Gabriola Island, BC: New
Society, 2006.

Chapter Eighteen

1. Paul Gipe and Richard Perez. *Wind Energy
Basics: A Guide to Small and Micro Wind
Systems.* New York: Chelsea Green, 1999,
p. 13.

2. Ibid., p. 73.

3. *Small Wind.* [online] American Wind Energy
Association. December 3, 2008. awea.org.

Chapter Nineteen

1. *Hydroelectric Power Use.* United States
Geologic Survey. [online] May 13, 2009.
ga.water.usgs.gov/edu/wuhy.html.

2. Scott Davis. *Microhydro: Clean Power from
Water.* Gabriola Island, BC: New Society,
2004.

3. *The Guide to Hydro Power.* [online] Canyon
Hydro. November 17, 2008.
canyonhydro.com.

4. Scott Davis. *Microhydro: Clean Power from
Water.* Gabriola Island, BC: New Society,
2004

5. Rex Ewing. *Power with Nature: Alternative
Energy Solutions for Homeowners.* New York:
PixyJack Press, 2006, p. 165.

Chapter Twenty

1. *Energy Efficiency and Renewable Energy* . [online] US Department of Energy. May 19, 2009. energysavers.gov/your_home/ space_heating_cooling.

Chapter Twenty-one

1. *IDA Fact Sheets and Practical Guides*. Fact Sheet #52. [online] International Dark Sky Association. May 13, 2009. darksky.org.

2. International Dark Sky Association. dark-sky.org.
3. *Energy Efficiency and Renewable Energy* . [online] US Department of Energy. May 13, 2009. eere.energy.gov/.

Bibliography

American Nursery and Landscape Association. *American Standard for Nursery Stock*. American Nursery and Landscape Association, 2004.

American Wind Energy Association. *Small Wind*. [online] December 3, 2008. awea.org.

Baskin, Yvonne, Paul R. Ehrlich and Jane Lubchenco. *The Work of Nature: How the Diversity of Life Sustains Us*. Shearwater Books, 1997.

Brochure on the Use of Cool Pavements to Reduce the Urban Heat Island Effect. [online] Town of Gilbert, Arizona. May 11, 2009. ci.gilbert.az.us/planning/urbanheatisland.cfm

Caron, Celine. "Regenerating Soils with Ramial Chipped Wood." *The Ecological Landscaper*, 7, 2000.

Chiras, Dan. *The Homeowner's Guide to Renewable Energy : Achieving Energy Independence Through Solar, Wind, Biomass and Hydropower*. Gabriola Island, BC: New Society, 2006.

Chronicle Online. [online] April 1, 2006. Ithaca, NY: Cornell University. January 26, 2009. news.cornell.edu/stories/march06/insect_value.ssl.html.

Cullina, William. *The New England Wild Flower Society Guide to Growing and Propagating Wildflowers of the United States and Canada*. Boston: Houghton Mifflin, 2000.

Davis, Scott. *Microhydro Clean Power from Water*. Gabriola Island, BC: New Society, 2004.

Dunnett, Nigel. *Dynamic Landscape Design, Ecology and Management of Naturalistic Urban Planting*. Dallas: Taylor & Francis, 2004.

"Earth-Sun Relationships and Insolation." [online] *The Encyclopedia of Earth*. May 15, 2009. eoearth.org.

Energy Information Administration. *End Use Consumption of Electricity 2001.* [online] May 11, 2009. eia.doe.gov/emeu/recs/recs2001/enduse2001/enduse2001.html.

Energy Information Administration. *Energy Kid's Place* . [online] May 12, 2009. eia.doe.gov/kids/energyfacts.

Ewing, Rex A. *Power with Nature: Alternative Energy Solutions for Homeowners.* New York: PixyJack Press, 2006.

Ewing, Rex A. and Doug Pratt. *Got Sun? Go Solar: Get Free Renewable Energy to Power Your Grid-Tied Home.* New York: PixyJack Press, 2005.

Fountain, Henry. "Concrete Is Remixed with Environment in Mind." [online] *New York Times.* March 31, 2009. April 3, 2009. nytimes.com.

Gipe, Paul and Richard Perez. *Wind Energy Basics : A Guide to Small and Micro Wind Systems.* New York: Chelsea Green, 1999.

Golany, Gideon. *Earth-Sheltered Habitat: History, Architecture and Urban Design.* New York: John Wiley & Sons, 1983.

Guide to Hydro Power. [online] Canyon Hydro. November 17, 2008. canyonhydro.com.

Guyton, Arthur C. *Basic Human Physiology: Normal Function and Mechanisms of Disease.* W.B. Saunder, 1971.

International Dark Sky Association. *IDA Fact Sheets and Practical Guides.* [online] May 13, 2009. darksky.org.

Jenkins, Virginia Scott. *The Lawn: A History of an American Obsession.* Washington, D.C: Smithsonian Institution, 1994.

McDonough, William. *Green Roofs: Ecological Design and Construction.* Grand Rapids: Schiffer, 2004.

Missouri Department of Natural Resources. *Earth Center Global Climate Change.* [online] May 11, 2009. dnr.mo.gov.

Moffat, Anne Simon and Mark Schiler. *Energy-Efficient and Environmental Landscaping Cut Your Utility Bills by Up to 30 Percent and Create a Natural Healthy Yard.* Hamilton: Appropriate Solutions Press, 1994.

My Watts Renewables Estimator. [online] Choose Renewables. December 3, 2008. chooserenewables.com/estimator_start.php

National Oceanic and Atmospheric Adminstration. *National Weather Service Windchill Chart.* [online] weather.gov/os/windchill.

National Snow and Ice Data Center. *Arctic Climatology and Meteorology.* [online] March 13, 2009. nsidc.org/arcticmet/factors/pressure.html.

Natural Resources Conservation Service. *How Windbreaks Work.* [online] October 29, 2008. nrcs.usda.gov/technical/ecs/forest/wind/how.pdf.

Sauer, Leslie. *The Once and Future Forest.* New York: Island Press, 1998.

Stein, Sara. *Noah's Garden: Restoring the Ecology of America's Backyards.* Boston: Houghton Mifflin, 1993.

Tallamy, Douglas W. *Bringing Nature Home: How Native Plants Sustain Wildlife in Our Gardens.* New York: Timber Press, 2007.

Thompson, J. William and Kim Sorvig. *Sustainable Landscape Construction: A Guide to Green Building Outdoors,* 2nd Edition. New York: Island Press, 2007.

Tukey, Paul and Nell Newman. *The Organic Lawn Care Manual.* Grand Rapids: Storey, 2007.

United States Geologic Survey. *Hydroelectric Power Use.* [online] May 13, 2009. ga.water.usgs.gov/edu/wuhy.html.

University of Arizona. *Global Humidity Zones.* [online] College of Agriculture and Life Sciences, November 11, 2008.

cals.arizona.edu/oals/soils/surveys/
legend.html.

US Department of Energy. *Energy Efficiency and Renewable Energy* . [online] May 19, 2009. energysavers.gov/your_home/space_heating_cooling.

US Department of Energy. *Energy Efficiency and Renewable Energy: Energy Savers.* [online] May 11, 2009. energysavers.gov/your_home/landscaping.

US Department of Energy. *Landscaping and Your Regional Climate.* [online] May 11, 2009. energysavers.gov/your_home/landscaping.

US Department of Energy. *Tomorrow's Energy Today for Cities and Communities.* National Renewable Energy Laboratory, 1993.

US Environmental Protection Agency. *Heat Island Effect.* May 11, 2009. epa.gov/heatisland/mitigation/trees.htm.

US Environmental Protection Agency. *Wastes, Resource Conservation, Composting.* [online] May 13, 2009. epa.gov/osw/conserve/rrr/composting.

Wasowski, Andy, Sally Wasowski and Darrel G. Morrison. *Building Inside Nature's Envelope: How New Construction and Landscape Preservation Can Work Together* . New York: Oxford University Press, 2001.

Wells, Malcolm. *Underground Designs.* Malcolm Wells, 1977.

Wilson, Alex. *Your Green Home.* Gabriola Island, BC: New Society, 2006

Index

About the Author

S UE REED is a registered landscape archi-tect, writer and workshop leader who has helped hundreds of homeowners create comfortable, livable, beautiful and energy-efficient landscapes. She has worked in this field for nearly 25 years, operating her own design practice since 1991. Her recent article on sustainable landscape design appears in the *Encyclopedia of Sustainability*, Volume II (2010).

Sue earned her master of arts degree in 1987 at the Conway School of Landscape Design and served as an instructor there between 1991 and 2007. As a teacher and a practitioner, she excels at conveying complex technical information and subtle concepts to her students, clients and readers.

Beside her house in western Massachusetts grows a mature dogwood tree that she planted as a tiny shoot in the lot behind her first office. Like Sue herself, the tree has been transplanted a few times but now has taken root in its permanent home.

About the Illustrator

KATE DANA's habit of doodling on elementary school desks led her to a long career in illustration and design. Her eclectic path through industrial and graphic design now focuses on sustainable residential landscape design. Kate enjoys life's adventures and riding old rusty bikes around Newport, RI, her seaside town.

If you have enjoyed *Energy-Wise Landscape Design* you might also enjoy other

BOOKS TO BUILD A NEW SOCIETY

Our books provide positive solutions for people who want to
make a difference. We specialize in:

**Sustainable Living • Green Building • Peak Oil • Renewable Energy
Environment & Economy • Natural Building & Appropriate Technology
Progressive Leadership • Resistance and Community
Educational and Parenting Resources**

New Society Publishers

ENVIRONMENTAL BENEFITS STATEMENT

New Society Publishers has chosen to produce this book on recycled paper made
with **100% post consumer waste**, processed chlorine free, and old growth free.

For every 5,000 books printed, New Society saves the following resources:[1]

39	Trees
3,548	Pounds of Solid Waste
3,7904	Gallons of Water
5,092	Kilowatt Hours of Electricity
6,450	Pounds of Greenhouse Gases
28	Pounds of HAPs, VOCs, and AOX Combined
10	Cubic Yards of Landfill Space

[1]Environmental benefits are calculated based on research done by the Environmental Defense Fund and
other members of the Paper Task Force who study the environmental impacts of the paper industry.

For a full list of NSP's titles, please call **1-800-567-6772** *or check out our website at:*

www.newsociety.com

NEW SOCIETY PUBLISHERS
Deep Green for over 30 years